Praise for The Glory Years

"Reading through 'The Glory Years' was a fun trip down Cardinals memory lane. I'd forgotten many of the great stories that Mel tells so well. These are the teams that made me say 'That's a Winner!' so many times. This book belongs on the bookshelf of anyone who is a fan of the Cardinals as well as anyone who is a fan of this fine game."

Jack Buck
Hall of Fame Cardinals broadcaster

"If Mel Freese didn't hit a literary home run with his recitation of the high spots for the Redbirds, take the word of a gaffer who saw them all 1926 through 1996 - that dear Mel hit a triple. Yeah, and scored standing! Congratulations, fellow SABRite!"

Bob Broeg
Hall of Fame baseball writer

"As a Cardinals broadcaster, native St. Louisian, and life-long baseball fan, I thought I knew a lot about the history of the Redbirds. The stories in The Glory Years are fascinating and the details are incredible. It's amazing how good so many of the teams and players have been."

Dan McLaughlin
KMOX radio, Fox Sports Midwest

"This wonderful book recaptures the championship legacy of the St. Louis Cardinals."

Erv Fischer, Historian
St. Louis Cardinals Hall of Fame Museum

Gary,
Merry Christmas
2000.
Bob

The Glory Years
of the
St. Louis Cardinals

Volume 1
The World Championship Seasons

by
Mel R. Freese

Palmerston & Reed Publishing Company
St. Louis, Missouri
StLouisBooks.com

The Glory Years of the St. Louis Cardinals
Volume 1 - The World Championship Seasons

By Mel R. Freese
©Copyright 1999 by Mel R. Freese

ISBN 0-911921-52-4

Printed in the United States of America

Published and distributed by: Palmerston & Reed Publishing Company
1524 S. Big Bend Blvd.
St. Louis, MO 63117
877-99-BOOKS (877-992-6657) toll-free
www.StLouisBooks.com

Library of Congress Cataloging-in-Publication Data
Freese, Mel R., 1933-
The Glory Years: The Championship Seasons of the St. Louis Cardinals/by Mel R. Freese.
    p. cm.
    Includes bibliographical references.
    ISBN 0-911921-52-4(pbk.)
    1. St. Louis Cardinals (Baseball team)—History. I. Title.
GV875.S3 F74 1999
                                99-088642

Cover photo: Stan Musial, compliments of Stan The Man, Inc., St. Louis, MO
www.stan-the-man.com

Dedication

*This book is dedicated to
my wife, Martha,
who has made me what I am.*

The Glory Years of the St. Louis Cardinals

Table of Contents

Acknowledgements

This book would not have been possible had it not been for Vince Schoemehl, Jim Hunstein, and Ken Christian of the publishing firm Palmerston and Reed. They were instrumental in commissioning me to write this book and to them I am gratefully indebted.

To Jim, I owe much thanks for his guidance and assistance as I was writing this book. He allowed me to participate in the choosing of the pictures, the layout of the book and in the marketing and promotion of same. We worked as a team in putting together this project. My sincere thanks to you.

I also am greatly indebted to Steve Gietscher, archivist of the Sporting News, and his assistant Jim Meier for the use of their facilities in doing my research during the summer of 1999. Without their help this book would have been much more difficult to write.

Also to the many writers, authors and publishers on whose work I drew references. Each of these books are listed in the bibliography and it is my most sincere thanks and appreciation for the publications they had which made my job much easier.

Another individual who deserves acknowledgement is Mark Stangl, president of the Bob Broeg St. Louis SABR chapter. He offered the resources of the chapter for help in editing and other assistance on the book. To him personally I am indebted for his help as well as the editing he did. Many thanks, Mark.

Finally, and most importantly, I thank my wife, Martha. She was extremely patient as I researched and wrote this book during the summer of 1999. My work often consisted of researching by day and writing at night. For nine weeks she had the responsibility of our household by herself. During that time we also experienced a family crisis which she handled without a whimper, like the real trouper she is.

Foreword

The Glory Years
The Championship Season of
The Saint Louis Cardinals

The ultimate in major league baseball is winning the World Series and only the New York Yankees have been more successful than the Cardinals in that pursuit. It took the franchise from 1892 to 1926 to win their first World Series flag, but once they mastered that art, their success was undeniable.

The Cardinals first saw the light of day as the St. Louis Browns in 1881. The following year they became a charter member of the American Association, a new major league formed in part to offer fans the beer and Sunday baseball prohibited by the older, more established National League.

Initially, Chris Von der Ahe, one of the club's founders and its first president, saw baseball as a source of customers for his St. Louis saloon and beer garden. However, he soon became entranced with the team and through his drive and determination made them one of the powerhouses of baseball for that era.

By the mid-1880s the Browns were riding high and won the league title from 1885-88. Unfortunately they won just one World Series Championship. The Browns tied the Chicago White Stockings (3-3-1) in 1985 and defeated them four games to two the next season. They lost to Detroit in 1887 and New York in 1888. In 1889 the club finished second to Brooklyn and then faded.

The team was picked up by the National League in 1892 and it did not fair well at all. In 1897 and 1898, they, finished last on records of 29-102 and 39-111, respectively. There first two and one-half decades in the National League found them normally in the second division. It wasn't until the 1920s the team began to consistently show some staying power.

After St. Louis captured its first pennant and World Series Title in 1926, they proceeded to win eight more pennants and five more World Series in the next 20 years. Only the Yankees could better that mark. It should be noted that in head-to-head play in the World Series, the Cardinals lead the Yankees, three series to two. The Cards beat them 1926, 1942, and 1964. The Yanks won the title, beating the Redbirds in 1928 and 1943.

From 1926 through 1953 the Cardinals finished below .500 in only two years (1932 and 1938). During that time they established themselves as the premier team in the National League, winning nine pennants, six World Series Titles, finishing second nine times, third four times and fourth twice. From 1941 through 1949 they were first or second each year as they captured four pennants and three World Series Championships.

There was a downturn in the 1950s, but a revival in 1960 and by 1964 they were winning pennants again. During this decade they would win three pennants and two World Series Titles. Then came a slump in the 1970s, although they did challenge in a few years.

By the 1980s the club was back on track and they won three more pennants and one more World Series Title. Since 1987 it has been a little sparse for the Redbirds, but with the likes of Mark McGwire, Ray Lankford, Fernando Tatis, and J. D. Drew, they hoped to rebound with the start of the 2000 season. All that is needed is for the arms of Matt Morris and Alan Benes be healthy and Rick Ankiel be all he is touted to be. General Manager Walt Jockety has made a couple trades for proven workhorse starters, so the pitching is rounding into shape.

The Cardinal history has been a rich one, filled with memorable seasons, players and stories. This book will take you through the championship years, with a chapter devoted to each season in which they won the World Series. We examine the highlights as well as the lowlights of each year. We talk about the obstacles that had to be overcome, major trades, the heroes and the goats.

For each year that is reviewed we look back briefly at the previous season to see how the team fared and what it took to bring them to championship status. We also follow up what the team did after its triumphant season.

The book covers the World Championship Years in chronological order, starting in 1926 and ending with 1982.

It is our goal and objective to retrace these nine seasons as the team fought for the title. We will take you through their triumphs, as well as their moments, and at times hours of pain. We will relive some of the great stretch drives, such as those by the Cardinal teams of 1926, 1934, 1942 and 1964.

However, all of it is pure Cardinal, and if you are a St. Louis fan I believe this book will give you many hours of enjoyment. For you older fans, it will rekindle some fond memories of days gone by, while for the younger fans it will introduce you to an era you may have only heard about. It is my sincere hope you will receive as much enjoyment in reading this book as I did in writing it.

- Mel R. Freese

Introduction

Night after night, St. Louisans filled Busch Stadium to its brim to watch Mark McGwire swat his tape-measure homers.

Sure, the Cards had been out of the 1999 pennant chase since the spring. And the more compelling history was written the season before, when McGwire toppled Babe Ruth and Roger Maris by hitting an unthinkable 70 home runs.

That breathtaking pursuit brought the region to its feet and kept it standing for months. And a year later, as McGwire pounded away toward another home-run title, the glow remained. This was not monotony, not in the eyes of the real fans. St. Louis knew it was seeing something exceptional, a power display that would stand the test of time - an accomplishment we would be sharing with our children and grandchildren about for decades to come.

And that's what baseball in St. Louis is all about. This sport is ingrained in the local culture. It is a key to our collective pride and essential to our sense of place. There may be millions of Americans, especially the young ones, who don't GET baseball. But St. Louisans do. And that makes them special.

It's only right that baseball's most significant individual achievement of the 1990s, McGwire's mesmerizing home-run assault, would take place in this city. It's only fair that McGwire would finish the job right in Busch Stadium, with the Maris family in attendance and the national spotlight glowing. Which baseball market has more loyal, durable and knowledgeable fans? Is there any place that appreciates the history and the heritage of our National Pastime more?

As co-host of a call-in show on KFNS, an all-sports radio station, I got to feel this appreciation on a daily basis. The arrival of the new millennium spurred much reflection on the 100 years that just passed and the thoughtful phone calls poured in.

Fans loved to debate the proper make-up of baseball's all-century team. They argued long and hard about who should be on the all-time Cardinals team. These fans refused to live for the moment; in fact, many callers lined up to support "Sunny" Jim Bottomley over the remarkable McGwire for the all-time Cards team.

After all, Sunny Jim had six straight seasons of 100 or more runs batted in and he twice led the league in doubles. This all happened in the 1920s, but the real fans couldn't dismiss such greatness. This is when the winning started for the Cardinals, the winning that makes fans here so proud, the winning that is celebrated in this book.

Folks around here don't forget the past, they embrace it. They understand that a lot of tremendous baseball was played before the days of artificial turf, radar guns, retractable dome stadiums, $90 million payrolls, Sega showdowns and fielding gloves the size of serving platters. They can speak reverently of Walker Cooper's steady work behind the plate and Frankie Frisch's speed and versatility. They can honor the great Orlando Cepeda and lament that his time here was so short.

Sure, Joe Morgan was a spectacular second baseman. He had power and speed and he played full-tilt. Yes, Jackie Robinson was both a courageous pioneer and a true superstar who won games with his bat and feet. But ask Cardinals fans about the greatest second baseman the major leagues have ever seen and they speak reverently of Rogers Hornsby's numbers.

This guy was unreal. How about a second baseman who drives in 152 runs in a season? Or a batter who hits 46 doubles and 42 homers in the same season? Or a batting champion who enjoyed three .400 seasons in a span of four years? Awesome.

Yes, that was a different era of baseball. But within his era, Hornsby dominated as few infielders ever have. And before he left town, he helped the Cardinals win it all, in 1926.

When Cardinals fans read that Nolan Ryan was named the starting right-handed pitcher on baseball's all-century team, they spray coffee.

Nolan Ryan? How about Bob Gibson, who once finished a season 22-9 with a microscopic 1.12 earned run average?

Fans young and old line up to rave about his competitiveness and ferociousness. Wasn't he the driving force behind those great World Series teams in the 1960s? Bob starred in a glorious era of pitching, a time when the great hurlers dominated.

(Baseball felt sorry for the hitters and lowered the pitching mound, hoping to reduce the leverage these hard throwers enjoyed. These days, as any fan knows, baseball should raise the mound and maybe move it closer, too. Gibson could probably take the mound today and outperform some modern pitchers.)

And don't get these fans started on Stan Musial. Fans around the country slight "Stan the Man" because he didn't play in New York, but romantic figures like Joe DiMaggio had nothing on Musial.

Stan won seven batting titles. He banged out 3,630 hits and hit a staggering .331 for his epic career. He drove in 100 or more runs 10 times in his career and he led the league in doubles eight times. Most significantly of all, he won. The Cardinals were a monstrous team in the 1940s, one of the most dominant in the history of the game.

St. Louisans remember those players and the rest. Musial. Hornsby. Gibson. Bottomley. Lou Brock. Ozzie Smith. Johnny Mize. Mike Shannon. Joe "Ducky" Medwick. Dizzy Dean. Curt Flood. Marty Marion. Willie McGee. Pepper Martin. Red Schoendienst. Ken Boyer. Jack Clark.

The names go on, the memories go on. Pennants. World Championships. The White Rat, Whitey Herzog, ordering double steals.

This is baseball as it oughta be in St. Louis. Remembered.

Jeff Gordon
St. Louis Post Dispatch, KFNS All Sports Radio

The Glory Years
of the
St. Louis Cardinals

Volume 1
The World Championship Seasons

by
Mel R. Freese

Palmerston & Reed Publishing Company
St. Louis, Missouri
StLouisBooks.com

ROW THREE L-R   Johnson, Alexander, Rhem, Haines, Sherdel, Sothoron, H. Bell, Clough, Keen, Reinhardt

ROW TWO L-R   Flowers, L. Bell, Blades, CO. Killifer, MGR. Hornsby, CO. Williams, Bottomley, Toporcer

ROW ONE L-R   Hafey, Vick, Holm, Southworth, O'Farrell, Thevenow, Warwick, Douthit

1926

A Struggle To Win

Prologue

The Cardinals had been in the National League since 1892 and through 1925, they had never won a championship. The last time the franchise came home first was during the 1880 glory days of Chris Von der Ahe's team, then known as the Browns. The Browns prevailed four consecutive seasons from 1885-1888. Then the team was switched to the National League and was in the second division much of the time.

It wasn't until 1921 that the team developed into a consistent winner, finishing third in 1921 and 1922 and fifth in 1923. They slipped in 1924 and were headed for a deep second division finish in the 1925 season, when President Sam Breadon fired manager Branch Rickey and replaced him with Rogers Hornsby. The team was 13-25 and mired in seventh place. Under Hornsby's leadership the team regrouped and finished fourth at 77-76.

Hornsby had been the hero of St. Louis fans ever since he joined the team in 1915. He won six straight batting titles 1920-1925, hitting over .400 three times and averaging .397 for the six seasons. Hornsby would retire with a .358 career mark, second only to Ty Cobb. Many consider him the greatest right-handed batter of all time.

During 1925 Hornsby hit .403 in 502 at bats during 138 games. He missed 11 games in July due to a muscle pull in rib cage area and the final three games of the season because of an injured toe. On September 28th, while taking batting practice, Hornsby fouled a pitch off his big toe and split the nail. He summoned reporters to see the bloody toe so it wouldn't be thought that he was sitting out to protect his .400 average.

He also led the league with 39 home runs, 143 RBIs, 381 total bases, as he won the triple crown, and was the first Cardinal to win the MVP award. Jim Bottomley provided excellent support hitting .367, a league high 44 doubles and 227 hits, as well as 21 home runs and 128 RBIs. Ray Blades hit .342 and 112 runs scored and Les Bell hit .285 with 88 RBIs provided good hitting support.

It was pitching that let the 1925 team down, as only Bill Sherdel and Art Reinhart pitched consistently and effectively. Sherdel led the league with a .714 win percentage on his 15-6 mark, 3.11 ERA and 17 complete games in 21 starts. Reinhart was 11-5 and 3.05 ERA, completing 15 of 16 starts. The rest of the staff turned in poor performances.

Jesse Haines was 13-14, 4.57 ERA with 15 complete games in 25 starts. Flint Rhem was 8-13, 4.92 ERA and had just eight complete games in his 23 starts as did Allen Sothoron who had a 10-10 mark and 4.05 ERA. Duster Mails was 7-7, 4.60 ERA, completing nine of 14 starts, while Leo Dickerman was 4-11 with a horrible 5.58 ERA and only seven complete games in 21 starts.

Thus, entering the 1926 season the Cards did not have a pennant winning caliber pitching staff, but there was high hope based on their finish under Hornsby. The Cards were picked to finish third. Pittsburgh was the preseason favorite to repeat with the New York Giants and Cincinnati Reds also in the hunt.

The team would rely on hitting for the 1926 season and hoped that young pitcher Bill Hallahan, who had been in spring training in 1924 and 1925, was now ready. They picked up Vic Keen from the Cubs, where he was only 2-6 with 6.22 ERA in 1925, although he had won 15 games the previous season.

They also picked up Sylvester Johnson, once with Detroit, by drafting him from the Vernon, California team. He had undoubtedly one of the worse records for any pitcher drafted. He was just 3-17, although he played for a last place team. He would be of little value in 1926, going 0-3 and suffering a broken toe and broken ribs. He would later pitch winning ball from 1928-1931 for the team.

The club also picked up Walter Huntzinger from the Giants, but he too proved of little value, going 0-4 before he was traded to the Cubs.

5

Still the club had high hopes entering the season. They figured Chick Hafey would blossom into a star and that young Taylor Douthit would become the regular center fielder. Douthit would turn into a .300 hitter for the team and play a brilliant outfield. He was recognized as one of the game's finest center fielders in his day. Never a power hitter, he would bat near the top of the line up and score more than 100 runs three times as he played regularly through 1930.

Meanwhile Sportsman's Park had been enlarged to 32,000 seating capacity with the leftfield foul line distance increased 15 feet to 355 and right field five feet to 320 feet. During the 1925 offseason the squabble that had been going on between Breadon and Browns' owner Phil Ball about the rent the Cards should pay at Sportsman's Park was finally settled. Thus the team could now concern themselves with winning their first National League pennant, but they faced a tough obstacle course.

There were rule changes to help the pitcher. Home teams had to place a rosin bag on the mound before the start of each game to help the pitcher get a better grip on the ball. Also, the sacrifice fly rule was re-introduced, tacking a few points on to batting averages.

Regular Season Play

The Cards began the season with high hopes, finishing 22-1 in spring training. On April 13th the team opened at home against Pittsburgh. The Cards ran up an early 6-0 lead then held on for dear life as Flint Rhem beat the Pirates, 7-6. Bottomley homered and Hornsby had a double and two singles.

St. Louis took three of four from the defending champions and the air was filled with electricity as the fans were talking pennant and the season wasn't even a week old.

The only loss in the opening series was in the second game and it was a double loss as Haines was hit on right instep and was lost to the team for two weeks. The Cards, already weak on pitching, could ill afford to have one of the pitchers on whom they would depend be out for any length of time.

In game three, Keen earned a five-hit shutout. Johnson pitched eight strong innings in game four, allowing just four hits, but left trailing 2-1. In the ninth, the team rallied on hits by Bell, D'Arcy Flowers, as a pinch hitter, and Clarence "Heinie" Mueller. During the rally, Blades was hit by a pitch with the bases loaded to drive in one run and Mueller got the game winning hit. Sothoron picked up the win with one inning of relief.

Mueller was a St. Louis boy and, while never a regular, had been with the team since 1920 and had always provided a solid line of play whenever in the game.

The team then went on the road and was just 3-7, going 2-1 at Pittsburgh, 1-2 at Cincinnati, and 0-4 in Chicago. The 1925 trend seemed to be resurfacing, when they were just 30-47 on the road versus a 47-29 mark at home. You don't win pennants that way and Hornsby knew it. He had his work cut out for him.

Hornsby's attitude was simple. He only wanted ball players with winning attitudes on the team. Hornsby accepted no middle effort. He fined Reinhart $50 for failure to obey orders on April 20th in Chicago, setting an example for the rest of the team. Follow orders and have a winning attitude or else.

The Cardinal pitchers completed 11 of their first 14 starts. Thus the area of most concern going into the season seemed strong in the early going although the team had just six victories in those games. Meanwhile their expected strong suit, hitting, was faltering with a team average of only .251, fifth in the league.

Injuries plagued the team all season, especially Hornsby. He would have his "poorest" season since 1919, as he batted "just" .317 with 11 home runs, 96 runs, and 93 RBIs in 134 games. He was bothered nearly all season with misplaced vertebrae. He also had a protracted bout with carbuncles on his neck, ears, and thighs that kept him in daily pain. While missing just 22 games, he played many at less than full speed. He knew the team needed him, and he was trying to be the role model for everyone else. He was the leader.

The team played poorly on their next home stand as they were 1-2 versus Cincinnati and 1-3 versus Brooklyn. On May 6th against Cincinnati, Hornsby collided with catcher Val Picinich at second and displaced the two vertebrae that would bother him all season.

The only win against Brooklyn was a 3-1 win by Rhem, as the team got all its hits (three) and runs in the first inning off Dazzy Vance. Doug McWeeney then held the Cards hitless for six innings and Rube Ehrhardt pitched a hitless eighth. But, on only three hits, the team won. Hallahan pitched a six hitter, but the Cards got just five hits in a 3-1 loss to Brooklyn. They were getting pitching, but no hitting. St. Louis was now mired in seventh place at 11-15, going nowhere.

The Cards celebrated Rogers Hornsby day on May 22nd, so designated by St. Louis Mayor Victor Miller. Hornsby was presented with the Most Valuable Player medallion and $1,000 in silver. Commissioner Kenesaw Landis, National League President John Heydler and Cardinals President Sam Breadon were at home plate to congratulate Hornsby. Mayor Miller proclaimed Hornsby one of the city's greatest assets. The Phillies cooperated with the celebration by losing 9-2 and the Cards were at .500 with a 19-19 record, not a pennant winning pace.

So far in the season, the pitching had been okay, but the hitting was only sixth in the league at .263. Rhem, a product of the Cardinals farm system, was 7-1 and Keen 6-1, while the rest of the staff was only 6-17.

The Cards turnaround in the 1920s can be traced to their farm system, developed by Branch Rickey. It was this system of owning farm teams that would eventually make the Cardinals the premier team of the league for most of the next three decades. Soon other teams would follow suit and start their own farm systems, but the Cards were years ahead of them. They had been developing their own talent for many years and most players on the 1926 club were from the system. Rhem was a good example. He came from a town in South Carolina named for his family, Rhems. He was only 8-13 as a rookie, but was a real comer in 1926.

From 1926-1953, the team would win nine pennants, and six World Series, finish second nine times, and have only two seasons under .500. While several trades helped along the way, the success was mostly built on players developed in the Cardinals' own farm system. At one time the Cardinals had the deepest and richest system in the majors.

After winning three in a row over the Reds at home the team began a long road trip by losing four in a row to Cincinnati. Eventually the team would right itself to finish at the road trip 14-8 and move themselves into contention.

Until Hornsby took over as manager, not a lot of attention had been given to the "Flying Dutchman" as Mueller was nicknamed. Under Hornsby's tutelage he blossomed and hit .313 in 1925 and was batting .296 in 1926. However, the team was still under .500 on June 3rd at 22-24 and Hornsby decided to platoon Wattie Holm with Mueller.

The injury jinx continued as Keen split a finger on his right hand from line drive off the bat of Charlie Grimm in Chicago. Hafey developed eye trouble in Chicago and was sent back to St. Louis. This would be a lifelong problem for him and it would shorten his career and playing time. Even though Hafey is in the Hall of Fame, one has to wonder how good he could have been, given good health.

Bottomley contended that Hafey was a better hitter than Hornsby, as he had played with both. But, during his career Hafey was bothered constantly by sinus infections and had four opera-

9

tions, two in one season, trying to correct the problem.

Finally, by June 10th the team crept over .500 at 26-25, but was still in fifth place. Then the Cards made the first of two deals that would alter the course of events. On June 15th they traded Mueller to the New York Giants for outfielder Billy Southworth, a proven hitter and fine defensive player. He was six years older than Mueller at 32, but Hornsby believed he would solidify the outfield. Southworth would later gain fame as the manager of those great Cardinal pennant winning teams of the early 1940s.

Pitching problems prevailed as Johnson and Huntzinger faded out of picture, and although he was winning, Sherdel couldn't pitch that often. Herman Bell picked up some of the slack with a couple of wins. Haines at this point was an in-and-outer, while Hallahan was possibly too young and not fully developed. Meanwhile Reinhart wasn't fooling hitters as he did in 1925 and Sothoron was used mostly in relief.

After the Cards swept the Giants, they became the dark horse team and pennant fever once again started to build in St. Louis. The team still had many problems, as the pitching had started to falter and Hornsby and Bottomley were both hitting 100 points lower than last year. Injuries nagged Hornsby all year, but no explanation could be found for Bottomley's decline.

The outfield now seemed set with the addition of Southworth who had hit .317 since coming to St. Louis with 11 home runs, 76 runs and 69 RBIs and only nine strikeouts. For the season, in 135 games, he would bat .320 with 16 home runs, 99 runs, 99 RBIs and just 10 strikeouts. Plus, he was an excellent outfielder. Douthit played a great center field and batted .308 while Blades and Hafey shared left field.

Bell was solid offensively and defensively at third, while young Tommy Thevenow played a great shortstop and was a clutch hitter. The iron man of the team was Bob O'Farrell, as he appeared in 147 games, of which he caught 146. He was a clutch hitter, an excellent handler of pitchers and had a rifle arm.

The team got hot in the east, winning 11 of 12 games, losing only to the Brooklyn Robins. (It would be several years before the team would be called the Dodgers. They were named the Robins in honor of their long time manager, Wilbert Robinson.) The Cards then took two from Philadelphia, three from New York, and four from Boston, returning home in the thick of a pennant race.

The team would now be home from June 24th until July 25th except for five days. Hornsby was doing a great job in handling the pitchers, and Sherdel was coming along. He had two straight shutouts, one over Brooklyn and one over Boston, running his string to 21 shutout innings including the last three innings he pitched against New York. In the Brooklyn game the the Robins had only two hits, both by Jerry Standaert.

In the past, Rickey had Sherdel in the bullpen part of the time, but Hornsby had him starting every fifth day. Haines was in and out and if Hornsby could turn him around he it would be quite an accomplishment. Much of the team turnaround could be attributed to a pickup the club made on June 22nd.

On that date the Cards picked up Grover Cleveland "Pete" Alexander on waivers from the Chicago Cubs, where he had landed in the doghouse. Three teams claimed Alexander -- Cincinnati, Pittsburgh, and St. Louis. But on the day he was claimed, St. Louis was lowest in the standings and therefore got him. At the time, few realized what he would mean to the team. He not only provided a strong right arm, but his presence and influence lifted the rest of the staff and team.

Alexander was known to drink alcohol, but had always made certain his off-field activities didn't interfere with his pitching. However, when his performance on the Cubs faltered, manager Joe McCarthy disciplined him by suspending him from the team. This shocked the fans, for in that day and age the fans knew little about the off-field activities of the ball players. Babe Ruth was the obvious exception.

When McCarthy handed down the suspension, it was the sixth time in 10 days Alexander wasn't in condition to pitch. He was barred from the Cubs' dressing room in New York and McCarthy said, "I can't let him jeopardize the rest of the team and will not have him around in that condition. He hasn't been winning. I don't known what will happen to him. He has been drawing a big salary from the club and was of no use, so there was only one course to take. I won't stand for cutting up any longer."

Cubs President Bill Veeck, Sr. supported McCarthy and a trade seemed imminent. Although Alexander was twice offered to Cincinnati in the last two years, he was turned down both times. The reasons were not stated. When he left the Cubs his record was 3-3 with a 3.48 ERA.

Alexander suffered from epilepsy for years and had used alcohol to try to combat the effects of the illness. However, his drinking had just the opposite effect and made his problem even more severe. By the time of his suspension in Chicago, his drinking had gotten completely out of hand. However, Hornsby had the confidence that Alexander could still pitch winning ball and be a great influence on the team and the pitching staff.

Alexander would finish the 1926 season with the Cardinals with a record of just 9-7 with 2.91 ERA, but his real contribution was in the tone he set and leadership he provided for the team. He started, he relieved, and he did whatever Hornsby asked him to do. His real glory would come in the World Series.

In that day, many players did not respect managers who had not played the game. In 1926 there were seven playing managers in the majors, just two in the National League. Besides Hornsby there was Dave Bancroft of the Boston Braves. The American League had Ty

Cobb, George Sisler, Tris Speaker, Eddie Collins, and Bucky Harris. All five would eventually go into the Hall of Fame.

Hornsby wanted no "second division ball players." If, to win, he had to use "some egg I think is dumber than four humpty dumpties," he would. Hornsby wouldn't use "snitches" to spy on players. He would know when somebody began to slip. "A ball player owes it to the club to deliver the goods. If he doesn't, he is either gonna shake his habits or we will shake him out of the league." That was Hornsby's philosophy and it seemed to work with the Cardinals.

Hornsby previously had a retiring disposition, but as a manager he was now forced to attend luncheons, banquets, and other social and civic functions. "He had to socialize and at least pretend to enjoy it," observed Bill McGougan of the St. Louis Post-Dispatch.

The excitement was running high in St. Louis, as the fans hungered for a pennant. Most weren't around for the glory days of the 1886 St. Louis championship, so they wanted a championship of their own. That was the year the St. Louis Browns, managed by Charlie Comiskey, won the American Association championship ove Cap Anson's Chicago White Stockings. Six years later, the St. Louis franchise were accepted in the National League and became the Cardinals. This was the most excitement in town since 1922 when the Browns battled the Yankees for the American League pennant. The Alexander trade plus the team's improved play really inspired the city.

Just when it looked like everything was going the Cardinals' way, disaster struck. Hornsby was admitted to St. John's Hospital for removal of a badly infected carbuncle on his thigh. Bill Killefer took over the team and Hornsby missed 10 days. However, on July 9th Hornsby, against Dr. Robert Hyland's order, inserted himself back in the lineup. George "Specs" Toporcer had filled in at second during his absence.

However, as J. Roy Stockton observed, Hornsby "has no more in a swing than a girl would." While hitting consistently, he lacked power. Later in the month he missed another week. He would return in early August to help the team with six straight victories over Brooklyn.

The weekend of June 26th, the Cardinals played by the Cubs at Sportsman's Park. The Redbirds won Saturday's game when Hornsby hit a three-run homer for his 2000th career hit, although the team had been trailing 6-2 until the seventh inning.

On Sunday, June 27th the two teams were scheduled to play a doubleheader. The game drew a record crowd of 37,196 screaming fans. Pennant fever was running high and the win on Saturday had served to fuel the excitement. Fans started lining up at 8:00 AM and additional police were needed to contain the crowd. An estimated 10,000 were turned away.

The remodeled park now had a seating capacity of 34,000, but thousands more crammed in, hanging over walls, perching perilously in other places, and draping around steel network, with many more crowded in rear of the stands. If their eyes were good enough, they could catch a fleeting glance of a batted ball, but not the field. This was a more enthusiastic crowd than seen at a World Series game.

The Cards had gotten Alexander for the waiver price of $4,000 and on Sunday, June 27th, in his first start, he defeated the Cubs in 10 innings 3-2. Cardinal catcher Bill Killefer had been Alex's catcher in Philadelphia and Chicago and knew how to handle Alex. The two had been regarded as one of the greatest batteries in National League history.

Although now 39, there was still fire and a competitive spirit in Alex. When he arrived in St. Louis he said, "This looks like a pennant team. I'm not going to say anything about myself, but don't let anybody tell you that this arm doesn't have a few more good ones in it. I'm tickled to be with the team and Hornsby and Killefer. All Rog

14

has to do is nod his head and I'll jump through a hoop for him."

The Cards dropped the second game of the doubleheader 5-0 as Southworth got lone hit off Sheriff Blake, who fanned 10.

St. Louis was now 38-30 and in third place, trailing Pittsburgh and Cincinnati. With Hornsby out of the lineup the team headed for Chicago and earned one victory with the second game rained out. Next they traveled to Pittsburgh for three games. They won the first game in Pittsburgh and the Redbirds thought they were on their way. But they were wrong. Rhem was hit hard in a 7-3 loss,. Alex lost 3-2 to Ray Kremer and Bell and Keen were bombed in a 13-2 loss.

The team returned home, hoping to nurse their wounds, only to run into more problems. They dropped their first game home to Cincinnati, giving them four defeats in a row. They split the next four with the Reds to stay in the race. The team sorely missed Hornsby. Pitching was faltering as Rhem was not as effective as earlier and Keen had a sore arm.

Haines picked up some of the slack with a July 10th win over the Braves for his sixth straight. Alex had been pitching good ball in each start, but due to a lack of hitting was only 2-2. Rhem was rocked in three straight games by Cincinnati, Pittsburgh and Boston. No one could explain the reason for the reversal of form. Bell was also slipping, but Reinhart picked up some of the slack.

As if things couldn't get worse, they soon did. Some of the Cards were violating the 18th amendment (the Volstead Act, a.k.a, Prohibition) and showing up at the clubhouse with hangovers. One sportswriter stated, "The genial proponent of the theory that Volstead laws were made to be broken, is said to have accompanied the club as a sort of steward-in-ordinary."

Another added, "It might well be remembered that not only the batting eye, but the employee's eye is apt to become considerably clouded after revelations of the sort. It might be said the barometer has been falling rapidly at Sportsman's Park, with indications of a storm."

15

The Cards had not been known as a "joy" club in recent years, but always had an athlete or two who must have his poison. The current violations could affect the Cards pennant chances. Hornsby was taking no action. He didn't feel an occasional "dip" hurt, but was quick to post "don'ts" if it interfered with the pennant chase. Rog believed the players were old enough to know how to live.

After this episode nothing more was heard of the violations of the Volstead Act. If any occurred, they were kept under wraps, or at least didn't interfere with the Cardinals play.

Heavily bandaged, Hornsby returned to lineup. The bandages covered boils on left thigh, a boil on his left ear, and a spike wound on his hand. However, he still climbed the railing behind the Cards third base dugout to go after an abusive Brooklynite. Before any punches landed several Cards players pulled him back.

Later in the month the Redbirds took three straight from the Giants in St. Louis and briefly landed in first place. From then on the lead changed hands almost daily.

After an 11-10 home stand, the team headed out for a long road trip. They would be gone until August 14th. Rhem seemed to be regaining his form and Keen should be ready for a regular turn soon. Rog didn't heed Dr. Robert Hyland's advice and returned to duty too soon. He did it because the team needed him, but he hurt himself and was forced to miss almost a week.

St. Louis took two of three from Philadelphia and after Rhem won the first game in New York 5-2, it looked like the team was on its way. Then the Cards dropped four straight to the Giants and lost ground. Bell's hitting streak stopped at 21 games. He had hit .519 during the streak. The Cards were still third at 53-48, 4 1/2 games behind 55-41 Pittsburgh.

Hornsby got back in the lineup and his spirit rallied the team to six wins over Brooklyn. Even though he was not at his best he

16

inspired the team. There was just more confidence in the men when he was on the field, ailing or not, hitting .400 or .250. In the six game series, Sherdel won the opener 8-4, but more with his bat than arm, as he had a double, triple, and a home run, scoring two runs and earning two RBIs.

St. Louis moved into second at 58-49 and trailed Pittsburgh by just 2 1/2 games. The Cards were slowly closing the gap.

The fighting Cardinal spirit allowed them to put their ills and ailments behind them. They were bolstered by the leadership, determination, and grit of Hornsby. Bottomley got a boil and had his side iodined and bandaged and was back in the lineup. O'Farrell had been in 104 of the Cards 107 games, batting .280 with many clutch hits. He was one of the key reasons the Cards were in the thick of the pennant chase.

Thevenow turned an ankle in Brooklyn, reinjured it in Boston, but stayed in the lineup. Les Bell got a severe cold in Boston, had 102 fever and was sent home. Dr. Hyland expected pneumonia, but Bell announced he felt better. Though weakened, he played in the Cub series. On that home stand, every team but Cincinnati would visit the Cards.

The Cards would play Chicago, Brooklyn, New York, Boston, Philadelphia, and Pittsburgh in that order. The home stand would conclude with a five-game set with the Pirates, starting on August 29. After that the Cards would go on the road, which included Labor Day against the Pirates.

Only the Cubs and Reds had an edge on the Cards for the year. They trailed Chicago, 11-8 and Cincinnati 11-7. The Cards had just completed a successful road trip, going 11-6 with only the 1-4 mark against the Giants to mar it.

Rhem seemed to be back in form and Haines and Sherdel were doing well. Alex continued to pitch very effectively, but got very little support. In game one against Chicago Alex lost 3-2 due to errors. Rhem took game two 7-2 as Bottomley hits number 16 and Bell got his 13th home run.

Keen had still not returned to his former effectiveness, but fans surely would welcome the sight of him embracing O'Farrell after a win. Each time Keen won a game he would rush to home plate and give O'Farrell a big bear hug, and the fans would roar with laughter and applause. This soon became a tradition which the fans had missed the past several weeks with Keen out of action.

Hornsby liked the team's chances and commented as the home stand was about to begin, "Where we have an advantage over other contenders is in our pitching. We have more reliable men then either Pittsburgh or Cincinnati, and if we can just show some of our natural batting power we ought to go out in front during this stand at home."

As the home stand began, St. Louis was second at 62-46, just percentage points behind Pittsburgh at 61-45. The Cards proceeded to win eight in a row. The city had been on a "percentage" spree, but it had nothing to do with interest rates or the Volstead Act. It had to do with a decimal and its vagaries as it pertained to baseball standings. It was all because of a near dead heat in the National League, and the Cardinals trying to push a nose ahead so it can be said that they are in first place.

St. Louis was getting baseball thrills unseen since the 1922 Browns challenged the Yankees for the AL pennant. Hornsby's surprise team had set the town on its collective end. Few expected Hornsby, in only his second season as a manager, to have the team in a three-horse race with Pittsburgh and Cincinnati down the stretch.

The Cardinals good playing also made owner Breadon happy, as they packed them in at the old ball park. Not only was Breadon happy, but were the stockholders, as they saw big dividends coming at the end of the year. It was also rumored that if the team won the pennant, Rickey would get upwards of a $50,000 bonus. This was quickly denied, so as not to upset Hornsby, who was not given a raise to manage the team nor qualify for a bonus if they take it all.

Before the team left for the last road trip, they were already ahead of the 1925 season's total attendance by 20,000. It was Hornsby who deserved the credit as he had this club clawing, scratching, and fighting for every game. They played the same brand of ball, with the same vigor, win or lose.

While he was the boss, Hornsby was also part of the team and that was what the players liked and admired. Everyone was treated equally and there were no secrets. For this attitude, Hornsby got a 100 percent effort from every player. The question was often asked, "Where would the Cards be if Hornsby was hitting his usual .400 and Bottomley .360?" Most think they would have been at least six to eight games in front, if not more. Fortunately, their off years were picked up by others.

Rog was in a slump, but continued to play as if he were hitting .400. He was his own boss. Hornsby was carrying a mental load, not so much managing the team, but contending with "front office" politics. Rickey, whom he replaced, secretly envied his success. He was constantly asking Hornsby if there were other players he should bring up and how about playing so and so.

Friends believed that Hornsby would ask for a showdown with Breadon. It was a real shame this had to happen when the team was going so well and was in the middle of a pennant fight. As of August 26th, good pitching had carried the day. During that stretch Sherdel, Rhem (now back on track), Haines, and Alexander each had three victories with Reinhart and Bell two each, the latter getting his in relief.

Entering the final five weeks Rhem was 16-5 and seemed headed for his first 20-win season. Sherdel had come on to be 12-7 with Reinhart at 5-4 and Alexander at 6-5. Again it should be noted that

19

Alexander had pitched very well in almost every start, but was the recipient of few runs. Keen was only 10-8 after a 9-2 start. His second half was a real disappointment. Had he matched his first half the Cardinals would be ahead by six or seven games.

St. Louis hitting had picked up and, while only third in the league, the team batting average is up to .286. As the team headed for the showdown of the "Little World Series" with Pittsburgh, they were 66-50 and Pittsburgh was 64-48.

The "Little World Series" was a five-game set beginning on August 29th between the Cardinals and the Pirates. Thousands arrived in St. Louis by excursion trains from Indiana, Oklahoma, Texas, and other points south and west. Chartered buses made their way into the city displaying Cardinal banners. The whole atmosphere was one of a real World Series.

Ticket scalpers were selling $1.35 ticket for $5 and in some cases as high as $15. Scalpers caught by the police were turned over to the federal government. It seems when they scalped tickets they violated two laws. First, the ticket must bear the name of the seller. Second, the seller must pay the tax on any ticket over $1.00. Needless to say, the tickets didn't have the name of the scalper, nor did the scalpers intend to pay tax.

The five-game set drew 113,113 with almost 37,000 for the Sunday doubleheader. As luck would have it, one game was rained out and the second ended in a 10-inning tie, 2-2, as darkness ended the game. The second game was held up 2 1/2 hours and then resumed. Then came another 30-minute rain delay. Thousands got drenched, but they sat through it all to watch their beloved Redbirds.

Alexander started and relieved. Roscoe Holm had been playing in place of the injured Blades and O'Farrell continued in his iron man role, as he caught all but eight games. It seemed that the Cardinals, inspired by Hornsby, always rose to the occasion when the going was the roughest. No matter how bleak it looked a new hero came through.

Since that six-game sweep of Brooklyn in early August, the team went 20-5 to push them into a tie with the Pirates.

The Cards had the steel of champions because of the never say die manner in which they play. The team was filled with real "go getters" It had been a race of high tension for two months, requiring steel nerves and the Birds had them. Reverses came, injuries happened, and weaker men would fall, but the Cardinals had overcome all obstacles.

After losing the doubleheader to the rain, the Cards played two doubleheaders with the Pirates. They lost the first game 3-0 to Ray Kremer, but Haines won game two. In the second doubleheader, Sherdel took the opener and Sothoron won the nightcap, while Reinhart won game five.

The dark horse in this series was Sothoron. The veteran spitballer had been all but forgotten by the fans. He had pitched some relief, but it had been a long time since Sothoron had pitched a creditable nine innings. Fans are still asking what possessed Hornsby to start him, and it has yet to be explained. Perhaps Hornsby had a sixth sense, contact with a medium, or read it in the stars. Whatever the reason, Sothoron responded with a brilliant three-hitter (one an infield squibbler). Hornsby played a hunch and it paid off.

The team moved on to Chicago and took a doubleheader with Alexander winning in a three-hit shutout, 2-0 and Rhem winning 9-1. At Cincinnati the team wasn't so fortunate as they lost 4-2 and 5-3. One of the games was lost when Hornsby made an error on a pop fly. Trying to catch the ball he fell on the back of his head and was momentarily knocked out. This error led to four first inning runs from which the team never recovered.

Cincinnati was in first with the Cards one game back. Alex had just pitched in Chicago two days before, but knowing how important the final game was at Cincinnati, he went to Hornsby and offered to pitch with two days rest. Hornsby accepted and Alexander responded with a win. The team jumped into a first place tie at 82-60.

The newspapers were calling Hornsby The miracle worker, the miracle man, or similar titles. He shrank from fan hero worship and disavowed the miracle worker title. The Cards played strong for him because he was one of them. His common sense has paved the way to victory.

Why had Hornsby succeeded when Rickey failed? Hornsby's system was simple. He had no rules, except that the men must be fit to deliver winning baseball. If the players couldn't do that, they were fired, traded, or given away. Hornsby was absolute boss. The players knew that. When he gave one of his few orders, the players obeyed quickly and absolutely. Hornsby also did away with as many signs as possible. The only ones he kept were hit and run and sacrifice.

He wouldn't have sulking or pouting players or those who showed signs of displeasure. They all respected him and displeasure never happened. When he took over, he said if a pitcher sulked or threw his glove into the air when he was taken out of the game, Hornsby would follow him to the club house and punch him in the nose. He never had to do it.

The players loved playing for Hornsby. They knew he was the boss and they accepted it and liked it that way. The Cards might bend, but they would never break. Knocked down they got up and fought again.

They lost a 3-1 series in Boston while Cincinnati swept Brooklyn. However, the Cardinals took five of six from Philadelphia and Cincinnati had trouble in New York.

In the Philadelphia series the Cards lost one game by the score of 3-2, but scored 59 runs in winning the other five. A new record was set on September 16th when Philadelphia used 22 players and the Cards used 14 for a total of 36. The final score by the way was St. Louis 23, Philadelphia 3. Hornsby snapped out of his slump, and went 17 for 40 in Boston and Philadelphia while Bottomley was 12 for 23 in Philadelphia.

On September 24th, Southworth homered to beat his old team, the Giants, and put the Cards three games up with two to go. The team had clinched its first title as the Cardinals and the first one for the franchise since 1888. The Cards dropped their last two games but still finished two ahead of Cincinnati and 4 1/2 up on Pittsburgh.

Loud speakers were placed in strategic locations in downtown so St. Louis could carry a telegraphed play-by-play account of the pennant clinching game. Thousands went into the streets to celebrate. It was like New Year's Eve.

However, there were some problems the team had to face. Some of the younger players had not done well on base running. Hafey ran through Killefer's signal in New York and was cut down at home plate. Douthit, who had great speed, hadn't learned how to use it. He strayed too far off base and was picked off several times, sometimes in crucial situations.

More problems loomed for Hornsby despite winning the pennant. His health had not been good all season, and he had great concern over his dying mother to whom he was devoted. Lastly, interference from Rickey was starting to take its toll. Rickey had given unsolicited advice to players and also had a federal prohibition agent snoop on Alexander and other tipplers on the road.

Hornsby finally told Breadon he wouldn't manage or play for St. Louis in 1927 if Rickey were still there. Hornsby told local baseball writer Herman Wecke he was fed up with: "that Ohio Wesleyan bastard."

After Labor Day, Breadon insisted the Cardinals play exhibition games, at Syracuse and Buffalo, enroute from Pittsburgh to Boston. Breadon could see the large profits to be made from a team in the pennant race playing in a minor league city. Hornsby didn't want to and said the players were tired and needed the rest. Also there was the chance of an injury jeopardizing the team's pennant and World Series chances.

Breadon kept pushing Hornsby for these games and Hornsby kept refusing. Finally, after much badgering by Breadon, Hornsby shouted at him, "All right, but I won't send the first team! Now get the hell out of my clubhouse!" Breadon left, quite upset at being thrown out of his own clubhouse and privately vowed he wouldn't forget that act.

While Killefer took a couple of extra pitchers and mostly subs to the exhibition games, Hornsby went to New York with the regulars. They attended a game at Yankee Stadium, and he posed with Babe Ruth sitting atop the dugout.

Thomas Rice, writer for The Sporting News, stated that bum teams do not win pennants in response to the criticism heaped at the Cardinals. They were being called an overrated club, one that played over its head. Some New York writers thought the Cardinals didn't belong in the same stadium with their beloved Yankees. Critics claimed St. Louis mulled through to the title.

O'Farrell, who later was named MVP, best summed it up when he said, "Hornsby was a great manager as far as I was concerned. That year in St. Louis, he was tops. He never bothered any of us, just let you play your own game."

J. Roy Stockton, fast becoming St. Louis' foremost baseball reporter, offered a contemporary appraisal. "Hornsby went from being 'a colorless ballplayer' to a 'dynamic leader', a chief for whom his warriors would go any limit to win." Stockton quoted an unnamed New York writer who had remarked that Hornsby "is one of the most delightful characters I have ever met."

"He is the squarest, bluntest, cussingest, and most convincing man I ever met in baseball." Stockton added, "He is stubborn, bull-headed, he uses very bad language, and has some peculiar aversions. He can't mention a colleague with a few decorative adjectives. But you can't help liking Hornsby. He is just an honest-to-goodness person without guile or subterfuge. People trust Hornsby. He contributed much less statistically to his team due to his poor health. A healthy Hornsby might have given the Cards a runaway - maybe 100 victories if he had hit ala the 1920-25 years. This was his lowest average since 1919. He lost 15 pounds during the season and weighed less than he had since 1915."

On September 27th, just days before the series was to begin, Hornsby received a wire telling him that his beloved mother had died. She had wanted him to remain with the team. He wired a relative that he would remain with the team and come to Austin, Texas after the World Series. He then sent a telegram to his wife to join him in New York.

The season had many hitting and pitching stars. Southworth and Hornsby both contributed heavily. After his slow start, Bottomley finished the season batting .299 with 98 runs, 40 doubles, 14 triples, 19 home runs and 120 RBIs. The doubles and RBIs were the league's high water marks. Les Bell also drove in 100 runs, with 33 doubles and 17 home runs while hitting .325.

Douthit finished at .308 with 96 runs and 23 stolen bases and O'Farrell caught 146 games, batted .293 with 30 doubles and 68 RBIs. Hafey and Blades did a good job of platooning left field and had a composite 111 runs scored and 81 RBIs. In future years Hafey would better those numbers by himself.

On the pitching side Rhem tied for the league lead with 20 wins, while losing just seven games. Sherdel was 16-12 and Haines came in at 13-4. Reinhart, starting and relieving was 10-5. Alexander finished at 9-7, although with better support, that could have been several wins higher. The disappointment was Keen who ended at 10-9, after being 9-2 before the first half of the season ended. A sore arm slowed him down, and he was of little value in the second half of the year.

The World Series

The team was poised and ready for the World Series and the Yankees. They knew going in, they were the underdogs, but relished the role. They had been that all season. All season long they had to overcome adversity and misfortune, and prevail they did. They felt the same way about the Yankees and the World Series.

Both teams entered the World Series as hitting clubs, as each had led its league in slugging and runs scored. While we would see some of this firepower in the Series, pitching would dominate as each team bettered its regular season ERA by about one run per game.

The attendance at game one was 61,658 as they saw Yankee pitcher Herb Pennock out duel Sherdel, 2-1. Pennock allowed one run and two hits in the first, then blanked the Cards the rest of the way. Meanwhile, the Yanks scored a run in the first as Sherdel walked three batters. They put across the clincher in the sixth when Ruth singled, was sacrificed to second by Bob Meusel, then was driven home by Lou Gehrig with what proved to be the winning run.

Game two drew an even larger crowd as more than 63,000 attended. The fans saw another pitching duel as Alexander hooked up with Urban Shocker. However, this time St. Louis got the better of it, edging the Yankees, 6-2. Alex held the Yankees to four hits, three in the second,   and fanned 10 batters. Southworth had a three-run homer and Thevenow hit a solo blast to pave the way for the Cardinal victory.

The Series now moved to St. Louis, deadlocked at a game apiece. The momentum seemed to switch to St. Louis with the next three to be played in their backyard.

On October 4th at 3:50 PM an onslaught of people awaited the Cardinals arrival from new York as they pulled into the Washington Avenue Station under Eads Bridge. Hornsby and his wife, Jeanette, got separated in the melee and she began to cry. So did little Billy Hornsby who was waiting in a car in the care of his nurse.

Cardinal red was displayed everywhere. No matter where you looked you saw banners, buntings, sashes, women's dresses, men's ties — all red. This was the biggest demonstration in St. Louis since the 1918 Armistice. In stark contrast, the Yankees came into St. Louis almost unnoticed and stayed at the Buckingham Hotel.

On Tuesday, October 5th a record crowd of 37,708 showed up for game three. There was a 21-station midwestern radio hookup, anchored by the Post-Dispatch-owned KSD carrying play-by-play, with Grahame McNamee describing the events as they unfolded.

Haines was matched with Dutch Ruether and the game was all Haines. He not only pitched a five-hit shutout, he was also the hitting star with a two-run homer. Reuther was somewhat of a surprise starter as he was just 2-3 for New York, after being 12-6 for Washington a year earlier. With a 2-1 lead, the St. Louis fans went wild and now had visions of the Cardinals wrapping up the title in St. Louis.

However, the Yankees and especially Ruth, had other ideas. Waite Hoyt was matched against Rhem in game four. Rhem was quickly dispatched in his only Series appearance, as he allowed seven hits in four innings. It was a little strange that the team's leading pitcher appeared only once in Series play and then not until the fourth game. However, with the likes of Alexander and Sherdel, Rhem was pushed out of the picture.

Each team had 14 hits, but 12 of St. Louis' were singles. The Cards did manage five runs off Hoyt, but the Yankees doubled that number as Ruth became the first player in Series history to hit three home runs in one game. The Yankees' heavy lumber put the

Cardinals to sleep in game four and doused any hopes they had of clinching the title in St. Louis.

In 1961 Rhem related what happened when he was pitching to Ruth. Hornsby had told him in the first not to give Ruth anything fast, so he hit a slow pitch on to the right field pavilion roof. Hornsby gave the same advice in the fourth, saying Ruth had been lucky before. This time the ball cleared the roof and broke a Chevrolet dealer's window across Grand Avenue. That ended Rhem for the day. Home run number three came off of Herman Bell.

Game five saw a rematch of the opening game starters as Pennock and Sherdel hooked up again. Once more it was a pitchers duel and once again Pennock got the better of the two. The two played through a nine-inning 2-2 tie, but in the 10th, Yankee rookie Tony Lazzeri hit a sacrifice fly and that brought home the lead run. Pennock held the Cardinals in check in the bottom half and the Yankees headed back to New York, ahead three games to two.

The dreams of St. Louis seemed to be fading. From thinking about winning in St. Louis, the team now had to return to New York with their backs to the wall, on the brink of elimination. The Cards would have to win two in New York to be World Champions.

Sportswriters were writing the Cardinals' obituary and sounding their death knell. But the Yanks still had the 39-year old master, Alexander, to deal with. Alexander was matched with Bob Shawkey, and the Cards rocked him for three runs in the first, keyed by a single by Bell. He was knocked out in the seventh when Bell hit a two-run homer. Alex was superb as he threw just 29 called balls in 104 pitches and fanned Ruth twice. The Series was now tied at three games each. The attendance was just 48,615 as many assumed the Yankees would win.

After the game Alexander said that, if needed tomorrow, "I can throw four or five of the damndest balls they ever saw. Maybe a couple of innings, but I won't warm up."

Sunday, October 10th, the final game day was dark and ominous. It should have been a foreboding for the Yankees. Intermittent rain held the crowd to 38,000, in a game that would become part of baseball folklore. This would be one of the golden moments of World Series history. Years later, 10 times the attendance would swear to being at the game.

Haines, winner in game three, and Hoyt, winner in game four, were the pitchers. Three Yankee errors gave the Cardinals three unearned runs in the fourth inning and Pennock relieved for the Yankees in the seventh. The Yankees had took a 1-0 lead in the third and picked up a run in the sixth.

In the bottom of the seventh, with Cards leading 3-2, Haines loaded the bases by walking Gehrig. In throwing his curve he had raised a blister on the index finger on his right hand. Every pitch hurt, but Haines wanted to stay in the game. Hornsby signaled to the bullpen in the far leftfield corner. Rhem and Alexander were there. Rhem said Alex had celebrated in his usual fashion the night before and was dozing with a pint of whiskey in his pocket.

Alex, seeing Hornsby's signal, grinned, "staggered a little, handed me the pint, hitched up his britches and walked straight as he could to the mound," said Rhem. Alexander has always contended he deliberately walked slow so as to make the rookie, Lazzeri, nervous and sweat. He knew Lazzeri would be anxious, so Alex thought he would just make him wait a little longer by taking his time walking from the bullpen.

Hornsby greeted Alexander and explained the situation. Hornsby looked at Alex and asked, "Do you feel all right?" "Sure, I feel fine," Alex responded. "Three on, eh. Well, there's no place to put Lazzeri, is there? I'll just have to give him nothin' but a lot of hell, won't I?"

The first pitch was a curve too far inside for ball one. The second pitch caught the inside corner for strike one. Then Alexander deliberately threw a curve inside, knowing Lazzeri would pull it foul and he did, hitting a line shot 10 feet foul. A fair ball and he was the hero and Alex the goat. The last pitch was a fast ball low and outside for which Lazzeri lunged, but couldn't reach. Strike three. The inning was over.

Later when asked, "How do I feel?" Alex said, "Go and ask Lazzeri how he felt. I feel fine . . . the strain naturally was on Lazzeri." Alex then retired the side in order in the eight while Pennock set the Cards down in the eighth and ninth. Alex held a 3-2 lead heading into the bottom of the ninth.

Earle Combs and Mark Koeing were easy outs, but Ruth walked. With Meusel and Gehrig the next two hitters, nobody expected Ruth to run. But he did. On the first pitch to Meusel, Ruth took off. O'Farrell fired a bullet to Hornsby, who had the ball waiting, as Ruth slid into the tag, ending the Series, giving St. Louis their first of nine World Series titles.

Hornsby hit just .250 in the Series with six singles, one double, and four RBIs, but fielded flawlessly. He had played the entire Series with severe back pain. Bottomley hit .345 with five RBIs and Les Bell, although hitting just .259, led the team with six RBIs.

On the pitching side, Alexander was the hero with two complete game wins, a 1.33 ERA, and the classic save in game seven. Haines also won two games and had a miniscule ERA of 1.08. Sherdel lost twice, but pitched very effectively, finishing with an ERA of 2.12. Rhem got into just one game and pitched only four innings and had a 6.75 ERA.

A big reception was planned at Union Station, but Hornsby, his wife, and son slipped off at Washington Station and took a train to Dallas and made connections to Austin. On Wednesday, October 13th he attended funeral services held for his mother.

In St. Louis on Tuesday evening, October 12th, 30,000 gathered in darkness at Sportsman's Park to honor the 10 Cardinals still in town. (Remember no lights were in the stadium at the time.) Mayor Miller presided. The crowd celebrated and frolicked. Remarkably nobody fell out of the upper deck and no one was hurt or injured.

Epilogue

Breadon was still smarting over being ordered out of his clubhouse in Pittsburgh and also from profiting little from the Buffalo and Syracuse exhibition games. He retaliated by not coming to the Cardinal dressing room after the seventh game victory to congratulate the players. This was not only an insult to Hornsby, but to the entire team. He also allowed only two tickets for each player (presumably to spite Hornsby).

He then offered Killefer the managing job in 1927, but Killefer remained loyal to Hornsby and turned down the offer. The plot got thicker. Rickey got a $25,000 bonus, but Hornsby received zero. The players had gotten $5,944.50 as their winners share, which was more than many made during the regular season. The losers received $3,723.00. This was still in the days when getting to the Series meant big money for the players, often equal to or better than most of their salaries.

Although Hornsby was the second highest paid player in the majors at $33,000, he had not gotten more money to manage the team. He told Breadon he wanted a three-year contract for $150,000. Breadon would only go one year at $50,000. He also insisted Hornsby (a notorious gambler) would never again go to race tracks, play cards, bet on horses, or associate with people connected to horse racing.

Hornsby shouted at Breadon, "Horse playing was nobody's damn business and Breadon could take his ball club" and (as Breadon delicately paraphrased it to Stockton later) "perform an utterly impossible act."

31

That was it for Breadon. He decided that Hornsby had to go. Breadon eventually traded him to the New York Giants for Frankie Frisch. The deal was very controversial and for some time Breadon caught a lot of flack over the trade. In time things would smooth out as Frisch become a favorite of the fans.

It must be remembered that the Cardinals had just traded away the man who brought them their first 20th Century championship. He was also the greatest righthanded hitter in the game and the best hitter in the National League. He was a real favorite of the St. Louis fans. So to say the fans were upset would be putting it mildly.

Many local fans took his departure as a devastating civic loss. Mark Steinberg, a member of the Cardinals board of directors and Hornsby's stockbroker, called the trade "an insult to the fans of St. Louis" and resigned from the board. James M. Gould of the Post-Dispatch vowed never to cover another Cardinals game at Sportsman's Park (and didn't for nearly 10 years).

Officials of the local chamber of commerce asked Commissioner Landis to block the transaction, whereupon Breadon withdrew his membership in that organization. At his downtown auto dealership, Breadon discovered crepe hanging above his office door. So many abusive calls were made to his home that he disconnected his telephone.

At Broadway and Olive, a hoodlum jumped onto the running board of the Breadon's' Pierce-Arrow and shouted insults until a traffic policeman chased him away. But Breadon, rode out the storm. A week after the Hornsby trade, he named O'Farrell the new manager. Killefer joined the Browns as a coach.

Frisch would soon win the hearts of the St. Louis fans, although Hornsby would be sorely missed for a long time, as he batted .337, scored 112 runs, had 78 RBIs, and led the league with 48 steals in 1927. But defensively, Frisch covered more ground. And the first piece of the Gashouse Gang was in place. Over the next eight years

Frisch would be part of four pennant winners and two World Series Champions.

The Cards were not picked to repeat in 1927, but won three more games than the year before, and in a tight race, even closer than in 1926, the club finished second, 1 1/2 games behind Pittsburgh.

On the plus side, in 1927 Alexander was great with a record of 21-10, 2.52 ERA, completing 22 of 30 starts, and relieving seven times. Haines developed a knuckleball and had a career year at 24-10, 2.72 ERA and tied for the league lead with 25 complete games. Sherdel was in 39 games, completed 18 of 28 starts and finished at 17-12 with a league high six saves. The rest of the staff was just 30-29, reinforcing the difficulty of winning a pennant with just three dependable pitchers.

Two other hitters had big seasons with the bat. Bottomley batted .303 with 95 runs, 31 doubles, 15 triples, 19 home runs, and 124 RBIs. Hafey batted .329, but was limited to 103 games because of illness. This was to be his history during his career.

The rest of the club had problems. Douthit fell to .262 and Bell slipped to .259 with just 65 RBIs. But the worse was yet to come. O'Farrell missed much of the season due to a sore arm and shoulder. He split catching duties with Frank Snyder, and wound up hitting just .264 with only 18 RBIs.

Shortstop became the real problem when Thevenow broke his ankle and was out for the season. Several players were tried at the position, and all were found wanting. The group made a combined total of 64 errors. Thevenow made 18 in 59 games and batted just .194, while Heinie Schuble had 29 errors in 65 games, hitting .259. With marks like that it is no wonder the Redbirds didn't repeat as champions.

What is amazing is that they missed only by 1 1/2 games, thanks largely to the pitching of Haines, Alexander, and Sherdel.

Rogers Hornsby

Bob O'Farrell

Flint Rhem

Grover Cleveland
"Pete" Alexander

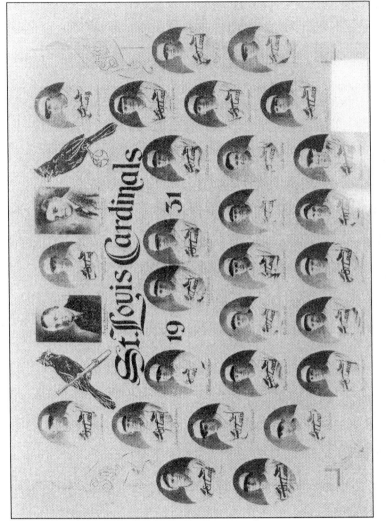

ROW FOUR L-R   Haines, Breedon, Street, Rickey, Grrimes
ROW THREE L-R   Johnson, Hallahan, Frisch, Wares, Lindsey, Rhem
ROW TWO L-R   D. Dean, Kaufmann, Gelbert, Mancuso, Wilson, Gonzales, Bottomley, Derringer, Stout
ROW ONE L-R   Martin, Orsatti, Watkins, High, Adams, Collins. Hafey Douthit Blades

1931

We Had It
All The Way

Prologue

In 1930, the Cardinals had climbed from mediocrity to the pinnacle of success by winning 40 of the last 53 games to finish first, two games ahead of Chicago and five ahead of New York. A spectacular stretch drive had placed the team in the World Series, but also had put a tired club there to compete against Connie Mack's powerful Philadelphia Athletics. St. Louis went down to defeat in six games.

The 1930 season is most remembered as one of the heaviest hitting in baseball history. The National League hit a combined .303, with only Boston and Cincinnati failing to hit over .300, although each batted a very respectable .281. The Cardinals set the National League mark for runs scored with 1,004, which still stands at the writing of this book in 1999.

The team had 12 men who batted over .300 with at least 100 at bats; 10 over .300 with 200 or more at bats. Rookies George "Showboat" Fisher and George Watkins hit .374 and .373, respectively, the two highest marks for rookies ever recorded. Franke Frisch led all others with a .346 mark and had 121 runs and 114 RBIs, while Chick Hafey hit .336 with 108 runs, a team high 26 home runs and 114 RBIs.

The pitching, needless to say, was not up to previous seasons. Their 4.40 team ERA was second best in the league and Bill Hallahan paced the staff with 15 wins and a respectable, for the time, ERA of 4.67. Burleigh Grimes, acquired from Boston early in the year, finished at 13-6 and a remarkable 3.02 ERA for the team.

Jess Haines was 13-8, Flint Rhem 12-8 and Sylvester Johnson 12-10. Herman Bell was 4-3 with a league high eight saves and the only other hurler with an ERA below 4.00 at 3.92.

The 1931 team had a lot to prove. First, they wanted to be the first National League team since the New York Giants of 1921-24 to repeat as pennant winners, and secondly they wanted to avenge their defeat in the 1930 World Series. They were hoping the A's, who were the favorite in the American League, would repeat, as they wanted another crack at them.

The Cardinals were picked to win the pennant, but this seemed a jinx, as no team had repeated in eight years. The Pirates won in 1925 and 1927, the Cards in 1926, 1928, and 1930 and the Cubs in 1929. The only National League teams to repeat so far in this century were the Giants of 1911-13 and 1921-24, and the Cubs of 1906-1908.

The Cards seemed to have the edge in pitching with Rhem, Grimes, Hallahan, Haines, Johnson, Jim Lindsey, and Al Grabowski. In addition, they had highly touted rookies Paul Derringer and Dizzy Dean. Grimes would be available all season, whereas he didn't do any real pitching for the Cardinals until July the previous season.

Regular Season Play

The Cards opened the season by sweeping Cincinnati and then won the first game at Chicago, but lost the second in which Cardinal Manager Gabby Street filed a protest. The Cardinals' Ernie Orsatti was on first when Bottomley hit a long fly ball. Cubs outfielder Riggs Stephenson raced back to make the play, but the overflow crowd touched it momentarily. The ball bounced out of his glove into the crowd. The umpire said the ball was caught fairly. Street protested.

Superb work by the Cardinal pitchers gave them an edge over their rivals. With so many good pitchers, the team was compelled to let Dean pitch the season with the farm team in Houston. After two weeks, the Cards had been in first place every day and were 11-3, after taking five of six from the Cubs, their most serious rival.

Club President Sam Breadon, in another of his tight moods, said Hafey couldn't play or be on payroll until he showed that his muscles were firm. If he played and was injured in line of duty and the team would have to pay him. If, however, he were injured during his five days of rehabilitation, that would be his misfortune. Remember those were the days of individuals owning ball clubs, and their word was final.

The fans would soon be cheering a new star if he could continue at his present pace. John "Pepper" Martin was a real crowd pleaser, besides being a great offensive and defensive player. Martin batted .363 in the International League and fielded brilliantly in the 1930 season. He got his chance to play when Taylor Douthit got hurt. Then Martin was forced out temporarily with a spike wound during a loss in Philadelphia.

While still in first, the Cardinal express was temporarily slowed down due to various injuries to players such as Bottomley and Charley Gelbert. Martin started slowly, dreading the day he would have to polish the bench when Douthit returned. But on the road he gained confidence and began tearing the cover off the baseball.

Martin's fielding prowess showed in an early game in Pittsburgh. With Grimes and Heinie Meine dueling into the 11th, it looked like Pittsburgh would win. Ben Sankey singled to right, Eddie Phillips sacrificed, and Tommy Thevenow singled to center. The fans started exiting, but they didn't count on Martin's strong arm. He threw Sankey out at home.

That play gave Martin the confidence he needed and he was a different player from that day on. In the 13th, Gelbert hit a triple and Martin told Street, "I'll hit one just as hard." He then got the winning base hit. The next day Martin had two singles, a double, a home run, and stole a base. It was going to be tough for Douthit to regain his job.

Martin had the more powerful arm, was more aggressive and while no one can chase fly balls with Douthit, Martin had not suffered by comparison to the brilliant regular of the team's championship days.

The only thing that seemed to be able to stop the Cardinals' march to their fourth pennant in six years was a three-game rain out with Boston. That made a total of 11 postponements in the first month. They had been able to play just 14 games. Street was not concerned as he believed he had pitching deep enough to handle the doubleheaders piling up.

Hafey returned to the lineup and resumed his normal fifth spot. Street hoped that with Hafey's bat in the lineup, the Cardinal attack would pick up. No one expected a repeat of the awesome offenses 1930, but plenty certainly thought the hitting would be better than it had been. It was the same story throughout the league.

Many were saying that the new ball was missing the jack rabbit and that meant managers would have to do more managing, according to Street. He made up his mind to just that after the series in Philadelphia, when the ball wasn't flying out of the park or up against the wall. During that series, there was only one ball hit over the rightfield wall and one against it.

Managers were going to have to change their style. Teams could not play seven innings waiting for a big explosion of runs then change strategies to playing for one run to win the game. They would have to play for one and two run innings right from the start. There weren't as many .300 hitters that season and the Cards had just three home runs in the first 18 games. Weak hitting slowed down the Cardinal express, but strong pitching kept them in first place.

On the eastern trip the team lost four of six games to Philadelphia, New York, and Brooklyn. Rain took care of the rest. Hafey got just two hits in three games at New York and was benched. He platooned with Orsatti until he regained his batting eye. Frisch, Watkins, Douthit, and Adams were hitting below their average. Only Bottomley was holding his own. The sacrifice fly rule was dropped, but that didn't account for the decline in averages.

Grimes said the Cardinals couldn't expect a repeat of their 1930 hitting performance. Fisher and Watkins were rookies and had out-

41

standing seasons. Fisher was gone and Watkins was struggling. All teams go through batting slumps and the Redbirds expected to bounce back.

The Cards were in first place every day since opening day, but the standings were close now as St. Louis was 18-8, New York 19-9, and Boston 17-12. In late May, the Cards started a long home stand by losing two of three to Pittsburgh, but bounced back to take five of six from Cincinnati. The Cards had trade discussions with Boston about Douthit for lefthander Tom Zachary, but the deal fell through. When Martin got hurt, the Redbirds were glad they hadn't made the trade, as they needed him in the outfield. He started to regain his batting eye.

Meanwhile Hafey started to hit as did Jim "Ripper" Collins, subbing for the injured Bottomley. Several Cardinals who were reserves could have been regulars for other teams. Once again the wealth and depth of the Cardinal farm system were paying off big dividends.

There is an old axiom in baseball, that good teams win the close games. The Cards showed this ability, by winning numerous games by one run in the eighth or ninth inning. By early June, the Cards lead was four games after they beat New York three of four and Brooklyn two of three.

The reserves and the bullpen were doing a good job. Douthit and Collins continued to impress when Martin and Bottomley were out with injuries. The latter was injured when he was beaned. Rhem saved games twice in one week by stopping the opponents after they loaded the bases. Allyn Stout saved the first game of the Brooklyn series and pitched two scoreless innings the next day as Cards tried to overcome a Brooklyn lead in game one of the doubleheader.

On July 15th, the Cards traded Douthit to Cincinnati for Wally Roettger. Douthit had a career .300 average. Although he never was a power hitter, he was regarded as a premier centerfielder. At the time of his trade he had nine straight hits, one short of the National League record, and was hitting .331. Roettger played with the Cardinals in 1928 and 1929 hitting .341 and .253 respectively. He had been traded to the Giants in 1930 and hit .283. At the time of the 1931 trade, Roettger was batting .351.

Injuries continued to plague the Cardinals as star shortstop Gelbert was injured taking batting practice before one of the games with the Giants. Nothing was mentioned about it at the time however he subsequently had trouble swinging and his average dropped 50 points. Finally he had to be taken from the lineup.

As a result the Cards suffered. They lost three straight to the lowly Boston Braves as various combinations at short and second didn't work. The Cards then tried Andy High at second, Frisch at short, Joe Benes at second, Adams at short, and High at third.

Street talked to Gelbert and promised to talk for him at contract time if he would return to the lineup despite his injury. He played brilliantly as Hallahan got his second consecutive shutout and the Cards salvaged the final game in Boston. They then swept a doubleheader from Philadelphia and on June 14th were three ahead of the Giants and four in front of the Cubs.

With Gelbert on the bench the team was a good hustling, but losing ball club. With him at short, the Cards showed new life and dash and looked like the champions of the circuit. He gave the team a spirited lift that doesn't show in the box score.

While Bottomley was out, Collins got red hot with the bat and hit .512 during a 12-game hitting streak with a 27 for 52 stretch that included six triples and five doubles. When Harry Seybold shut the Cards out 3-0 on four hits, Collins had three, including a triple.

The Cards re-acquired Jake Flowers from Brooklyn, marking his return to the team with which he made his major league debut. Since High and Benes didn't impress when Frisch and Gelbert were

43

injured, the team picked up Flowers. He could play anywhere on the infield and was a good hitter. Benes was then optioned to Houston.

About that time, the Cards developed some pitching woes as Haines was lost for about two weeks when a bone in his right hand was dislocated by a line drive off the bat of Brooklyn's Babe Herman. Perhaps not as effective as he once was, Haines still was counted on as a spot starter and long relief man.

St. Louis was still in first with a 37-20 record, but New York at 34-22 and Chicago at 33-24 were hanging tough. Cincinnati was last at 18-40. Bottomley was now back at first and Martin would lead off with Frisch batting second and Watkins hitting third.

After losing a game to Philadelphia the team bounced back to win a doubleheader, but each game was a struggle. In game one it took a three-run rally in the ninth to win 4-2. The night cap was won by the same score as Watkins hit three home runs and drove in all four runs.

The team's struggles continued in Brooklyn, where they faced Dazzy Vance. He retired the first 20 men before Watkins (who had fanned his first two times) bunted for a single. Bottomley then singles him to third. When Vance kept throwing to first, Watkins stole home for the only run of the game and Derringer held on for a 1-0 victory. Then they lost a doubleheader to Brooklyn 7-0 and 4-3 and the race tightened up. St. Louis was 41-24 and New York was 39-26.

In early July, St. Louis completed its road trip at 11-11 and still was 3 1/2 games ahead of New York. They opened the home stand with four against Chicago and unless they lost all four and New York won its next four, the Cards would remain in first place.

Brooklyn became a new challenge by moving into third after taking four of five from St. Louis and then sweeping the Giants at the Polo Grounds. They were just four games out, not a big deficit for such a heavy hitting team.

The good news on the road trip was that Rhem pitched excellent ball, winning three times, twice in Philadelphia and once in New York. For the year he could have a better record with more consistent hitting behind him.

Brilliant fielding was also the name of the game for the Cards on this trip, as Martin and Gelbert stood out. Martin made a catch in the Polo Grounds that many called one of the greatest of all time. Ethan Allen hit what looked like a sure double or triple to left center, but Martin made a leaping catch and held onto the ball as he turned a couple of somersaults, his spikes digging up the turf in the process.

The injury jinx struck again when Hafey injured a muscle in his back sliding into home plate at Philadelphia and was out for a week. When he did return, he complained that he couldn't bat, run, or throw. He didn't show his usual punch and power at the plate. On the good news side, Haines seemed ready to go again when he pitched effectively in relief against the Cubs on July 6th.

Approaching the mid-season point, St. Louis was still in first with a four-game bulge over New York, a five-game lead on Brooklyn and Chicago resting in fourth, 5 1/2 games back. The team had held the lead continuously since opening day. Their lead had been as wide as five games and as close as a few percentage points.

This team differed from other Cardinal pennant winners in several respects. The 1926 and 1930 winners both had to make gigantic runs at the pennant to win. Each club faced large deficits and only a spectacular drive enabled them to overtake the front runners and finish first.

After two thirds of the 1926 season, the Cards trailed by 4 1/2 games, but a 36-17 drive placed them two games in front of Cincinnati. The 1930 Cardinals had to come from even further back to win the pennant. After 99 games they were just 50-49 and it took a 42-13 finish to give them their final two-game edge over the Giants.

The 1928 team started slowly, floating between second and fifth until late June when they climbed into second place to stay. By the end of the month the team was in first place and would remain there for the balance of the season, withstanding a charge by the Giants in September when they won 25 games, but fell two short.

The 1926 team led the league in home runs, while the 1928 team hit over 100 and the 1930 club was the heaviest hitting Cardinal team of all time. The 1931 team hit just 60 home runs, but had 114 stolen bases, the most of any of the four championship teams. Despite the injuries to Rogers Hornsby in 1926, that team as well as the other two weren't plagued with the extent of injuries of the 1931 team.

While certainly each of the teams had its share of good pitching, each club was limited to the dependable pitchers they had. The real strength of the 1931 team is its depth of pitching. The team carried only nine pitchers, with eight having winning record and the ninth, Tony Kaufman, was 1-1 in 15 games.

The Cardinals opened the second half with a four-game set against the Chicago Cubs and a patched up infield. Gelbert jammed his heel in a game in Chicago. Flowers took over and was spiked so Adams replaced him only to get a charley horse. All of the sudden three infielders were down with injuries.

Flowers had to be reinserted in the lineup to play game one of the July 12th doubleheader, but his wound kept opening so despite the severe charley horse, Adams had to play in game two. Needless to say this weakened the defense, as Adams was not at full strength.

On the brighter side Haines returned as a starter and held Cincinnati to one run. Now, along with Hallahan, Derringer, Grimes, Johnson, and Rhem, the Cards had six starters. Some would start every fifth day and some, like Haines, every sixth day. In addition, several could be used in relief, as illustrated best by

Derringer, who made 12 relief appearances.

Pennant fever was once again gripping St. Louis and a new record crowd appeared for the Sunday, July 12th doubleheader with the Chicago Cubs. The people could smell a pennant and the passions were running high as the fans saw a fourth pennant in six years. Another trip to the World Series was in the offing.

But problems developed before game time as there was not sufficient police to control the crowd and the fans became unruly. Finally the crowd broke up, but the disturbance prevented infield practice for either team.

Due to the overflow crowd it was necessary to rope off sections of the outfield to allow the fans to stand on the grass to see the game. The crowd was only 70 feet from first base and almost as close to third base from the left field wall. The reason for the overflow crowd was two-fold. First, the aforementioned pennant fever, and secondly, the Cubs had been the best draw for several years. A natural rivalry, which continues to this day, had been born. It makes no difference the record of the two teams when they meet. Each gets a shot of adrenaline from playing the other.

The doubleheader saw a major league record for doubles, as a total of 21 were hit. Most sports people who saw the game, say perhaps six were legitimate hits. The other 16 would have been routine outs under normal conditions. The ground rule established for the game was that any ball that went into the crowd behind the ropes on the field was an automatic two-base hit. Ordinary pop flys became two baggers. It was a pitchers' and outfielders' nightmare.

Derringer, who had beaten the Reds, won the first game in relief against the Cubs. Johnson had returned to form by beating Cincinnati a few days earlier.

The day prior to the doubleheader St. Louis had notched it's 50th win. It didn't win number 50 in 1930 until August 2nd. The current team was three weeks ahead of last season's pace.

St. Louis at 52-31 was 4 1/2 games ahead of the Giants, six up on the Brooklyn team and 6 1/2 ahead of the fading Cubs. The Cards could only place two hitters in the top 20, with Roettger number eight at .334 and Collins number 19 at .312. It was the pitching that held them in first place. Haines was 6-2 and Hallahan came on at 9-6. Meanwhile Derringer and Grimes were both 10-game winners with a chance to win 20.

By the end of July, St. Louis was trying to put more distance between themselves and the rest of the pack. There is another old axiom; beat the stuffing out of weak ball clubs and break even with the good teams. Up to this point St. Louis had a big lead on doormat Cincinnati (last with a 28-53 record). They were ahead of the Cubs, even with Brooklyn, and already assured of a split with New York.

On July 19th the Cards widened the gap against the Giants by sweeping a doubleheader by identical scores of 2-1. In game one, the team got only four hits off Carl Hubbell, but made the most of them as Johnson held the Giants in check. In game two, Derringer bested Jack Berly, as the Cards rallied with two in the 9th to win the game.

As with most good teams, it took effort and performance from everyone to become a champion. The Cardinals were no exception. The reserves were earning their pay. Flowers had a home run, double and two singles in helping to beat Vance. The day before he hit a triple and two doubles as Grimes beat the Cubs.

Another reserve, Orsatti, played rightfield in the night cap and in the 9th inning, drove in the winning run with a double against New York, while Derringer fanned eleven for the second time this season. He was now 11-4 and Grimes was 11-6.

The last rookie to win 20 games was Wes Ferrell for Cleveland in 1929 when he notched 21 wins. Derringer was being touted as having an excellent chance to win 20 games. He figured to start another 14 times and, with 11 wins already, should crack the 20 barrier.

Gelbert was available for duty in the Giant series and his play sparked the club. Meanwhile catcher Jimmy Wilson, who had been out for a week with a sore finger, returned to the lineup. The Cards still were not hitting as they were capable, but their pitching kept the team number one.

As the team moved towards the last week of July they were 56-34 with Brooklyn second at 49-39, six games out. The Giants had fallen to third at 46-37, 6 1/2 back and the Cubs were 47-38, 6 1/2 back also.

Most baseball men were giving the pennant to the Cardinals, but Street wasn't taking anything for granted. As far as Street was concerned the team didn't have it locked until they had a 10 game lead with nine to go. He well remembered 1930, when his team came from 12 back to take it all. He was conceding nothing and wouldn't allow his boys to let up. He insisted they bear down all the way.

During their hot home stand the Cards were 4-0 versus Cincinnati, 3-1 against New York, 3-0 over Philadelphia, 3-1 against Chicago and a 1-1 record with Boston. The team would have a short road trip in the west, playing Chicago and Cincinnati and then a 15-day trip to the east where they would meet all the clubs.

During the road trip in August the team would played the contenders in succession. Street believed that if they played satisfactorily against the contenders, the club could take the title. They wouldn't clinch it mathematically, but they could put it virtually out of reach.

Before departing on their long road trip they split four games with the Braves and a doubleheader with the Cubs. Grimes beat the Cubs in game one 10-2, but Hallahan was the loser by the same score in game two.

In opening the road trip, Johnson lost a tough one to Chicago 3-2, but Derringer came back to take the nightcap 5-2. The Cards out hit the Cubs, 11-10, but bunched three in the second for two runs and five in the third for three more, snapping the Cubs' Charley

Root's six-game winning streak.

The Cards now headed to Pittsburgh, whose pitching staff had hurled four straight shutout wins and a total of 40 consecutive scoreless innings. They also must make the trip to Pittsburgh without Collins, their aggressive young first baseman. He tripped over first base running out a grounder in Chicago and was sent back to St. Louis with a sprain. He would wait their until the team returned to play Chicago again.

Bottomley was now back at first base temporarily. It was a rarity for a team to carry two players of such quality as Colllins and Bottomley only to sit one of them on the bench. It was almost certain that one of them would not be with St. Louis next season. Although Bottomley had been with the team since 1922, had given many great seasons, and was a fan favorite, he would probably be traded. Collins was four years younger. Street was re-signed for 1932, giving him a strong vote of confidence. His signing also spurred the team, as it showed management appreciated the job he did.

In game one against Pittsburgh, Haines defeated his old nemesis, Meine, 7-1. Meine had extended the scoreless string to 45 innings before St. Louis broke through.

The Pirates won game two 5-4 in 12 innings. For 11 innings Rhem and Larry French had battled to a 4-4 tie. In the 12th, Rhem argued a ball called by umpire Quigley, got mad, threw his glove in the air, and was ejected. Then he let go with a tirade and was eventually fined $50. Lindsey relieved and Pittsburgh got a scratch run to win. In the second game of the doubleheader, the Cards won 16-2 behind Hallahan. Bottomley tied a record in the second game by going six for six.

St. Louis returned home and Grimes picked up his 14th win as he shut out Chicago 8-0 in the first game of a doubleheader. The Cards also picked up the nightcap and almost killed Chicago's hope for a pennant. Their team was managed by Roger Hornsby, the old Cardinal star and manager. The Cubs did salvage the final game of the series on a one-hitter by Guy Bush.

Bottomley was making the most of his playing time. In addition to his big game at Pittsburgh he was four for seven in the double-header with the Cubs. He was 12 out of 17 since his return to the lineup, so even when Collins recovered he would probably stay on the bench for awhile. It was a good news - bad news situation. The better Bottomley hits, the more his value increases for a trade, but fans will then miss him even more.

Breadon, warranted or not, had a reputation that he liked to fire managers, but he contended that was not true. He said he just never had the right man. It wasn't Hornsby, O'Farrell, or Southworth, but when Street was reappointed on August 7, 1930 and the Cardinals were in fourth place, that seemed to spur the team and they went all the way to win the title.

Breadon said Street knew how to handle players, especially pitchers, and was an astute baseball man and diplomat. He was a good business man and could cooperate with the front office. The latter was very important, given the personalities of Breadon and Rickey.

As mid August approached the Cards big eastern swing was beginning. They polished off Brooklyn in a four-game sweep then split four with the Giants. The team was moving closer to putting the National League flag over Sportsman's Park once more. In 1930, the team was worn out from the stretch drive, but in 1931, the pitching staff was in fine condition and everything was working smoothly.

Against Brooklyn, Hallahan picked up his 13th win by defeating Vance, but Derringer couldn't get number 14, as he left after six innings, trailing 3-1. The Cards rallied to win with Allyn Stout, from Webster Groves, 4-0, the winner. Stout held Brooklyn to one scratch hit in three innings. Wilson said, "He has one of the best curves in the league. And against the Robins that day he made Derringer, a pretty fast man himself, look like a slow ball pitcher."

The pitching was solid with Haines at 10-2, Grimes at 14-7, Derringer 13-5, and Hallahan 13-8. Time was running out, though, for anyone to win 20 games, as each only had seven or eight more starts, depending on doubleheaders. Derringer had the best opportunity, but a slump right after mid-season slowed him down. He seemed to be back on track, but was still seven wins away from 20.

The hitting had improved and the club had three hitters in the top 16. Bottomley was hitting so well that Collins couldn't get back in the lineup. Against Brooklyn, Bottomley was 10 out of 18, including two doubles, a triple, and a home run.

The Cards lead grew to 8 1/2 over the Cubs, 12 /2 over the Giants, and 15 over the Robins. Street's main concern was that his team didn't get complacent or start to loaf.

The Cards main challengers were cutting each other up and no team looked like a repeat of the 1930 Cards. As the month of August drew to a close, the Cards seemed to hold a commanding lead. However, they remembered 1930, when they were eight out on August 23rd and still won it all. However, it didn't look like the Giants could repeat that performance. The Cards had just 34 left, while the Giants had 37.

The Cards were trying to get a double digit lead over the second place team to no avail. Although they couldn't improve on their lead, none of the challengers could make a real dent in it either. It was status quo and as the Cards won or lost a game, that was just one fewer on the schedule.

All season long, even when the team was not hitting, the pitching carried the club. Now that the hitting started to come around, the pitching was just another plus. However, Street did have some concern about the team's play after they left Brooklyn, where they swept a four-game set. Among the things they did wrong was throwing to the wrong base and leaving second base uncovered.

Adding to Street's concern was the decline in stolen bases. The stolen base was no longer a major weapon. The Cardinals would finish the season with a league-leading mark of only 114. The next nearest team was New York with 83, followed by Pittsburgh with 49. No other team would finish with as many as 50. Nearing the end of August Frisch had just 17 steals, and led the league. He would finish with a league high 28.

As August drew to a close St. Louis hung onto its 8 1/2 game lead, this time over New York. St. Louis was 78-44, New York was 68-51, Chicago at 67-56 was 11 1/2 out, and Brooklyn at 66-59 was 13 1/2 behind. The Redbirds had 32 games left to play and the Giants 35. If the Cardinals split their last 32 games, the Giants would have to finish 27-8 to overtake them.

The Cards showed they were a stronger team than the squad that won it all in 1930. Their hitting might not have been as robust, but in the 1931 season no team hit as it had the previous year. 1930 was a once-in-a-lifetime year. The depth in the pitching staff, starting and relieving, made the difference for the Redbirds. Add in the strong reserves the team was able to put on the field and the 1931 team was a solid ball club, up and down the lineup.

Despite a large lead, Street still refused to discuss the fall classic with sportswriters until the Cards clinched the flag. Street said it was a greater strain to have an 11-game lead than it was to fight for first place because you have to fight complacency, players being nonchalant, and taking for granted they have it won. Nonetheless, everyone was talking about who should pitch the opening game against the Athletics.

Street's answer to them all was simple. He said let's clinch the title then we can make these types of decisions. Street wanted to win the title as soon as possible. He said, "then I can think about my rotation for the Series, rest some of the regulars, get the pitching lined out, so we can beat those guys this time." Street firmly believed his Cardinals would defeat the powerful Athletics.

By the time the Athletics entered the 1931 World Series they had won 313 games over the three years, an average of 104 wins per season, with their lowest win total of 102 in 1930. They also won two World Series titles. They took four of five from the Cubs in 1929 and defeated St. Louis four games to two in 1930. They were no pushovers. They had pitching, hitting, power, and defense.

The Cardinals completed a great eastern trip at 13-4 by sweeping Brooklyn in four, splitting four with New York and Philadelphia, then taking five straight at Boston. This run pushed the team to a 9 1/2 game lead over the Giants. They then returned home to take three of four from Pittsburgh.

Not only did the pitching continue to be outstanding, the hitting had really picked up as Hafey and Bottomley were tearing up the league. They were in a four-way batting fight with Bill Terry of the Giants and Lefty O'Doul of Brooklyn. Bottomley had also shown considerably improved defense over 1930.

Meanwhile Gelbert and Frisch formed a great double play combination which made the infield play much smoother. Adding the play of Adams at third base, which at times was brilliant, the Cardinals had the best defensive infield in the league.

The outfield also deserved its share of accolades. Watkins and Roettger each performed very well, both offensively and defensively. Hafey was not only an excellent hitter, but an exceptional outfielder with a strong arm. However, the best was Martin. He was even better than the great Douthit. Martin possessed a magnificent throwing arm and was one of the most aggressive players in the league. He would challenge for any ball hit anywhere.

Added to all the above was the standout job that Wilson did handling the catching duties. He was not only a strong receiver, but did extremely well in handling the pitchers, as evidenced by their records. This did Street's heart good, as the Old Sarge was an ex-catcher himself.

With just a little over three weeks to go it looked like St. Louis had it all sewn up with an 11-game lead, but fate stepped in. The Cards had three open dates while New York won several make up games. Then the Cards lost three straight at Pittsburgh and all of a sudden, the lead had shrunk to 5 1/2 games.

Fans and sportswriters started asking if they were going to see a repeat of 1930, only in reverse. Were the Giants going to get red hot and then overtake the Cards as they sputter and stagger down the home stretch? Would this be payback time for the Cards?

The team really shouldn't have lost three games at Pittsburgh, but they did not play like the team that had been in first place since the outset of the season. In game one Grimes blew a 4-0 lead, helped by an error by Gelbert that paved the way for defeat.

In the second game of the series, old nemesis Meine defeated the Cardinals for a fourth time that year. This time, the score was 3-1 and Hallahan was on the losing end of the game. Another error by Gelbert, this time on a double play grounder and a misjudged fly ball by Martin led to the defeat.

In game three, Haines had a 5-0 lead but couldn't finish it. He left the game leading 5-4 and Lindsey came in. Lindsey had done a good job coming out of the bullpen that year and would finish the season with a 2.76 ERA and a team high seven saves, but this wasn't his day. The Pirates knocked him around and he took the loss in an 8-5 game.

However, an even bigger loss was that Haines might not be available for the Series as he felt something tear in his arm in the Pittsburgh game. He was sent back to St. Louis to see Dr. Hyland to determine how serious the injury was and whether Haines would be able to pitch in October.

The Cardinals had not come this far and held the lead since opening day to let it fritter away now. They gained some ground back with a doubleheader win at patsy Cincinnati while New York lost to Boston. All of a sudden the lead was back at eight games. The Cardinals had to be careful of the shrinking of their big lead. They sure didn't want to panic. The Cards had just 20 games left and at 86-48 had an eight-game lead. It looked like they were in, but anything could happen. The Cardinals would play the eastern teams at home then finish with a three-game set with last place Cincinnati on the road.

Just as the Cards made a spirited drive in 1930 to overtake the Giants, they put on a similar spurt in 1931. The difference was that this time they pulled away from all challengers, as they won 15 of their last 20 games to finish at 101-53, 13 games ahead of New York, 17 ahead of Chicago, and 20 in front of Brooklyn.

The final standings made it look like the team had a cakewalk, but that wasn't necessarily so. Although the Cardinals led every day of the season, it did get close and during the last two months the lead, on occasion, did shrink to as little as four or five games.

Every time they seemed to stumble slightly and it looked like someone might over take them, the team got a new shot of energy, ran off several wins in a row, and put some more distance between themselves and their nearest competitor.

On September 22nd at 2:22 P.M., the Cardinals clinched the pennant as the Reds beat New York at Cincinnati before St. Louis could clinch on their own by beating Philadelphia. There was great relief that it was all over. Now that the pennant was clinched, Street could turn his attention to the World Series. Indications were that with Haines not available for the Series, Street might start Derringer. He had a great start running his record to 10-3, then sputtered, but he righted himself and finished his rookie season at 18-8. It was a giant responsibility to place on the shoulders of a rookie, but Street believed the Derringer was up to the challenge.

Another problem facing Street for the Series was the availability of Grimes. He became ill after the last eastern swing and had been slow rounding back into form. He had a chance at 20 wins, but illness sidelined him and he had to settle for a 17-9 record.

Hallahan would probably pitch game two as he had been brilliant for the last six weeks. After a slow start, Hallahan finished at 19-9 for the season, tying Meine and Jumbo Jim Elliott of the Phillies for the league high in victories.

Other problems that worried Street were Frisch, Adams and Johnson as each had various illness or injury in the last month. Frisch really worried Street when on September 12th he became ill. It turned out to be a bad case of indigestion from some bad lobster. Frisch also has a sore thumb, but didn't let it affect his play. Street said that a lesser money player would be sitting on the sidelines.

Johnson contacted a bad case of poison ivy, but pitched three good innings of relief against Brooklyn on the home stand, so he should be ready. He also had shutout wins in the last weeks of the month over Cincinnati and Boston. With Haines and Grimes both sidelined, Johnson and Rhem, almost the forgotten man of the staff, were starting.

Street would probably use Johnson out of the bullpen. With two days off between the second games, and third he planned to use Derringer and Hallahan in games one and two then again in three and four. However, depending on their performance and the outcome, Street said that could change. It looked like Johnson would be in the bullpen, as not as many starters will be needed.

The Cardinals challenged Brooklyn to a mock track and field meet on September 21st and that was where Adams got hurt, but he would be okay for the Series. The meet consisted of circling the bases, bunting and running to first, 75-yard dash, and throwing for accuracy by catcher. Martin was extremely eager to participate, as he was considered the fastest runner on both teams, so he believed he could win many of the events.

With the exception of Van Lingle Mungo's victory in the 75-yard dash for pitchers, the Cardinals swept in the five field events. The results were as follows.

Circling the bases—Orsatti, 14:5; Denny Sothern (Brooklyn), 14.6; Watkins, 14.9

Bunting and running to first—Adams, 3.4; Watkins 3.6; Collins 3.7

Pitchers 75-yard dash—Mungo, 9.0; Stout, 9.1; Cy Moore (Brooklyn), 9.2, third

Accurate throwing for catchers—Gus Mancuso (Cardinals); Ernie Lombardi (Brooklyn); Wilson

75-yard dash, open for all—Frisch; Denny Sothern (Brooklyn); Orsatti

Scheduled 100-and 220-yard dashes were not held.

To Martin's chagrin he didn't win any of the events. Adams surprised all by winning the bunting and running contest, but when trying to win $50 more in base circling event he sprained an ankle rounding first base. In addition, on this day Street caught three innings and threw out Babe Herman trying to steal second.

The 1931 season featured one of the hottest batting contests ever, with the closest finish ever on record in the National League. Hafey was declared the winner at .349 (actually .3489) with Terry second at .3486, and Bottomley third at .3482. One basehit more from either Terry or Bottomley would have given either of them the title.

The World Series

The Cards were headed for their fourth Series in six years and hoped to even their Series record at 2-2. They had defeated the Yankees four games to three in that historic 1926 Series when Alexander fanned Lazzeri with the bases loaded in game seven and

Bob O'Farrall cut down Babe Ruth trying to steal to end the game and the Series. Then the Yankees swept the Cardinals four straight in 1928 and the A's defeated them in six games in 1930.

This was the first time the Cards had won back-to-back pennants and they were looking to upset the mighty and powerful Philadelphia Athletics. The A's were heavy favorites to defeat the Cardinals and to win their third championship in a row.

Both were good hitting teams as the Athletics batted .287, while the Cardinals hit .286 during the regular season. The Athletics outscored the Cardinals 858 to 815, hitting almost twice as many home runs. The Cards had 60 while the A's hit 118. The Cards top home run hitter was Hafey with 16, who also led the team with 95 RBIs and was the league batting champion at .349.

The Athletics possessed a devastating batting lineup and had three men who hit more home runs than Hafey. Mickey Cochrane hit 17 home runs with 89 RBIs, while matching Hafey's .349 mark. Al Simmons led the American League in hitting, batting .390 with 22 home runs and 128 RBIs, while missing 25 games because of various injuries and illness. Jimmy Foxx had 30 home runs, 120 RBIs and batted .291. The Athletics also had a premier lead off batter in Max Bishop, who batted .294, drew 112 walks, and scored 115 runs.

The two team's' ERAs were almost identical with the Cardinals checking in at 3.45, and the Athletics at 3.47. However, it should be noted that the National League ERA was 3.86, while the American League was at 4.38. Thus, the Athletics were almost a full run below their league ERA, while the Cards were less than a half run below their league ERA.

Each team entered the Series with confidence. If the years had taught A's manager Connie Mack anything, it was to not be overconfident. He wasn't, but he believed his team would prevail. They were then, and are today, recognized as one of the most powerful teams of all time. They had a 107-47 mark, finishing 13 games in front of a powerful Yankee ball club that outscored them by more than 200 runs.

It was on the mound where the Athletics prevailed. They had Robert "Lefty" Grove in his finest season at 31-4, 2.08 ERA. He had a three-year record of 79-15. George Earnshaw backed him with a 20-7 mark and 3.74 ERA, while Rube Walberg was 20-12 with 3.67 ERA.

The Cardinals had good pitchers, but none of that caliber to fire at the Athletics. Derringer was a rookie, Hallahan had his best season and although Grimes had a good year, he was ailing heading into the Series. During his career, Grimes had surpassed the 20-win mark five times, but his best days were behind him, even though he had pitched well for the Cardinals this season.

The Series began in St. Louis. The first game matchup on October 1st was Grove versus Derringer. Both were hard throwers, but Grove got the better of the match as he defeated the Cards 6-2. He allowed 12 hits, but only the two runs. The Cardinals got four hits and two runs in the first inning, then Grove shut them out the rest of the way. Derringer pitched seven innings and was touched for all six runs.

Game two was critical for both teams. A Philadelphia victory would send them home needing only two more for their third straight title. A Cardinals defeat would really put their backs to the wall and almost seal their doom. However, this was a team that had battled adversity all year. Also, the Athletics had not reckoned with the Cardinal rookie center fielder, Martin.

In game two, Earnshaw held the Cardinals to two runs and six hits, but Martin's daring on the bases gave the Redbirds both their runs. Martin hit a second inning double, stole third, and scored on a sacrifice fly. In the seventh inning, he singled, stole second, took third on an infield out, and scored on a squeeze play by Gelbert.

Hallahan was even better as he held the power-laden Athletics to three hits in pitching a shutout. Martin's base running and Hallahan's clutch pitching enabled the Cardinals to leave St. Louis in a dead heat with the mighty Athletics.

There was a three-day delay before the third game was played on October 5th. Grove was on the hill again for the Athletics and this time his mound opponent was the wily old craftsman, Grimes. Grove pitched eight innings and allowed four runs. Roy Mahaffey relieved in the ninth and gave the Cardinals their final run. Martin was five for eight against Grove.

Grimes was brilliant, as he pitched like a man 10 years younger. He held the Athletics hitless for the first seven innings. In the eighth, Simmons hit a two-run homer, but that was the only damage, as the Cards won, 5-2 to take a two games to one Series lead. The hitting star for the Cardinals was Martin with two hits.

Grimes had seemed a real risk, as he had gotten an attack of appendicitis in early September and was of little value the last several weeks of the season. It had cost him a chance for his sixth 20-win season. The Cardinals had used him in an exhibition game against the Browns and he was hit hard. Starting Grimes seemed like a very risky option, but he more than mastered the task.

In game four the Cardinals pulled a surprise and started Johnson, while the Athletics had Earnshaw back on the hill. Earnshaw, who pitched brilliantly in losing game two to Hallahan, was even better this time. He held the Cardinals to two hits, both by Martin, and he shut them out, 3-0.

Game five was now critical for both teams. It was just the reverse situation entering game two. If the Cardinals could win, they would return to their home park, up by one game with two to go. Even if the Athletics won, at least the Cardinals were going home and still had a good chance to take the title.

Hallahan, who pitched brilliantly in his shutout win in game two, was back, on the mound for the Redbirds, while Waite Hoyt was the Athletics' hurler. The former Yankee star had been 3-8 for Detroit, but then finished 10-5 for the Athletics. It was surprising that Walberg wasn't given the assignment. All of his duty in the Series would be in relief roles in two games.

The hitting hero of this game was again Martin, as he had three hits and four RBIs. He had a two-run homer, a run-scoring single, and a sacrifice fly. Meanwhile, Hallahan was once again brilliant, limiting the Athletics to one run despite nine hits. Once more the combination of Martin's hitting and Hallahan's pitching had given the Cardinals a victory. They were headed back to St. Louis with a three games to two lead. Attendance at each game was 32,295.

The Cardinal fans were ecstatic, as they could see another World Championship flag flying over Sportsman's Park. They jammed the turnstiles to get into game six on October 9th. Cardinals red was everywhere, as the crowd reached 39,405.

The date was October 9th and Grove was starting his third game in eight days. He had defeated Derringer in game one and lost to Grimes in game three. Derringer was once again his opponent and the Card's luck was no better this time than the first time around.

The game was scoreless until the fifth inning, when a Cardinal error opened the gates for four unearned runs. Two singles followed the error upsetting Derringer. He proceeded to walk four men, two with the bases loaded. That finished Derringer and the Athletics got four more off the Cardinal relievers in the seventh, two scoring on a dropped fly ball. Grove was even more dominating than in game one, holding the Redbirds to five hits and just one run.

Now it was all down to one game. This was the second time the Cardinals had been to the seventh game of a Series. They had won the first time around, in 1926.

Earnshaw, like Grove, was making his third start in eight games. Like Grove, he was 1-1 headed into his final start. His opponent was the wily old spitballer, Grimes, who had beaten Grove in game three. Could the old master summon up enough to turn the tables on Earnshaw?

Earnshaw held the Cardinals to five hits, but they made the most of them. In the first inning High and Watkins singled for a first and second situation. Watkin's hit was actually a blooped hit. Shortstop Bid Williams thought Simmons was going to catch it, and Simmons thought the reverse. The result, was a pop fly basehit.

Frisch sacrificed, moving the runners to second and third. Earnshaw then uncorked a wild pitch, scoring High and sending Watkins to third. Martin walked and promptly stole second. Orsatti fanned, but A's catcher Cochrane dropped the ball and had to throw him out at first. That was all Watkins needed, as he dashed for home and beat Foxx's throw. The Cardinals hadn't really peppered the ball, but they had two runs.

In the third, High again singled and this time Watkins got a legitimate hit, as he hit one into the right field pavilion for a two-run home run. After that, Earnshaw steadied himself and pitched a wonderful game, sitting down 15 men in a row.

In the meantime, Grimes shut down the bats of the Athletics. He carried a 4-0 lead into the ninth and now the Redbirds were just three outs from their second World Championship.

The ninth opened auspiciously for the Athletics as Simmons walked. Foxx then popped out and Bing Miller forced Simmons at second. It looked like it was all over.

Grimes was beginning to tire and he walked Jimmy Dykes. When Williams singled off High's glove the bases were loaded. At this juncture, Doc Cramer pinch hit for Walberg, who had relieved Earnshaw in the eighth. Cramer singled home two runs. Now Bishop represented the go ahead run.

Street made his move and pulled the tiring Grimes. He brought in Hallahan, a lefthander, to face the lefthanded hitting Bishop.

Meanwhile, in the Athletics bullpen, Grove was warming up and would go in the game if the Athletics tied or went ahead. Bishop's baseball forte was drawing walks and Hallahan had a tendency to be wild. Bishop ran the count to three and two then hit a screamer into center field, where Martin, on the dead run, caught the ball to end the game.

Once again St. Louis was World Champions, thanks to great pitching by Hallahan and Grimes and unbelievable playing, base running, and hitting by Martin. Martin was the hero of the Series, with 12 hits in 24 at bats, which included four doubles and a home run. He also stole five bases. His play was the difference in the Series. Going back to game two, he literally stole it for the Cardinals. Then his bat won it in game five.

The Cardinals hit just .236 in the Series and the Athletics only .220. Grove was 2-1 with a 2.40 ERA, while Earnshaw was even better at 1.88 ERA, but finished at 1-2. Hallahan had two complete game victories and a save in the seventh game. Shades of Grover Cleveland Alexander's performance in the '26 Series. Hallahan had a 0.49 ERA, while Grimes was 2-0 with a 2.04 ERA. Once again St. Louis was home of the World Championship.

Epilogue

It would be three years before we could say that again. The 1932 team slipped into a tie with New York for sixth place with a 72-82 record. Hafey was gone, traded to Cincinnati. Orsatti, his replacement, hit .336, but with little power, as he had only 44 RBIs. Martin had the sophomore jinx, hitting only .236. Collins was now the regular first baseman and hit 21 home runs and 91 RBIs, but his average fell to .279. Bottomley was now in a back up role in what was his final Cardinal season.

However, it was pitching that let the team down. Grimes had been traded to Chicago in the off season and early in the year Rhem was sent to Philadelphia. Derringer slipped to 11-14 and 4.05 ERA. Hallahan dropped to 12-7 and Johnson was only 5-14 with 4.92 ERA.

Rookie Tex Carleton was 10-13 with a 4.08 ERA. The one bright spot was Dizzy Dean, who had 3.30 ERA and was 18-15. With a better attack (the Cardinals scored 131 fewer runs than in 1931) Dean could have produced several more wins. Dean was a work horse, appearing in 46 games, completing 16 of 33 starts. More would be heard from him in years to come. It would be a couple of years before the Redbirds challenged for the flag, but surely they would be back.

Pepper Martin

Gabby Street

Paul Derringer

Burleigh Grimes

66

ROW ONE L-R   Medwick, Gonzales, Crawford, Whitehead, Mooney, Martin, Vance, P. Dean, Frisch, Haines, Hallahan, Durocher, Rothrock, J. Dean, Pippen
ROW TWO L-R   Haley, Walker, Delancey, Orsatti, Carleton, Fullis, Davis, Collins, Wares

1934

The Gashouse Gang

Prologue

In Cardinals lore, no team brings more reminiscences to mind than the 1934 Cardinals. Much has been written about the crazy and often zany antics of the famous Gashouse Gang. They fought with the umpires, the opponents, and when no one else was left, between themselves. When they took the field, it was no holds barred, as they fought, scrambled, chewed, and clawed their way to victory.

After winning four pennants, two World Series titles, and a second place finish in six seasons, the Cardinals had come upon hard times. The team had dropped to sixth in 1932 with a 72-82 mark. The following season the club was rocking along at 46-45 when club president Sam Breadon decided a change was in order. He fired the likeable manager Gabby Street and replaced him with Frankie Frisch as a player-manager.

Frisch, who had played under John McGraw, considered Street's tactics too hard boiled and was one of the few players to talk back to him. On taking over, Frisch announced, "I'm fed up with this team's carefree attitude and undisciplined ways." He forgot to mention he had created much himself of this and helped pave the way for the team's demoralization and Street's dismissal.

However, Frisch instilled a winning spirit in the team. He used the same hard-nosed tactics of McGraw and soon was being called John McGraw, Jr. As soon as he took over, the Cardinals had fights in Pittsburgh on two consecutive days. A new era was born. It was the beginning of the Gashouse Gang, although they wouldn't have that moniker hung on them until after the World Series.

The team ran more now and fire was in the air. Their uniforms were dirty. They were alive, loud, brash, and hustling. Frisch even let them have beer in the clubhouse. Two important members joined the team in 1933. After Charley Gelbert was injured in an off season hunting accident, the club acquired Shortstop Leo

Durocher from the Cincinnati Reds.

They then brought up outfielder Joe "Ducky" Medwick, who would soon become the hitting terror of the National League. From 1933-39 he was the most consistent, dominant hitter in the league. The team already had Dizzy Dean, the brash, boastful, hard-throwing righthander, who won 18 in 1932 and 20 in 1933. Each season could have seen a half dozen more in the win column, given better support.

One outstanding feat that Dean accomplished in 1933 was fanning 17 Cubs on July 30th, in a 6-2 win. That performance set a major league record for single game strike-outs. In addition, he had two doubles and two RBIs. He later went on the radio and ridiculed the Cubs, calling them bush leaguers. These statements would come back to haunt him. Against Chicago he had his only losing career mark at 13-17.

Bill Terry, manager and hard hitting first baseman of the Giants, made a statement in spring training that would come back to haunt him as well when he said brashly, "Are the Dodgers still in the league?

There was not only a Depression in the country and for the Cardinals as far as pennants, but the club's box office also lagged. The 1933 season saw the team draw its fewest people at 256,171,and lose more than $100,000, which did not sit well with owner Sam Breadon.

The Cardinals went to spring training with fire in their breast, ready to do battle. Although picked no better than third, the club believed it could go all the way. New York was the favorite to repeat with challenges expected from the Cubs and the Pirates, and now the newly inspired Cardinals.

During spring training, Dizzy Dean pestered Frisch almost every day about he brother Paul's pay. Diz said even though Paul was a rookie, he deserved more than $3,000. Diz said, "Paul is greater than I am, if that's possible." The club offered Paul the same pay as other pitchers. He "ain't no other ordinary pitcher" according to Diz. He was a Dean and for that he deserved $1,500 more or Paul would go back to Houston to work in a mill and make some real money.

Paul remained silent and the papers began calling him Harpo after the famous Marx brother comedian because of his silence. Branch Rickey finally told Diz, "Paul has one foot in Columbus." The implication was he better sign or he is on his way back to the mior league in Columbus, Ohio. Paul finally convinced Diz he should sign and Paul did so on March 17th for $3,000. However, this was only chapter one of the Dean saga and money.

Diz then proceeded to make his famous boast. He told the rest of the staff, "Paul and I will win 45 games and if the rest of you match it, we will go to the World Series." Some just shrugged it off, but others, like Tex Carleton, took exception and there would be bitterness forever between him and the Deans. Paul then added that he would win 25 just to prove he was better than Diz.

Regular Season Play

The Cardinals opened the season with a 7-1 win over Pittsburgh with Diz winning. In game two the Pirates beat up on Paul, but he wasn't the loser in a 7-6 defeat. Game three saw the Pirates bash Hallahan and others in a 14-4 loss. The Pirates left town saying the Cardinals were no better than a fifth place club.

In the next series, Carleton took the first game from the Cubs 2-1 on a five-hitter, grumbling about an untried rookie, Paul, ahead of him in the rotation. The feud was on.

The Chicago Cubs got their revenge on Diz for his statements after fanning 17 of them in 1933. They pounded his ears back in a 15-2 loss. After two weeks the Cards were 6-7, Diz was 1-2 and Paul 0-0 with 7.50 ERA. Carleton said gleefully, "He doesn't have a curve." Another said, "He's just a thrower." Added another, "If he weren't Diz's brother he'd be long gone."

Paul had a lot to prove and much respect to gain. Diz's braggadocio had hurt his younger brother. They would tolerate it from Diz, since they knew he would deliver, but Paul had to prove himself. The story on Paul was that he didn't have a curve, but could throw hard. Frisch would work with him and in time he did develop a decent curve.

Rumors of dissension on team were put down by Frisch. The claim was that he and the players didn't get along, but he denied it Part of the problem was that some of the players remembered him when he was just a player and didn't take his work quite as seriously as he did as the manager. The morale was "always hustle because you never know when somebody is going to run you down."

Frisch reorganized the lineup in Pittsburgh and the Redbirds won. Frisch put had Buster Mills in centerfield. He had a single, a double, and a triple in his last four at bats in Pittsburgh and got hits in his first three times up in Chicago. However, he soon faded out of the picture. Bill Walker pitched well against Cubs until the ninth. If he could regain his 1931 form it would be a real boon to the team.

Medwick was likened to Hornsby as a hitter. He was no stylist in leftfield, but he could hit. The nickname "Ducky" was pinned on him because of his stride; waddled like a duck. He was hot-tempered, egotistical, self-centered and ready to fight at the drop of a hat, but he could hit. When he went on a tear the Cards won seven in a row.

Just when it was looking like Walker was coming into his own, he was hit by a line drive off the bat of Medwick during batting practice on May 6th. He would be out for six weeks with a broken bone in his pitching arm.

May 11th was Ladies' Day at Sportsman's Park and Frisch knew in four days he had to cut the squad to the Depression limit of 21.

73

He wanted to give Paul one last chance. If he failed, it was back to Columbus, Rochester, or Houston. Frisch thought he could be a big winner, but needed some help. He told Paul, "pitch your own game. Don't try to emulate your brother." Paul followed his advice and beat Hubbell and the Giants in 10 innings 3-2.

On the day the squad was reduced to 21. Medwick and Carleton got into a fight. Medwick stepped in front of Carleton in batting practice and Carleton told him to wait his turn. Medwick, who liked just two things, hitting baseballs and money, took a swing at Carleton. The two tussled, until separated by teammates. Frisch made them shake hands and called it a draw, although Carleton had a black eye.

The reporters got wind of it and it added more fuel to the fire. The Cardinals got a reputation as a team of wild, high strung, pugnacious men who would fight among themselves if opponents were not available. They would soon be further described as a "hell-roaring, hard-riding bunch," able to out-holler, out-race, out-smart, out-throw, out-fight anybody, any place, anytime. The Gashouse Gang was born, in spirit of that name.

Frisch now had in place the lineup that would be used in most of the games. Leading off was Martin, playing third base and a charter member of the Gashouse Gang. Second was right fielder Jack Rothrock. Of all the Cardinals entitled to a year to remember, none deserved it more. He had never been on a good team. He worked hard, bore down, and played every game.

Frisch played second and hit third. He was the hardest boiled egg in the Redbird nest, but two thirds of the players didn't rate him high as a manager, some of that still a hangover from his playing days. Cleanup was Medwick. He was rough-edged, selfish, and struggling with feelings of inferiority, and always felt he had to prove himself.

He and Durocher battled for which was the most disliked on the team. Joe's fight with Carleton had lowered his standing, not because he fought, but because he bucked the line. If you criticized Medwick he wanted to fight you. His favorite pre-game activity was to stand at the opponents batting cage and harass them. He was fast, but a dumb base runner was often missed signals. In the field he varied between sloppy and good. But he was a favorite of the fans.

Ripper Collins played first and batted fifth. He was a former coal miner, for whom the Cards made first base available by trading Jim Bottomley after the 1932 season. He loved the camaraderie of the team and greatly enjoyed being with the Deans and Martin. He was always ready for a good time. In 1934, he would have his career year.

Spud Davis hit sixth and did the catching. He seemed out of place, as he was quiet and reserved. He could only stand so much strife. Near the end of the season Diz was ranting about how hard it is to win for a team that couldn't field, hit, or wouldn't fight. Then added he ought to whip the whole bunch. Davis, with about 20 players listening, shouted, "Shut the f... up!"

Hitting seventh was Orsatti who played centerfield. He liked flashy clothes and believed he looked a little like Valentino. He considered himself a ladies' man. He was called the "Dashing Daigo" and the "Hollywood Wop." Political correctness hadn't been invented yet.

Hitting eighth was the scrappy little fighting shortstop, Durocher. He was a great bench jockey, impertinent, and the best pool player. He was a natty dresser and a ladies man, later marrying movie star Laraine Day. On the field he was a great shortstop and a spark plug on the team. Later, he became a very successful national league manager at Brooklyn, New York, Chicago, and HOuston, six total of 3,739 games.

Two key reserves were Burgess Whitehead, a soft spoken, well bred southern gentlemen, who was the only Phi Beta Kappa in baseball. The other standout rookie was Bill DeLancey, a catcher, whose projected brilliant career was short circuited due to health problems and he died onhis 35th birthday from tubercolosis.

Eight pitchers were used. Diz and Paul would and did fight anybody. Then there was Hallahan, who had some good years and not so good seasons for the team. His nickname was "Wild Bill" not because of his lifestyle, but pitching style. Carleton could have been a better pitcher, except his endurance ran down during the hot St. Louis summers. Also his immense hatred of the Deans worked to his disadvantage. When told of Diz's prediction he and Paul would win 45, he said, "that loudmouth will be lucky to win 15". Walker was the fifth starter and would be invaluable in September, but for now was out until late June with a broken wrist. The bullpen was the refuge center all year. Near the end of the year it became the old folks home with 40-year old Jess Haines and 43-year old Dazzy Vance. The rest of the bullpen was Jim Mooney and, yes, the two Deans.

Diz would start 33 times, complete 24, and relieve in 17 games, while Paul started 26, completed 16 and relieved 13 times. The two appeared in 89 games, almost 60 percent of the team's total. They combined for 45 wins and nine saves. Like them or not, crazy or not, they were invaluable.

Certain players weren't initially sold on Frisch. They felt he clamped down too hard in view of his past association with them. They said he had become ultra officious. But all were with him now as they realized they could get into the big money (World Series) if they followed him. With the current salary scale, World Series checks could equal or exceed the season's pay for many of them. If they didn't follow him they also knew they would be playing at Houston, Rochester, Columbus, or someplace else.

Many of the papers had said it would be a lean year for the Cardinals. By June 1st, they were changing one letter in that statement. It was now a Dean year for the Cardinals. Diz was 6-2 and Paul 4-0, together accounting for almost half of the team's wins. Maybe Diz wasn't too far off on his prediction.

Frisch was trying to get Diz to fan fewer so that he could conserve his strength and pitch more. He would listen sometimes, then rebel and go back to his old ways. Carleton was starting to go the distance and was at 4-3 as St. Louis moved into first, one game ahead of Pittsburgh and two up on the Giants. The Cardinals' merry pace started to stir pennant talk.

During the month of June the Cardinals were only 13-14 and they slipped out of first down to third. However, Diz won six and Paul five of the games, as they pitched in 18 of the team's 27 games. Carleton was 2-3 and Hallahan a hapless 0-4. One New York writer said, "You can joke about the Dopey Deans, but there the only reason people come to the ball park in St. Louis. If the Cardinals played them every other day, they would win the Pennant." Someone temporarily hung the nickname of "Gunga Dean" on Paul.

Diz continued to pester Frisch about getting Paul a raise. He had not given up since spring training. Suddenly on June 1, with a four-game series to begin in Pittsburgh, Diz and Paul got "sore" arms, Diz in "sympathy strike" for Paul because he was underpaid.

Frisch told the boys if they weren't pitching, to get out of their uniforms and leave the dugout. So they dressed in their street clothes and watched the game from the stands. After a one-day strike, it was settled and they went back to the team, ready to pitch.

As a fighting manager, Frisch didn't even spare the umpires as he badgered them to keep his club at a high fever pitch. In early June, the Cards were 29-18 and in first place. The team was 11-0 against Philadelphia and Cincinnati, but only .500 against the rest of the league, but certainly enough time left to correct the situation.

For fighting spirit and competitiveness, there was no other team like the Cardinals in the National League, or the American for that matter. Frisch was the front runner as a competitor and fighter. The manner in which Frisch led the team was emphasized on June 6th when the Cubs were in St. Louis.

77

In the 12th inning, Medwick was thrown out at home plate on a close call. Frisch ran as fast as he could and in a mix-up seemed to jostle or shove umpire Charlie Rigler. Rigler threw off his mask and only missed hitting Frisch in the face because the latter threw up his arm in self defense. Both were fined $100 by the league. This incident showed that the Cardinal manager was dead set on winning and that his heart and soul were set on winning as many games as possible.

As an owner, Breadon had a reputation that he usually got his man, either manager or player. Throughout the winter he had his eyes focused on Charles (Chick) Fullis of the Phillies to platoon center with Orsatti. When Watkins held out in the spring, he was traded to New York for George Davis. Fullis didn't work out for Philadelphia, so they traded him to St. Louis for Kiddo Davis. Previously the two were involved in a similar trade. In 1932, Fullis was sent to the Phillies for Davis. Now Davis was back where he started.

Paul and Diz accounted for 17 of the Cardinals first 33 victories with Paul at 8-0 and Diz at 9-3. While Paul still didn't have a great curve, most players admitted they didn't know how to hit him. He had what they called a "sailor" ball. It seemed to dart out from the lower clutches of his hand when he came down side armed.

At that time, the team had only three capable pitchers on the staff, the Deans and Carleton. Hallahan had no complete games and the Cards were not certain when Walker would pitch again. Medwick was hitting .365, while Collins was hitting .342 with 14 home runs and playing great defense.

St. Louis was experiencing its hottest summer since 1871 with 30 straight days over 100. On June 24th, with the temperature at 102 Diz decided to have some fun. He gathered old paper, sticks, scorecards and other rubbish along the grandstands. He then placed it in front of dugout, built his fire, then rubbed his hand over it, so as to keep them warm.

He had the entire stands roaring with laughter. Then he got two blankets and he and Mike Gonzales wrapped themselves in them and began an Indian war dance. By now the people were rolling in the aisles and the applause was deafening. Then he pretended it was starting to rain, feigned opening an umbrella, and headed for the dugout amidst a thundering ovation.

Some of the staff resented the attention given the Deans, even though they had more than half the team's victories. Some of the resentment was professional or even petty jealousy. More generally it was because Diz wouldn't let anyone talk for him. When on his one day strike, Diz reportedly said then that Hallahan was getting 40 percent more pay than he was and wasn't earning it. Diz said, "I want to be traded". Haines even got into the dispute when Frisch pulled him from a game he thought he would win. Pitching help was available since the Cards had picked up veteran Brooklyn pitching ace Dazzy Vance in the off-season.

The Cardinals lost the last two at home to lowly Cincinnati, finishing the home stand 12-9, before heading for a long road trip. Pitching continued to be a problem, as Carleton and Hallahan couldn't go the distance. Only the Deans were dependable starters. Diz was 13-3 and Paul was 10-1.

There was some heckling of Cardinal officials by fans and sportswriters for the Cards selling minor league star pitchers Bill Lee for $25,000 to the Cubs and Fritz Ostermueller for $30,000 to the Red Sox. They said the Cards should have passed up the $55,000 and kept the pitchers. On the other hand, it was believed that the Cardinals had enough pitching and the farm teams could use the money. They didn't realize the problems that would develop.

Hallahan finally got a complete game victory, this one over the Cubs and turned in a good performance against an improving Cincinnati team. Carleton also got a complete game win at

79

Chicago. The team was growing stronger, as they continued to fight the pitching problem that plagued them since spring.

While Diz picked up win number 14 at Cincinnati with 10 strikeouts, Paul was knocked out on July 18th for the third straight game. Paul was upset at the bad day he was having and in the third inning he walked to the Cincinnati bench to challenge a heckler. It was really Ray Kolp, but Paul challenged Derringer. Paul was restrained by his teammates, but Diz then challenged entire team, "to come out and fight." The whole affair was only a "chinfest".

For the 1934 All Star Game, at the Polo Grounds in New York, Bill Terry was top vote-getter and Carl Hubbell was number one among pitchers, with Diz second. It was in this game that Hubbell gained immortality by fanning future Hall of Famers Babe Ruth, Lou Gehrig, Jimmy Foxx, Al Simmons, and Joe Cronin in order. Frisch and Medwick were both honored for the National League team.

The Cardinals won six in a row despite Paul with a sprained ankle and Hallahan with a dislocated finger. Walker came back and allowed eight hits in a win over Boston, while Vance picked up the triumph in the nightcap with a seven-hitter. If those two could hold up, they would make a good addition to the Deans, Carleton and the seemingly rejuvenated Hallahan. Mooney was also impressive in relief.

On July 20th, Carleton held the Braves hitless until the seventh when Wally Berger hit a home run. It was the second time this season Carleton had held them hitless until the seventh inning. Diz picked up his 17th win in the Boston series while Vance got his 2000th strikeout. When Dean retired the last 13 batters, added to the 20 by Carleton, that made 33 in a row retired, or the equivalent of an 11-inning perfect game.

As August drew near, the Cardinals hoped that the best was yet to come. They had a team with a lot of misery and injuries. Medwick was nursing a sore shoulder, which had affected his hitting and throwing. Martin had a sore arm and Frisch a charley horse. You never knew the lineup from day to day. However, the fans felt the team was doing pretty well considering the circumstances.

The Cardinals' next road trip had mixed results. They started off by losing a series in Philadelphia, then got hot in Brooklyn and rolled to seven straight victories, including a split of four at New York. Terry called the split a "moral victory" for the Cardinals. Strange that a first place team saying a split with a third place team is a "moral victory".

The team then moved on to Pittsburgh and lost the first two, with Diz's winning streak broken. After that loss he was now 18-4, Paul was 11-4, and Carleton was 11-8. The fans, however, were disappointed at the Cardinals play and put them on the "pan". They were especially upset about their play against Pittsburgh.

When the team came home, they won the first two games of a four-game set with the Pirates. Then things went sour. The Cardinals dropped a doubleheader with the Deans pitching. The catcalls and jeers began. The fans had expected a double win, and got a double loss. They thought the Cardinals would make one-handed grab of the few good balls the Pirates would hit in game one, and then game two would be a cake walk too. The Cardinals would score several runs and all Diz had to do was throw his glove on the mound and the game would be over.

It didn't happen that way. The crowning play of the day really made the Cardinals look silly. There was a high hopper down the first base line which Collins snared near the edge of the grass and stood there as one run scored and the batter reached first safely.

Some thought Paul didn't get to first to cover because he favored his sore ankle. Others thought Collins didn't get there because . . . . well he didn't get there. They lost game two. Diz didn't pitch after all. Hallahan, Vance, and Walker were bombed in game two. The entire team got razzed because of the poor play.

The good news was that the injuries seemed about over. Hallahan's dislocated finger had straightened out (about as straight as his curve, some have suggested).

Paul was at 12-5 and Diz was 19-4 while Collins was hitting .340 and Medwick .333. New York (66-38) had a three-game edge on Chicago (62-40) and 6 1/2 games on St. Louis (58-43). The Gashouse Gang seemed to have run out of gas, its motor stalled.

While the Cardinals were on a treadmill, Collins became an accepted home run hitter. Fans took notice and gave him the nickname "Ripper" for the way he hits the ball. Collins and Mel Ott were about the same size. Collins was 5' 9" and 165 pounds, while Ott was 5' 9" and 160 pounds. The other big home run challenger, Berger, was 6' 2" and more than 200 pounds.

Medwick continued playing with a sore shoulder, although it hurt both his hitting and fielding, which was never great anyway. When Martin was sidelined with a sore side, Frisch took over third and really began hitting the ball. Burgess Whitehead moved to second.

Things were looking up for the team on August 11th when Carleton picked up his 13th win in an 17-3 blasting of the Cubs. Then the bottom fell out as the Deans lost a doubleheader the next day to Chicago. Paul was defeated in game one and Diz lost in game two. Three of Diz's five defeats had come at the hands of the Cubs, whom he had last defeated when he fanned 17 on July 20, 1933. However, Diz picked up two wins within 24 hours at Cincinnati. On August 8th he blanked them, 8-0 then the next day pitched the 10th through the 12th in relief to win number 21.

To add to the already growing legend of Diz and his capers were new two stories. One concerned his birth date the other his name. Diz proceeded to tell St. Louis sportswriter J. Roy Stockton how his birth date mix-up came about.

In New York three reporters each came to him separately wanting a story. First was Tommy Holmes of the Eagle so Diz told him January 16, 1911 at Lucas, Arkansas. Then came William G. McCullough of the Brooklyn Times-Union and he wanted an exclusive story, so Diz told McCullough he was born February 22nd at Bond, Mississippi. The last was Roscoe McGowen of the New York Times and he too wanted an exclusive so Diz told him he was born at Holdenville, Oklahoma on August 22nd. Each had a scoop and their bosses were happy.

Stockton said he knew Diz better than any writer and was never sure of the right date or right place, although he thought it was the one Diz told Holmes. The legend that Diz didn't know where or when he was born started because of the three different stories.

He had several versions of how his name came to be. He had enlisted in the army using Jay Dean, because he didn't like the middle name, Hanna. As soon as he got out of the service he took the name Herman, from his half brother. Then in 1929 he was pitching for the Public Service Company of San Antonio and his best pal on the team, was Jerome "Jelly" Harris, who was the catcher.

Harris missed a fastball and fans yelled derisively, "Take a bow, Jerome". Harris didn't move, but Diz did. He took a bow. The more he heard the name, the more he liked it. So when he reported to Houston in 1930 for spring training and on meeting Rickey, Diz introduced himself as Jerome Herman Dean. Prior to the Chicago series the Cardinals had an open date and the Deans had a family reunion planned. Their older brother Elmer was to join them. He was the top peanut vendor at Houston's Buff Stadium. Diz wanted a better job for his brother and got Rickey to find him a job. He thought it was going to be a minor job in the front office. It turned out to be a headliner's spot in concessions.

Rickey had even ordered a press release saying that when the Cubs series started on August 10, Elmer "with the big league delivery" would be in the grandstand at Sportsman's Park flinging peanuts.

"Cards buy a third Dean Pitcher— And it's a Nutty Idea," said a page one story. "The Dean Brothers—Two Nuts and One Goober". said another. Pat, Diz's, wife was furious. "The boys are trying to pitch the Cards to a pennant and you make them look like clowns with Elmer throwing peanuts." So Elmer was sent back to Houston to sell his peanuts.

With just over six weeks to go the Cardinals trailed New York by seven games. They were in third, with Chicago sandwiched in between. Diz was 21-5 and Paul was 12-6, but was once 8-0. Carleton was 13-8 and pitching very effectively. Medwick batting at .333 and Collins at .324 continued to be the team's leading hitters.

After the doubleheader they had an open date, but Diz and Paul were tired. Diz said they had won 34 games, over half of the team's victories. Stars had rights and they weren't going to Detroit for the exhibition game. So the Deans didn't show up. On August 14th in the clubhouse, Frisch, after a meeting with Breadon and Rickey, told Diz he was fined $100 and Paul $50 for missing the game.

Diz said, "you can't fine me." Frisch told him he could and it would stick. Diz then told Frisch he and Paul would quit the team. When it was time to go on the field, Frisch ordered them both out to play and they refused. He told them to take off their uniforms and in a fit of anger Diz tore them up. Frisch suspended both players.

Breadon and Rickey supported Frisch and said "No two kids were going to run the ball club". Breadon added that they couldn't come back until they "gleefully" abided by the rules.

When the players got their checks, the fines were deducted and an additional $36 was taken from Diz for tearing up two uniforms. The suspension was costing Diz $50 per day and Paul $23 a day. To make matters worse, the fans did not support them.

Fans were saying they were "selfish, brats, spoiled, ungrateful, great pitchers who though they could get away with anything". The fans had turned against them. On hearing this Diz decided he and Paul would return and agree to the club's terms. Frisch said Paul could come back immediately, but because Diz was the ringleader he was suspended for 10 days

Diz told Frisch if he had known the exhibition game was for kids he would not have disappointed them for anything. He had been so disgusted about losing that Sunday game he didn't care at that time if he ever saw another ball game.

Diz was ready to pitch now, not 10 days from now. He told Frisch he would leave it up to the fans all over the country, but what he forgot was that he had turned them against him with his antics. He then decided to appeal to Commissioner Landis, so Diz drove for seven hours to Chicago.

August 16th Paul was reinstated, $120 poorer, $50 from the fine and $70 from three days loss of pay. All he had to do was repent publicly and sign a document that Rickey had prepared that would have made "a high school boy blush". Paul wanted to pitch, so he did what he was told. On Friday, August 17th Paul pitched seven good innings in relief and got his 13th win in a 12-2 victory over the Phillies.

Finally, on Monday August 20th there was a meeting with Landis, Breadon, Frisch, the two coaches, travelling secretary, treasurer, trainer, Durocher, Haines, several administrative assistants, and two torn uniforms. One the other side was Diz. He acted as his own council.

When the meeting ended Diz capitulated and the team, after some haggling, reinstated him. His total loss was $486. It broke down to $100 fine, $36 for two torn uniforms and $350 pay loss for seven days. Diz said, "How can a guy get by if people keep taking his money?" He accepted blame for everything. Fans sent in over $1,000 to reimburse him, but he returned all the money.

When the whole debacle began, the players lined up behind Frisch in almost 100 percent support. They vowed to give 200 percent effort instead of just 100. During Diz's absence the Cardinals were 6-1. While, they probably couldn't win the pennant without him, the team rose to the occasion and the adrenaline flowed to give them the spark to show him that no one player, no matter how great, was above the team.

Now it was back to baseball, but another crisis came. This time the Deans weren't involved. It had been the Cardinal practice to renew the manager's contract in late August and make a public statement. This year it didn't happen. The front office said it was changing its policy and a new manager would not be named until after the season. Quietly it was being said the Cardinals wouldn't finish higher than third and perhaps a new leader was needed.

Fans thought that Breadon believed Frisch had been here long enough and would be let go at season's end. The team was in a tizzy. An unsigned manager, the Dean debacle, and quarreling in the clubhouse all this while trying to fight for a pennant. Also, Breadon and Rickey both thought Frisch's treatment of the Deans was a little rough and high-handed.

The Cardinals started a long road trip by taking two from Chicago, with Diz winning number 23 on August 31st and Hallahan gaining the victory the next day. The Cardinals moved into second with these two victories, just five games out. However, a doubleheader loss on Labor Day to Pittsburgh while the Giants took two from the Phillies, dropped the Cards back into third, seven games out. Paul lost the opener, 12-2, while Diz was defeated 6-5 in the nightcap.

By now Diz had forgotten his "hatred" of Frisch over his recent difficulties and frequently was his manager's bridge partner. Waivers were asked on Hallahan, but withdrawn when both the Giants and the Phillies claimed him. Diz was 23-6, Paul 14-8, and

Carleton 14-10, while Walker has come alive and to reach 8-3. Medwick and Collins continued to spearhead the attack at .333 and .331, respectively.

Just when it seemed like everything was settled and things would go smooth, a new disturbance would pop up. It seems like this team just couldn't stand peace and calm. This disruption came when St. Louis fans saw this depressing headline in the Post-Dispatch: "Seven Game Lead Too Big to Overcome. Redbirds Now Concede." That was the view of the "bitterly disappointed" owner, Breadon.

He was so upset that he was telling friends he would sell the team if he got a fair offer, say $1.5 million. Rickey supposedly was acting as the club's agent. One story said a wealthy New Yorker would buy the team for $1.2 million, transfer it to Newark, New Jersey, and move the Yankee farm team to St. Louis. This would require league approval as well as approval of the Yankees, Giants, and Dodgers, since it would mean a fourth team in the New York metropolitan area.

There were many ramifications that had to be considered. The Cardinals' three largest farm teams, Rochester, Columbus, and Houston were key forces in this issue. Each were valued at $500,000 and each had a new park worth about $200,000. This raised the value of the Cardinals to about $3.5 million. Against this backdrop the Redbirds fought on, as they pushed into second place just four games out of first. New York was 85-50 and St. Louis was 80-53.

The attitude of the team, except for Carleton, changed toward Diz. They realized that without him, there would be no pennant. The club now rallied around the Dean brothers as they made their valiant drive down the stretch. Three weeks earlier the majority of the club was ready to trade Dizzy, but not now.

On September 10th, Diz beat the Phillies 4-1, pitching a five-hitter. They next day they lost the first game to the Phillies, 5-0, but won the nightcap 6-4 as Diz saved the game for Hallahan by striking out Dolph Camilli, Bucky Walters, and Jimmy Wilson with two men aboard in the seventh inning.

On September 12th, Diz appeared in his third straight game, relieving in the eighth inning with the score tied 1-1, the bases loaded, and nobody out. He got Ethan Allen to pop up to short center, but Orsatti with his gimpy legs couldn't get to the ball. Two runs scored and the Cardinals lost 3-1.

Twice in the game Medwick was thrown out at home plate, each time because he loafed. Medwick waited too late to start running off second on a two-out single and the next time from first on a one-out double that rolled to the wall in left center. Despite it being a must win game, he showed no remorse either time in the dugout.

The Giants won 3-2 over the Pirates as Hubbell took number 20 giving them a 5 1/2 game bulge. The Cardinals obituary was being written.

On September 13th, for 11 innings, Paul Dean and Freddie Fitzsimmons dueled to a scoreless tie. Then in the 12th, the Cardinals scored twice and Paul retired the side for a 2-0 victory and 21 consecutive scoreless innings against the Giants. The Cards were 4 1/2 back.

If a blue flag flew atop the scoreboard in the Polo Grounds that told the fans the Giants had won. On September 14th the Giants hoisted that blue flag as Schumacher beat Walker 4-1. To add insult to injury he hit a home run also. It looked like the Redbirds were dead. They were 5 1/2 games out of first with just 16 to play.

Saturday's game was rained out so a doubleheader was scheduled for Sunday, September 15th. The Cardinals trailed 3-1 in the seventh and Diz was lifted for a pinch hitter. The team rallied to score three runs with Frisch getting a bases-loaded single off Schumacher, who was pitching in relief. Carleton retired all nine batters he faced.

In game two Paul came back with just two days rest to face Hubbell. The score was tied 1-1 going into the 11th when Martin homered. The Redbirds then added an insurance run on Rothrock's single, Frisch's sacrifice, and a base hit by Medwick. Paul set down the heart of the Giant lineup for his second win over them in four days. In 23 innings, the Giants had scored only one run off Paul.

The Cardinals were just 3 1/2 games out, as they had taken the season's series with the Giants, 13-9. Diz and Paul each won six games. Breadon wired congratulations to Paul after the game.

On September 21st, the Cardinals had a make-up doubleheader scheduled with Brooklyn. In the first game, Diz was red hot and didn't allow a hit until the eighth inning when Buzz Boyle beat out a slow roller to short. Then in the ninth he eased up and allowed two singles. But the Cardinals smacked out 17 hits in the 13-0 win.

In game two, Paul carried a 3-0 lead into the ninth inning. He had a no-hitter going into the bottom of the ninth, but not without the help of two great catches by Medwick, who robbed Boyle of a double in the sixth. He made an even better catch off the bat of Sam Leslie in the eighth.

First up was Jimmy Bucher, pinch-hitting for Al Lopez. Bucher was called out on strikes. Then Johnny McCarthy, pinch-hitting for pitcher Ray Benge, popped out to Frisch. Boyle was up next, and he hit another screamer, which Durocher knocked down. If Boyle was safe at first, it would be scored a hit. On a bang-bang play, Boyle was out and Paul had his no-hitter. He had walked the second hitter in the first inning and then retired 26 men in a row.

After the game reporters were asking Diz how it felt to be shown up by his younger brother. Diz told them he was glad for Paul and then added, "Shucks, if I had known Paul was going to throw one, I'd throw'd one myself."

The Cardinals had September 22nd off and headed for Cincinnati, while the Giants dropped a 3-2 decision at Boston. The lead was down to 2 1/2 games. The Giants split a doubleheader in Boston, while the Cards did the same in Cincinnati. No change in the margin, but two more games off the schedule. Time was running out for the Redbirds.

On September 24th, the Giants had an open date while the Cardinals played a make up game with the Cubs. Walker rose to the occasion and defeated them 3-1, bringing the lead down to two. St. Louis went home to play their last six against Pittsburgh and Philadelphia, while New York would play Philadelphia and Brooklyn.

On September 25th, Diz beat the Pirates 3-2, while the Giants, who had beaten Philadelphia 15 of 20, lost 4-0. The lead was one game. The next day the Phillies did it again, 5-4, beating Hubbell this time. The Cardinals could tie for first, but Paul lost 3-0 as Waite Hoyt pitched a two-hitter. Still one game out.

The Giants and Cards had each lost 58, but the Giants had won two more. If the Cardinals won their last four against Cincinnati while New York took two from Brooklyn, the season would end in a tie. There would then be a three-game play-off to determine the pennant winner.

On September 28th, the Giants had another open date, so all they could do was sit and bite their nails, hoping and praying for a Cardinal loss. Diz didn't grant their favor, as he posted his 29th win and sixth shutout, beating Cincinnati 4-0.

On September 29th Paul took the mound and Cincinnati's measure, gaining his 19th win in a 6-1 victory. Meanwhile, Brooklyn and 23-year old whiskey-loving fireballer Van Lingle Mungo stopped the Giants, 5-1. For the first time since early June, the Cardinals were in first place.

On September 30th Diz, with just one day's rest was back on the hill. If he won, regardless of what the Giants did, the Cardinals were the champs. Diz was the old master as he shut out Cincinnati 9-0 for his 30th win. It made no difference that Brooklyn beat the Giants 8-5 in 10 innings. The Cardinals had the NL pennant.

New York had beaten the Dodgers 14 of 20 until the final two games. Now the Giant's manager Terry was reminded of his statement early in the year, "Are the Dodgers still in the league?" It had come back to haunt him. Terry said he could see the Cardinal victory coming three weeks ago. They never gave up. They just kept coming and coming. Some blamed the loss on the overwork of Schumacher, Hubbell, and Fitzsimmons. However, they didn't pitch anymore than the Deans.

Since September 5th, the Cardinals were 19-5 and Diz and Paul appeared in 16 of the games with Diz winning six and Paul five. During that time, Walker had four wins, and Carleton and Hallahan had two each. The Cardinals had won with basically five pitchers down the stretch. The hitters deserved their share of laurels as Collins led the league with 35 home runs, batted .333, scored 116 runs and had 128 RBIs on 200 hits.

Medwick finished with 119 runs, 40 doubles, a league high 18 triples, 18 home runs, 106 RBIs and a .319 average. Rothrock played every inning, including the final game with both wrists taped. He finished at .284 with 106 runs, while Martin led the loop with 23 steals. It was truly a team effort, in addition to the heroics of the Dean brothers.

The Cardinals became a hot team after overtaking the Giants in early September. Frisch was called "miracle man'. Frisch said, "It's the greatest team I ever saw. The gamest, best bunch of fighters that ever won a league title." Frisch rose above all the rhubarbs and problems, including the Dean debacle, to show that he was boss. In the end he had the support of everyone.

The World Series

St. Louis would face Detroit in the World Series. Mickey Cochrane, the Detroit manager, had vowed not to pitch Schoolboy Rowe in game one if Diz started for the Cardinals. He said he didn't want to put that kind of pressure on a young pitcher, although Diz was actually younger than Rowe. Instead he started Alvin Crowder, a late season acquisition, who had been 5-1 for the Tigers.

Crowder was no match for Diz. In fairness, five Detroit errors didn't help. The final score was 8-3 in favor of St. Louis. Medwick was the hitting hero, going four for four with a home run. The Cardinals had stormed into Tiger Stadium and with their rough, tough, slashing style of play, had bowled over the Tigers.

The next day, October 4th, the Tigers were ready for the ruffians from St. Louis and Rowe was the master, stopping them 3-2. The Cardinals got six hits off Rowe in the first three innings, scoring singletons in the second and third. With two out in the third, Medwick was thrown out trying to score from second on Collins single.

Once again Medwick had gotten a late start causing him to be out. He tried to score anyway, by crashing into Cochrane. He knocked Cochrane over, but the catcher held onto the ball. Cochrane had to leave the game with two deep spike cuts on his right leg. Attendance at 43,451 was about 1,000 more than game one.

St. Louis was the ball club of the heartland, being the farthest south and west. Fans came from all over the Mississippi Valley, Arkansas, Texas, Oklahoma and points south. They were dyed in the wool Redbird fans. This was their team.

This series would see no days off between games, so game three was played the next day. Paul drew Tommy Bridges, a 22-game winner. Only Rowe, with a 24-8 season, stood ahead of Bridges on the Detroit staff. Paul was in constant trouble for the first five innings, as Detroit left 11 men on base, but could not score. In the meantime the Cardinals beat up on Bridges with Martin getting a double and triple as they built a 4-0 lead. The Tigers scored their only run in the ninth. Collins and DeLancey each had two RBIs.

The Cardinals had a 2-1 lead and if Walker could take game four, the Cardinals, with Diz pitching game five, could win the Series at home.

By now the Tigers knew they had a tough opponent on their hands. The Cardinals played hard. They took the extra base and when sliding into a base, they came with spikes flying at you or hit you like a Notre Dame tackle. Medwick had bowled over Cochrane and in game three Martin did the same to short-stop Billy Rogell.

The Tigers had other ideas and after the Cardinals broke on top 1-0, knocked out Carleton with three runs in the third. Meanwhile the Redbirds got to Eldon Auker for four runs in the first four innings, but he blanked them after that. The score remained tied until the seventh when Detroit pushed ahead 5-4, then added five more in the eighth. The Tigers raked five Cardinal pitchers for 13 hits in a 10-4 victory.

Both teams had numerous players with injuries, but they all played on. However, the Cardinals almost lost their crown jewel in the fourth. With runners on first and third and no outs, Frisch sent Diz in to run for the slow-footed Davis. Martin grounded to Gehringer who flipped to Rogell for one out and he fired to first for a double play, instead the ball hit Diz in the head and knocked him out.

Diz was carried off the field and Frisch was taken to task by the press for risking injury to his star pitcher. The legend has always contended that a headline read, "X-rays of Dean's head show nothing". If such headlines actually did appear, they were not in a St. Louis or Detroit paper. What was written was by columnist Arthur Brisbane: Of 123,000,000 people in this country, 99 percent are more interested in Dizzy Dean than the president of the United States.

Now game five loomed critical and Diz was ready. The Cards didn't want to return to Detroit, down three games to two. Some questioned whether Diz would be able to pitch, but he said he shouted, "I'm ready to beat those Tigers again."

The game was scoreless until the second when Dean walked Greenberg and Pete Fox doubled, scoring Greenberg. Many believed if the ailing Orsatti had been in center instead of the sometimes clumsy Fullis, the ball either would have been caught or at least held to a single. In the sixth, Gehringer hit a long home run for a 2-0 lead. One out later, Rogell singled to center and took third as the ball went through Fullis' legs. Rogell scored on Greenberg's sacrifice fly. With Orsatti in the lineup the only run might have been Gehringer's home run.

The Cardinals got a run back on DeLancey's home run in the seventh, but could score no more. They had two on in the ninth and the fans were hoping for another home run from DeLancey, but Bridges fanned him on three called strikes, all curve balls. The Series had drawn 100,000 for the three games, but St. Louis was now headed back to a hostile Detroit crowd, down three games to two.

More than 10,000 fans greeted the Tigers at Detroit's Union Station, given them a welcome reminiscent of what the Cardinals had received after beating the Yankees in 1926. The crowd was revved up as they saw a World Series title coming to Detroit, their first ever. Game six would pitch their hero, Rowe, against Paul Dean.

The Cardinals grabbed a 1-0 lead on Rothrock's double to left and Medwick's single to right in the first. The Tigers tied it in the third when Jo-Jo White walked, went to third when DeLancey's throw got away from Frisch, and scored on an infield hit by Cochrane. In the fifth the Cardinals jumped back in front on an infield hit by Durocher, Paul Dean's sacrifice, Martin's hit, Goslin's error, and an infield out by Rothrock.

The Tigers weren't finished as they came back in the sixth. White walked, took third on Cochrane's hit, and scored when Paul Dean muffed Gehringer's soft roller for an error. Goslin bunted but Cochrane was out at third, although photographs tend to show he was safe. This was a turning point in the Series. After Rogell flied out, Greenberg singled to tie the game.

In the top of the seventh, Durocher doubled and Paul Dean singled him home for a 4-3 lead. Now Paul had to hold the Tigers for two innings to set up a seventh game battle for the title. In the ninth the Tigers had one more chance. They had men on first and third with Greenberg at the plate. The crowd was ranting and raving, going wild, waiting for the big guy to bust one. All he could do was hit a weak infield pop fly. The cards won and the stage was set for a seventh game showdown.

Auker, a 15-game winner during the regular season, and the winner of game four, was the Tigers' mound choice. Naturally there was only one pitcher to go for the title game. Diz. It was a rout as the Cardinals scored 11 runs, while Diz pitched a six-hit shutout. The Cardinals blew the game open with seven runs in the third, highlighted by Frisch's bases loaded double. Collins had a four for five game with two RBIs.

For one last time there would be an altercation between a Cardinal and Tiger player. In the sixth with two outs Medwick tripled to the center field wall and slid hard into third baseman Marv Owen. Owen had tripped and accidentally came down on Medwick's left leg. Medwick kicked back twice and Owen was ready to fight. The umpires separated them as both dugouts emptied.

All the frustrations of the day had boiled over for the Tigers. Medwick put out his hand to shake, but Owen refused it. When the inning ended Medwick went to his left field position, but the fans began pelting him with debris and empty bottles. That was in the days when beer and soda was sold in glass bottles, not paper cups.

Twice he tried to take his position and twice he was driven back because of the debris. Commissioner Kennesaw Landis decided to have Medwick removed from the game for his own safety. The Cardinals had what seemed like an insurmountable 9-0 lead and Dean was pitching magnificently, so it didn't seem to matter if Medwick was in the game or not.

No further incident occurred and the game ended with an 11-0 win and the Cardinals the World Champions as Diz and Paul each won two games. An interesting question arose: What if the Tigers had made a comeback and the Cards needed the powerful bat of Medwick? Would he had been permitted to return? Worse yet, what if Landis' removal of him had cost the Cardinals the title?

Dan Daniel had covered Honus Wagner in the 1909 Series, and although that was a tough bunch, he thought the Cardinals of 1934 were even tougher. They were a breed of player that played, rough, tough and always came at you in both gestures and actions. He wrote historically, the "Gashouse Gang" playing the nice boys from the right side of the tracks. The name didn't catch until seven months later.

On May 14, 1935, in the World -Telegram, a column by Tom Meany referred to the Gashouse Gang, as did a cartoon by Willard Mullin, who had dressed a group of thugs in Cardinal uniforms. The name took hold and would stay in vogue until 1937.

Epilogue
The Cardinals looked to repeat in the 1935 season, with New York and Chicago expected to furnish most of the competition. The Pirates were a surprise and finished a strong forth with 86 wins. Much of the year the Cardinals bounced between third and fourth, but in August took over first and were making the forecasters look correct.

It seemed like the Cardinal express was roaring again and nothing could stop it. The Chicago Cubs had other thoughts. They put on a Cardinal-like drive and won 21 straight games to claim the title. The Cubs beat Paul in the first game of a doubleheader, 1-0 and took Diz's measure, 6-2 in the nightcap. They then won the next day for their 21st consecutive win. That iced the cake and gave them the title by four games over St. Louis.

The Cardinals had finished 1934 at 96-58 and actually bettered that mark by one in 1935. Their team was even stronger, as they had young Terry Moore in center field, a position he would own for they next 13 years for the Cardinals. He soon would be recognized as the best center fielder in the league, if not in baseball.

Medwick and Collins had big years as did Martin. The Cardinals traded Carleton to the Cubs, but got great pitching from the Deans, Walker and Hallahan. Diz had promised in spring he and Paul would win 45 again. They won 47. However, they couldn't overcome the Cubs' 21-game win streak and thus finished second. It would be another seven years before they would be World Champions again.

Dizzy Dean

Joe Medwick

Ripper Collins

Paul Dean

ROW THREE L-R Crespi, Triplett, Dusak, Sanders, Moore, Lanier, M. Cooper, Krist, Dickson, Moore, Yatkeman

ROW TWO L-R Weaver, Beckmann, Brown, H. Walker, Beazley, White, Slaughter, Gumbert Pollet, W. Cooper, Cross, Ward

ROW ONE L-R Marion, Musial, Hopp, Gonzales, Southworth, Wares, Kurowski, Narron, O'Dea, Peters(Bat Boy)

1942

The
St. Louis Swifties

Prologue

Of all the Cardinal pennant winners, the 1942 team is considered by many to be the cream of the crop. This team represented the culmination of general manager Branch Rickey's farm system program. This team had it all. They hit for power and average, had air tight defense, and ran the bases with reckless abandon. But most of all had one of the finest pitching staffs ever assembled.

The staff consisted of Mort Cooper, Max Lanier, Johnny Beazley, Harry Gumbert, Ernie White, Murray Dickson, Howard Pollet, Howard Krist, and Lon Warneke. Only the latter was not an alumnus of the Cardinal farm system. Waiting in the wings were Johnny Grodzicki, George Munger, Harry Brecheen, and Max Surkont.

The team led the league in runs scored, hits, doubles, triples, RBIs, average, slugging percentage, shut outs, and ERA. While the team was only second in stolen bases with 71, they ran the base paths like they owned them. Rarely did the Cardinals fail to go from first to third on a single, score from first on a double, or score from second on a single.

Speed was up and down the lineup, including the catcher, Walker Cooper, Mort's younger brother. They didn't necessarily use the speed for stolen bases, rather to stretch singles into doubles and doubles into triples. Their daring on the base paths caused many an opponent to make a hurried throw, commit an error, or throw to the wrong base.

The Cardinals had lost a heartbreaker in 1941, winning 97 to the Dodgers' 100. Catastrophic injuries kept the team from taking the title. Injuries are part of the game, but the Cardinals had more than their fair share during 1941. The fewest games any Dodger regular played was 128, and that was by catcher Mickey Owen. Three played 148 or more.

The Cardinals had a range of 104 by catcher Gus Mancuso to 155 by Marty Marion. However, after Marion's 155 games and Frank

"Creepy" Crespi's 146 games at second, the numbers drop precipitously. Johnny Mize missed 29 games with various injuries. Jimmy Brown missed 23 games with a broken nose and other injuries. Enos Slaughter missed 42 games due to a broken collarbone and catcher Cooper was limited to 63 games because of a broken shoulder. Terry Moore was beaned and missed 33 games.

Despite all these injuries the team fell short by just 2 1/2 games. Many sports experts think the Cardinals still could have won had they brought Stan Musial up two weeks earlier. In just 12 games he batted .426.

While the 1942 team would miss Mize's big bat, they felt that a combination of Ray Sanders and Johnny Hopp would make up the difference. While they hit a composite .255 and drove in 71 runs, it was their fielding and speed which made the difference. As good as the 1941 pitching staff was, this one was deeper and stronger.

The infield would have Jimmy Brown and Crespi at second with George "Whitey" Kurowski at third. Brown also spent a considerable amount of time playing third. He finished the season, appearing in 145 games. Cooper caught 125 games this season and would hit .281 with 65 RBIs. Just a warm-up for the next two years.

It was in the outfield where the Cardinals would stand out. Their trio of Moore, Musial, and Slaughter would go down as one of the finest outfields of all time. All three were fast, great fly chasers and Moore and Slaughter had rifle arms. Musial, although a former pitcher, lacked their arms because of a shoulder injury. He would recover in time and had a more than adequate throwing arm. Moore hit .288 for the season, Slaughter .318 and Musial .315 as a rookie.

Manager Billy Southworth said the Cardinals were shooting for it all in 1942 after the near miss in 1941. He called the Cardinals pitching staff the best in either league. In their first 19 spring training games, the staff allowed just 52 runs. Mort Cooper said he would win 20 games this year or throw away his uniform.

Musial didn't hit in the spring, which gave rise to speculation that he was a "flash in the pan". Southworth planned on putting Hopp in left and Sanders at first if Musial fizzled.

Southworth chirped, "The Birds are the team to beat in '42. Sure we are gonna win. Who's going to beat us?" Southworth was not a pop-off normally like Leo Durocher, Frankie Frisch or Jimmy Dykes. When he looked at the talent on his team, he couldn't see how they could miss winning it all.

He said Harry Walker, younger brother of the Dodgers' Dixie Walker, was a real find. If Musial fizzled he could move Walker into the outfield and use Hopp at first with Sanders and also have Hopp as a spare outfielder. Musial had been labeled the next Chick Hafey, Walter Roettger, or Joe Medwick, but so far in spring training he'd been a bust.

Southworth told reporters Musial had solved all types of pitching last September, but the rookie couldn't hit a lick this spring. Maybe that old bugaboo that has cut down many a career, the change of pace, had got him. Only time would tell. Musial was to relate years later, that he never could hit in Florida and always thought St. Petersburg was a terrible place to bat.

The Cardinals were installed as the pre-season favorites, even though Brooklyn won the pennant in 1941. Most sports people believe the Cardinals would have won it all in 1941 had it not been for the unusually large number of injuries the team suffered.

After the Cardinals finished the exhibition season at 21-9, the St. Louis fans had pennant fever once more. They had gone eight seasons without a pennant winner, although there were four second place finishes over those years.

Regular Season Play

The Cardinals opened the season by taking two of three from the Cubs at home, then lost two of three in Pittsburgh. Except for an

11-6 rout of the Cubs, the team was not doing a lot of hitting. Mostly good pitching was carrying the ball club. Slaughter was classified 1A in the military draft because he and his wife separated and were in the process of getting a divorce. The team could lose him in the next 60 days. Although they had good depth, it would be a major setback to their pennant chances.

The Cardinals continued to receive good pitching, but little hitting. They lost three one-run games during the last week of April. The team lost 3-2 to Pittsburgh and 2-1 and 4-3 to the Cubs. On Sunday April 26th, they lost game one, 2-0 and the second was called after 11 innings because of darkness with the score tied 4-4.

In Chicago on April 24th, Southworth pulled Musial after futility against southpaw Johnny Schmitz. He also sat out the April 26th shutout loss to lefthander Ken Heintzelman. It was the second time that year he shut them out. In the early going Southworth was reluctant to play Musial against lefthanders.

Southworth said the team was just in a slump. There were too many good hitters on the club for this to continue. However, pennant fever was dimming because of the Cardinals slow start. But it was still early in the season for fans to be turned off.

Cooper, Warneke, Gumbert, Lanier, Beazley, and White all pitched good baseball, only Pollet had not contributed, as he had a sore arm. On the positive side, Slaughter, Moore, Sanders and Brown were hitting, but home runs were at a premium. Brooklyn was 11-3, while the Cards were fifth at 5-6.

Some of the early raps on the Cards were; they wouldn't hit lefties, they don't look like a championship team, Warneke can't finish what he starts, and Cooper lost his fastball when they operated on his arm. Southworth was red-faced because of these comments. Musial was hitting just .275 with three RBIs in the 13 games he played.

The pitching staff said Moore was the best friend a pitcher ever had. The catches he made in the outfield belonged in the Hall of Fame. He had saved many a game for many a pitcher. He shook off his head injury and headed for what he hoped would be a banner season. The Cardinals pitching has allowed just 3.3 runs a game, best in the league. If only the hitting would pick up.

Moore was considered the finest centerfielder in the National League, if not in the majors. His career average was .284. While he couldn't hit with Joe DiMaggio, he could certainly field with him. Moore only finished grade school then got a job to support his mother. He was the youngest of six boys and never thought about playing ball until he was 16 years old.

Moore began his ball playing as a pitcher, but hurt his arm and had to move to the outfield. He started playing in the Industrial league with the Bemis Bag Company of St. Louis where he worked as a flunkie, as he called the job he had.

After the first month Brooklyn was first at 17-7 and St. Louis climbed to fourth with a 12-12 mark, five games out. Philadelphia trailed the pack with a pitiful 7-19 mark. Six of the Cardinal defeats were inflicted by lefthanders. On May 18th, they lost a doubleheader to Cincinnati. Ray Starr beat Cooper 1-0 in game one while Bucky Walters took Beazley's measure 3-0 in game two. The only bright note was the recent hitting of Musial. He had six RBIs in six games and his average was up to .319.

The figures continued to puzzle the experts and the fans. The Cardinals were the best in majors at runs allowed, with only an average of 3.1 per game. On the other hand, they had the poorest fielding average in the league, and had completed the fewest double plays. Offensively, they had the third best team batting average, and trailed only Brooklyn, Pittsburgh, New York, and Boston in runs scored.

The Cardinals lead the league in doubles and triples, but were sixth in home runs. This speedy, wild running team was only fourth in stolen bases. Musial, Slaughter, Moore, Brown, O'Dea, Sanders, and Cooper were all at or above .300, but still the team had been shutout five times.

The team in recent years had been a slow starter and this season seemed to be no different. The club was just 2-7 against left-handers. Musial slumped again, falling to .292 with just 10 RBIs in 23 games. Meanwhile Hopp was out with a broken thumb. When he recovered he would be in the lineup someplace. He had a lot of hustle and spirit in him and maybe the team missed his come-on-and-get-'em stuff.

The Army continued to keep an eye on Slaughter, as he took his physical. His loss would further stifle an already weak attack. One fan moaned, "If Uncle Sam takes Slaughter, the Cardinals will tot-ter." He had been a .300 plus hitter the last four years and was high in runs scored and RBIs, although not a big home run hit-ter. His loss would be devastating.

As May rolled to a close, the Cardinals went on a five-game win-ning streak; three in New York, the only game in Brooklyn, and the first game of a home stand against Cincinnati, which Musial won with a three-run home run. However, their fortunes soon changed as, on May 24th, the team dropped a doubleheader to the Reds.

Johnny Vander Meer held them to five hits in game one, winning 3-2. In the nightcap Ray Starr beat the Cardinals for the second time, holding them to three hits in a 2-0 loss. The defeat by Vander Meer was the Cards' ninth loss to a left-hander. Southworth fined one player, but wouldn't name him. All he would say was, "I'm through killing players with kindness."

The Cardinals were in third place at 20-17, 5 1/2 games behind first place Brooklyn, 27-11. Slaughter and Walker Cooper led the team in batting, hitting .321 and .319 respectively. The pitching continued to hold strong with Mort Cooper at 4-3, Beazley and Lanier at each 3-2 and Warneke and Gumbert with two wins apiece. Better records could be had by all with more batting support.

The events of late May rekindled what happened to the 1941 team. White gained a victory, but was nursing a sore arm. Hopp replaced the injured Sanders at first and added spirit to the club. Crespi was ailing and Brown shifted to second with Kurowski taking over at third. Musial injured his leg sliding in a May 31 game in Chicago and had to be carried off the field. Southworth still vowed that his team would take it all, but fans were now lukewarm about a pennant.

By early June, the club had settled in second place. The Cardinals took three of four from the Giants in New York as Pollet beat them 4-1 while Cooper won the nightcap, 2-0. The only loss was to another lefthander Dave Koslo, although they did defeat Carl Hubbell.

Slaughter and W. Cooper continued hitting over .300 while Musial moved up to .299. Hopp now appeared to be back at first to stay. It was still the pitching carrying the team. M, Cooper was 6-2 and Beazley was right behind at 5-3. Warneke was 4-2 and Lanier and Pollet each were 3-2. They were 29-20, but Brooklyn was setting a blistering pace at 37-14.

For years Ken O'Dea played a secondary role as back up catcher. First it was to Gabby Hartnett in Chicago and then for seven years to Harry Danning in New York. In St. Louis, he played fairly regularly, mostly against righthanded pitching. He and Cooper formed an excellent catching tandem, although the latter would eventually surface as number one.

First it was hitting that was slowing down the Cardinal pennant express, then it was the weather. During the period of June 6th through June 13th the team played only three games. Rain in St. Louis caused numerous cancellations. A three-game series with Brooklyn was wiped out. Owner Sam Breadon was very unhappy, as he lost an expected 65,000 in attendance.

The attendance had not been great as the team struggled, so this was a real blow to him. One game was rescheduled as part of a doubleheader on Saturday, July 18th. That meant the Cardinals and Dodgers would play back-to-back doubleheaders in July. Attendance would depend on the status of the pennant chase at that time.

They were able to get in the game on Saturday, June 12th against the Phillies, but only after a 40-minute rain delay. Sunday's doubleheader was postponed. The only other games played were against the Giants in a June 6th doubleheader. The Cardinals won all three games with Cooper taking two of the victories.

More problems surfaced for the team, albeit they were off the field. Estel Crabtree who was an excellent reserve in 1941, batting .341, was optioned to Rochester on May 25th where he was made manager. Supposedly he and Rickey were in complete accord on the transfer. The Cardinals decided to recall Crabtree, figuring they could use his bat off the bench. However, a snag developed.

It seemed Crabtree had been optioned out twice 12 years ago when playing for Cincinnati and the transfer in May was his third time. This meant he either had to remain with Rochester through the draft period or become a free agent. The haunting question was: Who overlooked the fact that he had been optioned out twice a dozen years before.

Reportedly Crabtree was upset with the story given to the Rochester papers. It said he was sent there to be manager and could not play regularly because he wasn't in condition to do so. He contended he did not intend to play regularly when he was sent there and his condition was no different than a year ago.

The Cardinals sent former St. Louis Browns catcher Ray Hayworth to Rochester to replace him. One reason advanced was that Hayworth's salary was about half of Crabtree and that he could better earn his pay by playing on the big club. Breadon said that was the sole reason for removing him as manger, as he would be more valuable to the Cardinals as a pinch hitter and reserve outfielder.

This led to a deeper problem - the growing feud between Rickey and Breadon. Rickey was in the last year of a five-year contract and there was strong speculation whether he would be back with the Cardinals the next season or not. A major example was that Breadon replaced Ray Blades as manager with Billy Southworth in 1940 without telling or discussing it with Rickey.

The loss of Rickey could be devastating. He was the mastermind of the farm system and the Cardinals' great success for the past 20 years or so was attributed directly to his efforts. The other thought was that the system was in place and could operate without Rickey's hand. It should be remembered he could develop a farm system for someone else and provide a competitive team to the Cardinals. This was what he would eventually do with the Dodgers making them the powerhouse of the 1947-1956 period in the National League.

The club vendetta that started in 1940 when Cardinal pitcher Bob Bowman beaned Medwick just days after he had been traded from the Cardinals to the Dodgers had not cooled. Until the Dodgers whipped the Cardinals four out of five at Ebbets Field, the Cardinals had held the upper hand on them. During the series in late June the flare up occurred again.

Medwick, who was on a 25-game hitting streak, was on first, when a Lanier pitch got by Cooper, who recovered and fired to second where Marion tagged Medwick out. Medwick slid hard into Marion and claimed Marion hit him harder than necessary when he tagged him. Marion, normally mild mannered, was ready to fight, but Crespi charged from the dugout and floored Medwick and a free-for-all developed. Dixie Walker tackled Brown and he suffered a twisted leg that took him out of the lineup.

This episode was reminiscent of the Gashouse Gang of the '30s. Medwick and Crespi were ejected and each fined $25 for staging a fight without a license. Ironically, the battle occurred on the second anniversary of the beaning of Medwick.

The only game the Cardinals won was by Cooper 1-0, his seventh in a row and fifth shutout. He was 9-3 and on a pace to win 20. He could lead the league in wins, shutouts, and strikeouts. The history of the National League is such that you needed a 20 game winner to win the pennant. Two of his three defeats have been by scores of 1-0. He could have been 11-1.

Following Cooper's victory he sent a telegram to team physician Dr. Robert Hyland, "This is the anniversary of elbow operation and I shut out Brooklyn today, 11-0. Please accept my heartfelt thanks and deep gratitude for the job well done by you a year ago today."

In that lone victory, Musial had a triple and a home run, boosting his average to .315. Judson Bailey of the Associated Press, listed Musial as one of the most prominent players "overlooked" for the All Star Game. It was the only time in Musial's career that he failed to play in the mid-season classic.

The Cardinals were 7 1/2 out as July approached then went just 5-7 on road trip, including a doubleheader loss to Boston. The only saving feature was Cooper's eighth consecutive victory, sixth shutout, and 10th win. The glow in the Cardinals pennant candle was barely a flicker, as the team fell further behind.

1942 had been a year of frustration for the Redbirds, who had been picked to win it all, and some thought by a handy margin. Added to the consternation was the still unsettled problem of Crabtree. Commissioner Kennesaw Landis stepped in and gave Crabtree his free agency, with the stipulation he could play for the Cardinals if he desired.

At that time the situation was still up in air. Rickey had gone to visit Crabtree but failed to get his signature on a contract. Crabtree did not show any resentment toward the Cardinals and pointed out they had always been fair with him in their dealings. He just felt that the Rochester fans should be given the real story of what happened. It was assumed that everything would be cleared up to Crabtree's satisfaction.

As the All Star game neared it looked more and more like another Dodger pennant. They built an 8 1/2 game lead over the Cardinals and it looked unsurmountable. While the Dodgers continued playing at over .700 pace and seemed to have few problems, the Cardinals' problems continued to grow.

The Cardinals were far off their 1941 pace. A year ago at the same time they were tied with Brooklyn for first place. Pitching and hitting problems continued. White and Pollet were both troubled by sore arms, with the former not resembling the 17-game winner of a year ago, and the latter not delivering on the promise showed late last year. Lanier was able to pitch in only one game in two weeks as he was also bothered by a sore arm.

Hopp and Sanders were sharing first base, neither was hitting as expected. Hopp, a .303 hitter in 1941 was in the .220s most of the year, while Sanders was inconsistent. Slaughter fell to .274, Cooper to .282, and Moore was at .268. Only Musial with his .330 average was providing any constant batting punch.

Cooper's nine-game winning streak ended and he stood at 11-4. Only Warneke and Beazley were able to provide any additional pitching support at this juncture. Warneke was 6-3. Beazley, starting and relieving, was 7-4. He would be primarily a starter the rest of the way. In fact, from the time he became a full time starter to season's end, Beazley would be 15-3.

If the Dodgers were to play just .500 ball the rest of the way they would win 94 games, and based on the current performance of the challengers, it would be enough to give Brooklyn the pennant. Should Brooklyn maintain its current pace, they would win 110 games, tying the 1909 Pirates and 1927 Yankees. The only team with more wins was the 1906 Cubs at 116.

When Warneke was sold to the Cubs on July 28th, it brought out those hunting for Breadon's scalp. The old cries of cheapskate, penny pincher, miser went up. The fans believed what little chance the team had for the pennant had just been killed.

Breadon, trying to appease the fans, said, "He lost something". Fans didn't buy it. Warneke was 6-4 with 3.29 ERA when sold. Breadon denied that he has given up any hope of catching the Dodgers, but that was what the fans claimed. Once again the trades of Medwick and Mize in 1940 and 1941, respectfully, were brought up.

It came back to the same old story about Breadon and the fans. His basic philosophy was trade or sell a player while he still had value to get more for him. With the Cardinals vast farm system, that strategy worked pretty well for them. Should the well run dry, it would be a different story.

Warneke was the highest paid Cardinal, and many believed that was the real reason he was unloaded. In his five prior seasons he had won 77 while losing 45. If all pitchers performed like that it would mean 97 wins and a pennant in most years.

At the midpoint, the Cardinals were 47-30, eight games behind Brooklyn. On July 9th, Beazley pitched a 9-0 win over New York. The next day St. Louis scored two in the ninth to beat the Giants again. They used so many pinch hitters that day, the game ended with Moore playing third and Kurowski at short.

On July 11th, Pollet failed for the fourth straight time, losing to Hubbell and the Giants. After a doubleheader win against the Pirates, the Cardinals had gone 13-7 in the past three weeks, but still lost ground to front-running Brooklyn.

The Cardinals completed a long and prosperous home stand in late July by taking three out of four from Brooklyn. They finished 17-5 on the home stand. Then it was out for a trip to Philadelphia, Brooklyn, Boston, and New York and back home for another long home stand.

On July 18th, 19,395 saw the Cardinals and Dodgers split a doubleheader, with White winning the first game, 7-4 and Lanier losing the nightcap, 4-3. On Sunday, July 19th, the Cardinals swept a doubleheader from the Dodgers with Cooper picking up one of the victories, but he left the game with elbow problems. There were concerns he could be out a week to 10 days. The team could not afford to lose him for any length of time.

The Cardinals held a 7-6 edge on Brooklyn for the season. Musial said, "The Dodgers, particularly when managed by Durocher, always brought out the best in our team. We seemed to rise to the occasion whenever we played the Dodgers."

Walker Cooper's 15-game hitting streak ended in the first game of Sunday's doubleheader, but brother Mort picked up his 12th win and was 12-4. Beazley was 10-4, but the two lefthanders that were so heavily counted on Pollett and Lanier, were just 4-4 and 3-3, respectively. The good play in the Dodger series cut the lead to 6 1/2.

The hitting improved as Kurowski was a surprise at .325, third best in the league while Musial was right behind at .320. Cooper was at .308 and Slaughter was at .298 with a team high 54 RBIs.

Brooklyn had its sights on two targets. First, it wanted to win the pennant, but secondly, it wanted to become the second winningest team in National League history, if not the majors. The team carried 11 pitchers and all were over .500. It didn't look like any team could catch them, as they continued to play over .700 baseball.

The Cardinals were just 12-22 in one run games and therein lay the difference between first and second place. The death notice of the Cards was predicted for about September 15th, the anticipated clinching date for the Dodgers. That didn't mean the Cardinals hadn't done well; Brooklyn had just been exceptional.

St. Louis lost two of three in Brooklyn and then split four with the Giants. Cooper got his 13th victory but not without much mental and physical anguish. Many were concerned that his altered pitching motion would have the same affect as what happened to Dizzy Dean. It was only his second victory since the All Star break.

On the positive side Lanier was back on the winning track, posting his seventh win. Many fans were still harping about the Mize trade, as neither Hopp nor Sanders were hitting as expected. Both fielded well, but that had not made up for the loss of Mize's big bat. Mize would finish the season at .305 with 26 home runs and a league-high 110 RBIs.

The Cardinals were best in team average, doubles, and triples and second in runs scored, but still nine games off the pace. Cooper was 13-5, Beazley 11-5, Lanier 7-4, Gumbert 5-5, White 4-4, and Pollet 4-5. It was easy to see where this club would be had White and Pollet performed as in 1941. As mid-August approached the Cardinals had an excellent 62-38 record, but were 9 1/2 games behind the Dodgers who stood at 73-30. From this point forward through, the Cardinals would be 44-8, an .846 pace.

One thing the Cardinal team had going for them was youth. Musial was the youngest at 21, with most the players under 25. Moore was the only regular who was 30 and Gumbert, a veteran relief pitcher, was 31.

In mid August the team was still 8 1/2 games behind. Walker, the Cardinals rookie outfielder, took a liking to a clattering Spike Jones novelty song, "Pass the Biscuits, Mirandy." It soon became the team's victory song. It was played and sung after each win. The trainer, Dr. Harrison J. Weaver played the mandolin and Musial handled a slide whistle or kept time with coat-hanger drumsticks. A new Cardinal band was being formed, which would lead the parade down the stretch drive.

About the same time Mort Cooper decided to change uniform

numbers. He had been one of four National League pitchers to wear number 13. The others were the Cubs' Claude Passeau, the Dodgers' Kirby Higbe, the Pirates, and Luke Hamlin. Cooper had never won more than 13 games in a season, so he decided when he got number 13, from that point on he would wear the number uniform of the victory he was going for that day, provided it didn't belong to another teammate.

Kurowski had been a rookie find and although his hitting would tail off, he was still a key factor in the pennant drive. Until his arm injury gave him problems in the late '40s Kurowski provided a powerful right-handed punch in the lineup for the next several seasons. Marion, always a defensive whiz, had been off to a slow start, hitting below .200 as late as June 5th. Often he had been lifted for a pinch hitter, but the past two months saw him bat .318, raise his average to the mid .270s and become one of the best clutch hitters on the team.

Krist was 11-3 with a two-year record of 21-3. He would be 34-8 for the 1941-43 seasons, then he went off to the service for 1944-45. When he returned, he never regained his form, a fate that would befall numerous other Cardinal pitchers. Beazley was 14-5 and Lanier won his eighth game to five losses and seemed like the Lanier of old. Musial was batting .320 while Slaughter was at .318 with 78 RBIs.

Despite all this the Cardinals still trailed the mighty Dodgers by 7 1/2 games and time was running out. Less than six weeks of the season remained. No matter how well the Redbirds played, the Dodgers played just as well.

In late August, Hopp went on an eight-game hitting spree and seemed to have taken over the first base job. Hopp looked like the old Gashouse Gang sliding into third on his letters as he stretched a double into a triple. Musial and Slaughter continued to challenge Pete Reiser for the batting title. Reiser had been injured when he crashed into the wall in St. Louis in July, ironically chasing down a long hard hit ball by Slaughter. The Cardinals continued to hang on by their fingernails.

Mort Cooper won his 15th game wearing number 15. However, when he appeared in the first game of a doubleheader on August 23rd wearing number 14, he suffered his seventh loss, snapping an eight-game Cardinal winning streak. Beazley got his 15th win also and Marion continued his rejuvenated hitting, but the club remained 6 1/2 games back.

Murry Dickson was taken out of the bullpen and pitched a four-hit win over Pittsburgh. Another good development for the team, the Cardinal drew over 51,000 for a three-game set with Pittsburgh, with 17,000 for the Sunday doubleheader.

Breadon shared Rickey's concern, not only about the attendance, but whether there would even be a 1943 baseball season due to the war. In numerous polls taken of the servicemen, more than 95 percent said they did not want the baseball season cancelled. They said they had sacrificed so much, that to lose the baseball season would be the proverbial last straw. They wanted major league baseball to go on. Based on that, it was decided there would be a 1943 season. The record shows that the war news had a direct affect on attendance. When the news was bad, attendance fell. When the news was good, it rose.

Despite an excellent 78-43 record the Cardinals still trailed Brooklyn (84-36) by 6 1/2 games with just 33 to play.

The Cardinals had a brilliant August, going 25-8. They played at a .660 clip since June 1st. On June 1st, the team was 25-18. On July 1 they had climbed to 38-27. They were 60-36 by August 1st and on September 1 were 85-44. But was there enough time left to overtake the Dodgers?

The Cardinals took three out of four from the Dodgers in St. Louis in a nerve-wracking series. Lanier won game one (the fourth time he had beaten Brooklyn this season), while Cooper won a gru-

117

elling 14-inning game for number 16. In the 13th inning Brooklyn scored, but the Cardinals tied it and only a great play by Brooklyn's Herman, turning a hard hit ball into a double play, allowed the game to continue. In the 14th, Wyatt was replaced by Larry French (the loser in game one) and he suffered his third loss of the season, all at the hands of the Cardinals.

Kurowski opened the 14th by beating out a bunt. Marion sacrificed, but reached first when Kurowski beat the throw at second. Morton Cooper attempted to sacrifice but Kurowski was forced at third. Brown walked to load the bases and the infield came in. The crowd was going wild, smelling victory. Moore hit a hot shot and third baseman Lew Riggs fell fielding the ball. He fired home, but Marion beat the throw and Cooper had his 16th victory.

It was another nail-biter in game three as it took Beazley and the Cardinals 10 innings to win, 2-1. The ending was similar to game two. Brown was on third with two out and Max Macon (a left hander formerly in the Cardinal system) went all the way for the Dodgers. Coaker Triplett topped the ball between third and pitchers' mound and Macon tripped fielding it. He fired home, but Brown in typical Gashouse style, bowled over catcher Mickey Owen to score the winning run.

After three wins the Cardinals were jubilant and loose, while the Dodgers were serious and dour. It should be the other way around. All four games were hard fought. The fifth inning of the last game spelled doom for Lanier. Five hits drove him out and Curt Davis won. After the game when questioned why he didn't pitch White or Pollet, Southworth's answer was simple. "Both have been inconsistent and had arm problems. Next to Cooper and Beazley, Lanier has been my best pitcher."

There was much second guessing about starting Lanier with just two days rest. However, Southworth stuck by his decision, though many thought Pollet, Dickson or White should have been given the opportunity. The team was playing great ball, really driving. It was like the old Gashouse Gang.

The doormat Philadelphia team came to town and lost three straight to St. Louis while the Dodgers split a pair with Pittsburgh bringing the lead down to three. The the Dodgers won on August 31st while the Redbirds were idle and the lead went back to 3 1/2 games. However, the remainder of the schedule favored Brooklyn.

The latest word was that Slaughter would finish the season then go into the Army in January. The Cardinals attendance really picked up with 91,000 for the four Dodger games and a twilight doubleheader with the Boston Braves. Attendance was now 460,000 and Breadon wore a broad grin on his face.

The Cardinal farm system continued to pay dividends and Beazley was the latest example. His record was better than in any of his four years in the minors.

St. Louis had long been maligned as a "bad baseball town" (strange compared to today when it is considered number one). Some traveling secretary sarcastically said, "we couldn't pick up breakfast money." There were a lot of red-faced executives after the 91,000 attendance for two twilight doubleheaders and two night games. The Cardinals would have drawn 125,000 if all four Brooklyn games had been single night games. The last six Brooklyn games in St. Louis drew 146,000, almost one-third of the year's total attendance.

Medwick, once the darling of the St. Louis fans, heard the boo birds throughout the Dodger series. It all began in game one. Marion was given an error on a high throw on a Medwick grounder. Medwick protested loudly that it should be a base hit. This turned the crowd against him and for the rest of the series they hooted and jeered each time he came to the plate, as well as when he was in the field. He was in a five-way fight for the batting title, so the hit was important to him. Only 10 points separated Medwick at .316 from Reiser at .326. Musial, Slaughter, and Boston's Ernie

119

Lombardi were sandwiched in between.

Amid all the pennant clamor, the final chapter of the Crabtree affair unfolded. Rickey told a Columbus, Ohio sportswriter that Crabtree would rejoin the Cardinals in Pittsburgh later in the week. A few hours later Rickey had to send another wire advising that Southworth just talked to Crabtree and he changed his mind. He won't be joining the Cardinals in Pittsburgh.

Rickey had offered Crabtree the same salary as the prior year and gave him a couple of weeks to think it over. He never did reply to Rickey. Crabtree underwent a serious kidney operation in 1940, was never been able to get back to full strength and was sensitive about his health. He found it impossible to play regularly with Rochester and inside information said he couldn't eat or sleep because of managing duties. He did not rejoin the Cardinals for the season, even though they had a chance at the pennant.

Pennant fever was running high as the rampaging Redbirds swept a doubleheader from Pittsburgh at home. They had won 26 of their last 31 and by the time they arrived for the two game showdown in Brooklyn on September 11th and September 12th, the club was only two games out of first place. The Cardinals were 8-3 against Brooklyn in St. Louis, but only 3-6 at Ebbets field.

If the Redbirds could win both games they could win the pennant, as momentum and drive would be in their corner. If they split, it dimmed their chances, but there would still be hope. Should they lose both games, well . . .

As the Cardinals approached the Brooklyn series they were 91-45, a record that would win in practically any other year. Brooklyn was 93-43. With only 18 to go the Redbirds were still down by two. Their top four pitchers were Cooper (18-7), Beazley (17-5), Lanier (12-7), and Krist (11-3).

On September 11th, Cooper beat Wyatt, 3-0, for his 20th win of the season. It was the fifth time he had beaten the Dodgers and he allowed them just 10 runs in 53 innings. If the Cardinals could win the next day, they would be in a first place tie. Lanier drew Macon as his opponent and in another hard fought game, Kurowski hit a two-run homer to give Lanier his fifth win over Brooklyn, 2-1. In game three, Beazley carried a 1-0 lead into the ninth when the defense faltered and the Cardinals lost, 2-1. But, Moore hit a home run in the nightcap off Rube Melton to give the Cardinals the win by the same score. Rookie Bill Beckmann, just recently called up, pitched six strong innings of relief for his only win of the season, which was also his last major league victory. He had pitched for the Philadelphia Athletics from 1939-41 and produced a 20-25 record. Beckmann was a native of St. Louis. The season series ended 14-8 in the Cardinals favor with Cooper and Lanier sharing 10 of the victories.

Tragedy almost struck the Redbirds after coming from so far back to tie the Dodgers. As they detrained at the old Broad Street station in Philadelphia, Beazley tangled with a redcap because he wouldn't allow him to carry his bag. Beazley said the redcap cursed him and hot tempered Johnny threw his bag at him. The redcap drew a knife and cut Beazley on the thumb. There went the pennant. everyone thought.

Meanwhile the Dodgers dropped a doubleheader to Cincinnati, extending their losing streak to five in a row. St. Louis was in first place for the first time that season. Lanier used to call Southworth a great guy who was a good manager, but now said he was a great manager who was also a decent guy. He had the ability to handle young players, lift their spirit, help lift them out of a slump, bear down when he had to. He got undivided loyalty from his players. Southworth had said when Brooklyn was playing over .700 ball, "they haven't had their slump yet, we had ours."

With just 11 games to go the Cardinals had a 1 1/2 game lead.

They were 96-47 while Brooklyn was 94-48. The hitting race had come down to Reiser, Lombardi, Slaughter, all at .320 and Musial at .317. Musial said in his book if someone had told them that when they had a on- game lead with 12 to go, Brooklyn would win 10 of their last 12 and still not win the pennant, he wouldn't have believed it. The Cardinals went one better. They were 11-1 in their last 12.

When the Redbirds left St. Louis they were 4 1/2 games out of first, and when they returned on September 21st they were 2 1/2 games ahead.

Even though the Cardinals had a 2 1/2 game lead, Southworth was not talking World Series until the team clinched the pennant. He realized how far his team came back from and his lead was a lot smaller, although just a few games remained. He had been around baseball long enough to know anything could happen.

The Cardinals battled right down to the wire, winning five of six from Philadelphia and Boston, but none of the games were easy. They were all hard fought and nail bitters. To clinch the 1942 pennant the Cardinals needed only a split with Chicago on the final day of the season. The Dodgers, fighting to the bitter end, defeated Philadelphia on the final day for their eighth straight win and ended the season with 104 wins.

Most of the National League was rooting for the Cardinals, as they greatly despised Durocher, (the Brooklyn manager) while Southworth was liked and respected. The Cardinals didn't back into the pennant. They beat the Cubs 9-2 and 4-1 with White the winner in the opener and Beazley taking the nightcap.

The final standings saw St. Louis at 106-48, the most wins ever by a Cardinal ball club, and the Dodgers at 104-50. Lombardi won the batting title with a .330 mark, although he batted just 309 times. Under today's rules Slaughter with a .318 average would be the winner and Musial the runner up at .315. Slaughter had 591 at bats and Musial 467.

Mort Cooper was voted the league MVP with his 22-7 mark, 10 shut outs and a sparkling 1.77 ERA. All three figures led the league. Beazley finished at 21-6, giving St. Louis 43 wins from the two strong righthanders.

The World Series

In the World Series, the Yankees were heavy favorites to upend the St. Louis Swifties, as New York sports cartoonist Willard Mullin had named them. The Yankees had been hoping for a subway Series with the Dodgers, but thought they could beat any team the National League offered. The last time a Yankee team lost in the World Series was in 1926, when the Cardinals captured their first National League pennant and first World Series win.

In game one, 14-game winner Red Ruffing held the Cardinals hitless for 7 2/3 innings while the Yankees piled up a 7-0 lead against Cooper, Gumbert and Lanier. It certainly looked like the prognosticators were correct, that the Yankees would steam roll the Cardinals. Moore got the Cardinals first hit, a single in the eighth inning, but nothing else happened.

The ninth inning started auspiciously enough as Hopp flied out. Sanders (batting for Kurowski, who had fanned three times) walked on four pitches. Marion tripled in the first run and O'Dea, pinch hitting for Lanier, singled home Marion. Crespi ran for O'Dea and Brown singled. That was all for Ruffing and in came Spud Chandler, who had won 16 that year. Moore greeted him with a single to score Crespi. Slaughter's infield hit loaded the bases and if Musial could hit one to the roof, the Cardinals would have a victory.

Earlier in September he had hit a grand slam against Pittsburgh to win the game. Could fate repeat itself? Musial hit the ball hard, but right at first baseman Buddy Hassett for the final out. The Yankees

123

had won, but they also found out that the Cardinals wouldn't roll over and play dead. The Redbirds had shown what they were made of.

The Cardinals four-run ninth in game one had shown the Yankees were not unbeatable. Beazley and Tiny Bonham hooked up in a pitching duel with the Cardinals on top at 2-0 going into the seventh inning. The Cardinals had scored in the first on a single by Brown, Moore sacrificed, but was safe at first when Bonham failed to nip Brown at second. Cooper then doubled them both home. In the seventh Hopp singled and Kurowski tripled him home for a 3-0 lead and apparent victory.

Beazley weakened in the eighth as Roy Cullenbine singled, stole second, and scored on DiMaggio's single. Cullenbine played for the Browns in part of 1940, 1941, and the start of 1942 before goin to the Yanks. Charlie "King Kong" Keller then hit a two-run home run to tie the game. In the bottom of the eighth the first two men went out easily, but Slaughter doubled and Musial singled for what would prove to be the winning run.

However, there were still more excitement and thrills to come. In the ninth inning Bill Dickey singled and Tuck Stainback ran for him. Hassett singled and Stainback took off for third, but a great throw by Slaughter cut him down and the momentum was back with the Cardinals. They came into this game knowing they had to win. They didn't want to head to New York, down two games to none. The series was now tied and the scene shifted to Yankee Stadium.

In game three, White was unhittable, allowing just six singles. However, it also took some great catches by Moore, Musial, and Slaughter to keep the game scoreless. The Cardinals scored their first run in the third when Kurowski walked. Marion attempted to sacrifice, but the Yankees argued the ball hit him in the batter box, so he was forced to bat again.

On his next try Marion beat out an infield hit. White sacrificed and Kurowski scored on an infield out. In the ninth, the Cardinals got their second run when Brown singled, and Moore sacrificed but was safe when Brown beat the throw at second. Slaughter singled scoring Brown and Musial was intentionally passed, loading the bases. The Cardinals had a chance to break the game open as there were no outs, but Cooper flied to short center and Keller caught Hopp's fly and threw Moore out at the plate.

Game four was a slugfest with the Cardinals winning 9-6. Neither starter, Cooper nor rookie Hank Borowy figured in the decision. Lanier won with good relief pitching while Atley Donald was tagged with the loss. Walks benefitted the Cardinals as Hopp and Marion scored in the fourth and Musial and Slaughter in the seventh.

In the fourth they got six runs on six hits as Musial had two. He opened with a single and closed with a run scoring double. Cooper couldn't stand the prosperity and was blasted out in a five-run sixth. Gumbert and Pollet also worked in that frame.

The final game was won by Beazley over Ruffing, as Kurowski hit his now famous two-out, two-run homer in the ninth inning for the final margin of 4-2. Paul "Scooter" Rizzuto had homered in the first and Slaughter tied it in the fourth. Singles by Red Rolfe, DiMaggio, and Keller in the fourth put the Yankees back on top, but Moore and Slaughter singled in sixth and Cooper brought Moore home with a sacrifice fly.

Beazley had a tough fifth inning caused by two Cardinal miscues. With one out Ruffing, got an infield hit, then an error by Hopp put Rizzuto on and Marion's error let Rolfe aboard to load the basis. Beazley rose to the occasion, getting Cullenbine to pop out and DiMaggio to hit into a force play. So once again the Redbirds were world champions and the Yankees lost for the first time since the Cardinals had defeated them in 1926.

Musial, Slaughter, and Cooper all delivered timely hits during the series, while Marion was simply a wizard in the field. He certainly showed why he was called Mr. Shortstop. Cooper outshone Dickey while Moore and Slaughter were brilliant in the outfield. Someone had said before the series that the Cardinals ran the bases like they were on bicycles. After the series, a Yankee said, "no, it was like they were on motorcycles."

When the Cardinals defeated the Yankees in game two, it was the first time a western club had beaten the Yankees in World Series play since the Cardinals had done it in 1926. In the interim the Yankees had clean sweeps over Pittsburgh in 1927, the Cardinals in 1928, Chicago in 1932 and 1938, and Cincinnati in 1939. Twenty wins in a row and it was finally broken.

Everyone in St. Louis was happy and jubilant. Thousands crowded Union Station to welcome the returning heroes. Breadon was elated and now looked forward to several more championships seasons. Southworth said if he had to do it over, he would not have platooned Musial early in the season. He would have played every day and may have had an even better year.

Epilogue

The Cardinals lost two thirds of their outfield to the service, as both Moore and Slaughter went into the Army. They also lost reserve infielder Crespi, but a far greater loss was Beazley. However, the Cardinal farm talent was deep and soon they would have the likes of Brecheen, Munger, and Al Brazle as part of the pitching corps.

Thanks to their extensive farm system the Cardinals were able to field a team far superior to any other in the league. Walker became a regular in the outfield, with the other outfield position manned by Danny Litwhiler, acquired from Philadelphia. Lou Klein came up from the minors and took over at second, while Ray Sanders became the regular first baseman.

The club won 105 games in 1943, but unlike 1942 they had a runaway. After lounging in second during April and May they climbed into first in early June and were never headed. The club kept increasing its margin, until at the end they were 18 games ahead of second place Cincinnati.

Musial won the first of his seven batting crowns at .357 and the first of his three MVP awards. He also led the league in hits, doubles, triples and slugging. He scored 106 runs to start a string of 11 straight seasons of 100 or more runs scored. Cooper had a big year, hitting .319 with 81 RBIs and Kurowski had 70 RBIs and a .287 average. Klein did a good job at the top of the batting order, hitting .287 with 91 runs, 28 doubles, 14 triples and 62 RBIs.

The pitching as usual was brilliant. Cooper was again a 20-game winner, tying for the lead in victories with a 21-8 record. Lanier was 15-7 and Krist 11-5 to complete a three-year run of 34-8. Pollet was 8-4 before being called into service. Pollet completed 12 of 14 starts and led the league with a 1.75 ERA, followed by Lanier at 1.90 and Cooper third with 2.30. The Cardinals led the league with a 2.57 ERA.

Newcomers from which more would be heard distinguished themselves quite well. Munger was 9-5, Brecheen was 9-6, Brazle in an early season appearance was 8-2, completing eight of nine starts. Dickson came on at 8-2 and then left for the service, but did get a special pass to pitch in the World Series.

Even though the Cardinals had won the World Series in 1942 and ran away with the NL pennant, the Yankees, winners of their third straight pennant and seventh in the past eight seasons, were installed as favorites. This time they turned the tables on the Cardinals, defeating them four games to one. Cooper won the only game for the home town team. Still the team had back-to-back pennants, with the promise of more on the way.

Marty Marion

Terry Moore

Johnny Beazley

Branch Rickey

1942 - The St. Louis Swifties

ROW FOUR L-R   Yatkeman, Donnelly, Wilkes, Litwhiler, Sanders, Dr. Weaver, M. Cooper, Lanier, Musial, Brecheen, W. Cooper,

ROW THREE L-R   Byerly, Schmidt, Keely, Fallon, Hopp, Bergamo, Kurowski, Ward,

ROW TWO L-R   Marion, O'Dea, Martin, Gonzales, Southworth, Wares, Garms, Jurisich, Verban

ROW ONE L-R   S. Cooper, B.Scanlon (Bat Boys)

1944

The All-St. Louis
World Series

Prologue

The Cardinals followed up their magnificent 1942 season with a year that was almost as good, winning 105 in 1943 and finishing 18 games ahead of second place Cincinnati, despite losing Terry Moore, Enos Slaughter, Johnny Beazley, Frank "Creepy" Crespi, and Erv Dusak to the war effort.

The Cardinal farm system enabled the team to carry on better than any other club. The only disappointment came in the 1943 World Series, when the Yankees defeated the Cardinals in five games.

On the bright side, Mort Cooper won 20 or more for the second consecutive season and Stan Musial took his first of seven batting titles with a .357 average. He also earned his first of three MVP awards.

Entering the 1944 season things looked quite bright for the Cardinals. They were attempting to become the first team in National League history to win 100 or more games in three consecutive seasons. They were the odds on favorite to win their third consecutive title.

The club added a few veterans in trades to bolster the team, but lost Al Brazle, Murry Dickson, Howard Krist, Howard Pollet, Ernie White, Jimmy Brown, Lou Klein, Harry Walker, Johnny Wyrostek, and George Munger to the service. For any other team, losses such as these would be completely demoralizing, but the Cardinal's farm system helped St. Louis withstand the change.

Beginning in 1942 there was an ongoing discussion as to whether baseball should continue with the war going on. One reason cited against continuing was that young men in America should not be *playing* baseball, while millions of others were fighting elsewhere. A second and more pragmatic argument, held that there were not enough quality players available for the game.

In a survey conducted on the subject, an overwhelming number of American servicemen (approximately 95 percent) wanted to see major league baseball continued. They said it was one of the few great joy they had from home. They didn't care if the players were 4F or not. Major League baseball was a real morale booster. The 1942 opening day lineups saw a 60 percent turnover from opening day of 1941.

A new draft policy would benefit the game. There was to be a slowing of call-up of men over the age of 26. However, while this was the national policy, local draft boards still had the final okay. An individual between the ages 26 and 29 could be classified 2A, which was a classification for a person found to be in a job necessary to the support of national health, safety, or interest. Each case would depend upon the interpretation of this phrase by the player's local draft board.

As the 1942 season began, the Cardinals were expected to have another runaway pennant, similar to 1943. General Manager Branch Rickey was so confident of victory that he predicted the Cardinals would win by 36 games, double the margin of the clubs 1943 finish games. That was quite a millstone to hang around the neck of manager Billy Southworth.

Major league teams were filled with 4F players, although the Cardinals had fewer than most. They had 10, while their St. Louis counterpart, the Browns, had 18. It certainly looked like 4Fs would decide the pennant races in both leagues.

The Cardinals had three players on the infield that were classified as 4F. First baseman Ray Sanders had a cardiac condition, his heart occasionally skipped a beat. George "Whitey" Kurowski had a trick right arm, which was missing a piece of bone. Second baseman Emil Verban had a perforated ear drum.

Pitcher Mort Cooper was classified 4F due to a back ailment. The other 4F players on the team were pitchers Harry Brecheen, Blix Donnelly, Bud Byerly, Ted Wilks, Ken O'Dea and outfielder Augie Bergamo. Five of the Cardinal 4F players were pitchers.

Verban, the new second baseman, tried to pattern his style of play after the former Cardinal great and his hero, Frankie Frisch. He was a line drive hitter, a good fielder, and stuck out very few times. He did not hit for power, but for the season, Verban would fan just 14 times in 498 at bats.

Regular Season Play

The Cardinals justified the forecasters prediction by reeling off five straight wins to open the season. Max Lanier opened with two complete game victories, and Brecheen had a complete game win, while Munger picked up two victories in relief. He followed Cooper and Gumbert in their starts for the victories.

The Cardinals then showed they were human by losing two to Cincinnati, 10-3 and 1-0 in 13 innings. Southworth called the 10-3 loss, "the worse Cardinals game I have ever been in charge". Al Jurisch, a promising right hander pitched very effectively, but was the loser in the 1-0 game. The Cardinals then took the next four games to run their record to 9-2.

Johnny Hopp took his physical at Jefferson Barracks on May 16th. Musial had his physical transferred from Donora, Pa. to St. Louis and was scheduled to have it on May 16th at Jefferson Barracks. The loss of these two players could prove devastating to the team. The war was even thinning the farm system.

In early May, the Cardinals trimmed their squad to 23 players, sending Byerly and third string catcher Sam Narron to Columbus. Narron thought that with the shortage of catchers in the big leagues there would be a spot for him. Rather than reporting to Columbus, the 30-year old Narron retired to his farm in Middlesex, North Carolina.

A new ruling arrived from Washington. Men over 26 could not called for duty in the next four months, which could save the season for many teams. Hopp was 27, and the new policy would help the Cardinals keep him, but Musial was 23, so he still could be lost. For several seasons preceding 1944, the Cardinals came up with key pitching finds. In 1941 it was Ernie White, then Johnny Beazley in 1942. In 1943, Alpha "Cotton" Brazle came along at an opportune time. He filled a "psychological" spot, authorized by the league due to war losses and finished the season with a record of 8-2 and a 1.53 ERA. He appeared in 13 games and completed eight of nine starts.

The latest find seemed to be the young right hander, Al Jurisch. Although he was only 1-2, he was pitching terrific ball. He lost 1-0 and 3-1, while winning 1-0. The team had scored only four runs for him in 30 innings of pitching.

The Cardinals lost the lead for a day on May 6th when Cincinnati righthander Bucky Walters pitched his second shutout win of the season over them. They quickly regained the lead the next day with a doubleheader win over the Reds. Musial was off to another great start, hitting in the first 14 games, before being stopped in the Cincinnati series. As the second week of May approached, the Cardinals were 12-5, ahead of the surprising Philadelphia Phillies team at 9-5 and Cincinnati at 9-6.

Musial was hitting .429 to lead the majors while Brecheen, Wilks and Munger were each 2-0 and Lanier was off to a 4-0 start. Meanwhile Cooper was struggling, at 1-2.

With the season just one month old, there didn't seem to be any real challenger in sight. The Cardinals were slowly starting to pull away at 18-6. Cincinnati trailed them at 13-9 followed by Philadelphia at 12-9. Cooper was rounding into form, while Lanier, Jurisch, Brecheen, and Munger gave the Cardinals great starting pitching. Wilks would have been starting for any other team in the league. Rarely did the Cardinals get a poorly pitched game.

The biggest worry for the team was that they might lose both Musial and Danny Litwhiler to the service. However, Southworth believed they would still win, but by a lesser margin. His goal was to build up a big a lead as possible, to buffer against possible player losses.

The war might do what the National League teams had failed to do for themselves for the previous three years; slow down the Cardinal pennant express. Musial was accepted by the Navy on May 16th and the team expected to lose him within six weeks. Gumbert was accepted by the Army and awaited a call up from the Houston draft board. Munger took his physical on May 23rd at Jefferson Barracks and expected a call to duty within the next six weeks. The team was facing the loss of a star outfielder, a star starting pitcher, and a key man in the bullpen.

More bad news came as Cooper, only 2-3, was temporarily on the shelf with a bad elbow. The loss of Munger and Gumbert would really hurt if Cooper didn't come around. Brecheen and Munger were both 3-1, while Musial and Litwhiler were each hitting .344. As mid-May passed, the Cardinals were 21-9 with Pittsburgh second at 15-10 and Cincinnati third at 17-12.

The fans were upset with the Cardinal management about the May 16th game against Philadelphia. It seemed the Philadelphia team had to catch an 11:15 train so no inning could begin after 10:15. The game was stopped after seven innings with St. Louis ahead, 6-4. The fans argued that the Cardinals were aware of the situation, so they should have started the game earlier than the regular starting time of 8:30. The game could have been finished if it had started at 7:30.

Fans were also complaining about the price of food, beverages, and scorecards. For years, many fans believed that charging for a scorecard was akin to a restaurant charging for its menu.

The Cardinals were idle much of the next week with two open dates and two rainouts at Brooklyn. They did play the final game of the series before making their first assault on the Polo Grounds.

Dizzy Dean predicted the Cardinals would win the league title by

25 games and have the pennant locked up by September 1st. At that time the team was 24-10, with Pittsburgh at 18-12 and Cincinnati at 19-14, giving the Cardinals a four game edge. Brooklyn's Dixie Walker was trying to take the batting crown from Musial and was hitting .424, while Musial was hitting .364. Litwhiler, Sanders, and Kurowski were each over .300. Cooper had rounded into form. Lanier was 6-0, Wilks was 3-0, Munger was 4-1, and Brecheen was 3-1.

The Cardinals continued to push for a larger lead to soften the possible loss of personnel to the service. They expected to lose Musial within the next 30 days. On their eastern tour, the team lost four of five to New York and Boston at one stretch. They rebounded to split a four-game set with each club. They won the only game in Brooklyn and took three of four in Philadelphia for an 8-5 road mark.

They lost two tough 1-0 games in Boston and Philadelphia as their lead held at four games. They had pushed it to five, but let it slip back. Southworth continued his attempts impress upon the players the importance of building of a large lead, as they expected to lose Munger, Musial, Litwhiler, and Gumbert.

Lanier lost some of his effectiveness, but was picked up by Cooper, who was coming on strong. Verban split the tip of his index finger, and was dropped from first to eighth in the hitting order. Southworth then replaced Verban with George Fallon, but he didn't hit either, so Verban got back into the lineup.

St. Louis suffered more injuries when a finger on Munger's right hand was badly bruised. He was able to return to duty after a short break and was used in relief on June 4th. Meanwhile Marion was forced to miss a game in Philadelphia because of a stomach disorder. The rest of the team seemed to be healthy.

Most of the other National League teams seemed to be falling by the wayside with only Pittsburgh and Cincinnati in the hunt. Pittsburgh trailed by four games and Cincinnati by 4 1/2. Of the

Cardinals previous seven pennant winners, only two teams won by large margins. The 1931 club won by 13, much of that accomplished in the last six weeks of the season, and the 1943 team by 18. All the other pennants races had been dog fights.

There was a possibility that the first ever all St. Louis World Series could take place, as the St. Louis Browns led the American League, and were threatening to win their first pennant. Both teams would prefer all night games in the World Series, and both clubs also wanted more night games in the regular season. At that time, all major league teams were limited to a maximum of 14 night games. The Cardinals were averaging 9,000 for day games, but 12,000 for night games.

The Cardinals came home on June 5th with a 5 1/2 game lead which they hoped to improve during the home stand. This Cardinal team was the closest of any team to pre-war performance. Then the Cardinals received some good news. Litwhiler (age 27) was reclassified as 2A, which could delay his being drafted. The team was hoping for a similar ruling for Gumbert and maybe some type of delay for Musial and Munger.

On June 10th, the Cardinals beat Cincinnati, 18-0, in the most one sided shut out since the Chicago Cubs defeated the New York Giants, 19-0 in 1906. Cincinnati used the youngest player ever to pitch in the majors. Lefthander Joe Nuxhall made his debut and in one inning walked five, allowed two hits, and gave up five runs. He returned to the minors, but would be back in the big leagues in 1952 and remain until 1966, winning 135 games.

It seemed as if June was the month for the Cardinals to set or come close to records or be involved in unique games. In the 18-0 win over Cincinnati, the Cardinals set a major league record for runners left on base at 18. They also hit their first home runs since May 30th when Cooper, Kurowski, and Litwhiler hit homers in succession on six pitches from Clyde Shoun. It was the 17th time in major league history that three home runs in a row had been hit.

In a doubleheader against the same Cincinnati club the next day, the Cardinals reeled off nine double plays to beat the old National League mark by two, falling one short of the major league mark held by Washington against Chicago White Sox on August 18, 1943.

By mid-June the Cardinal lead was 5 1/2 games over Pittsburgh and seven over Cincinnati. Walker continued to run away with the batting lead at .421, while Musial was a distant second at .346. The pitching was where the Cardinals shone. Munger was 7-1, Lanier was 6-2, Brecheen was 4-1, and Wilks was 3-1. Cooper had won his last two and was now 4-3, while Gumbert was 3-2.

On June 15th, the Cardinals sold Gumbert to one of their chief rivals, Cincinnati, for $25,000. One reason suggested was that Gumbert could be drafted at any time which he wasn't. Gumbert went 10-8 for Cincinnati to finish at 14-10. Some fans were angered and threaten not to come to the ball park, calling club president Sam Breadon "cheapskate". But Breadon's policy for decades had been to sell or trade a player while he still had value to make way for younger players. Gumbert was 34 and considered expendable.

The Cardinals farm system allowed the team to trade and replace players quality since the 1920s. While this system would work for a few years yet, by the end of the 1940s the farm system would slip in quality. By the 1950s, the game would change and the Cardinals' farm system would no longer the most dominating in baseball. Partially as a result of the weakened farm system, it would be another generation before the Rebirds would bring a championship to St. Louis.

The fan boycott didn't pan out and immediately after the Gumbert deal, the Cardinals had their two best attendance days of the year. On June 16th, a night game with Pittsburgh drew 18,645 and a doubleheader the next day with Pittsburgh brought in another 16,292.

The Cardinals were now 36-16, seven ahead of Pittsburgh and 7

1/2 up on the Giants. Walker was hitting .413, but his lead had shrunk as Musial was hitting .383. Hopp, Sanders, Litwhilter, Cooper, and Kurowski were hitting between .285 and .324 with the latter two over .300. Munger led the team at 8-1 and Lanier was a close second with a 7-2 mark. Cooper was creeping up and was now 5-3.

Munger got his notice to report to the Army on June 26th. He asked that his induction be changed to Jefferson Barracks. This would give him another start or two. He was 10-1.

Schmidt was ordered to take his physical on July 5th at Ashville, North Carolina. He also requested his physical be transferred to Jefferson Barracks. On the good news side, Musial was advised his call up could be delayed 30 to 60 days. He could play most of the season. Breadon said he had the best pitching staff in the service-- Munger, White, Beazley, Pollet, Brazle, Krist, Dickson, and Grodzicki. Also in the service was an outfield of Moore, Slaughter, and Walker.

The Cardinals had gone 12-2 against western foes (Chicago, Cincinnati, and Pittsburgh) since their eastern trip. They also had two 5-5 ties with Pittsburgh. The Cardinals had played to seven tie games in the past two seasons, six of them against Pittsburgh.

Fans started talking about the possibility of not just a 25-game or more margin, but of breaking the 1906 Chicago Cubs record of 116 wins. The Cardinals were on a pace to win 111, as they were 41-16, 9 1/2 games ahead of Pittsburgh, 11 ahead of New York and Brooklyn, and 12 up on Cincinnati.

The race for the batting title was narrowing, as Musial was aiming for his second consecutive crown. He was at .368 and Walker was hitting .385. Sanders, Litwhiler, Cooper, Kurowski and Hopp were hitting between .282 and .313, as Hopp had moved up among the league leaders. Brecheen was now 5-1 and Lanier was 7-3 while Cooper won again to reach 6-3 and looked like the 20-game winner of 1942-43.

The Cardinals quest of a new major league win mark received a severe jolt when the Phillies dealt them three straight losses. The first on June 28th, when the game suspended in May was completed. The Cardinals were leading when the game was originally stopped. They lost that game and two more. One of the defeats was at the hands of an ex-Cardinal farm hand, lefthander Ken Raffensberger, who shut them out. The Cards were blanked for 36 straight innings by Philadelphia pitching before they scored a run for Cooper in the second inning on June 30th. The team rebounded after the Philadelphia debacle to take four straight from visiting Brooklyn.

The Cardinals maintained their 9 1/2 game bulge on Pittsburgh with Cincinnati now 10 1/2 games out. The Cardinal players kept changing, but the lead remained constant. The batting race was almost a dead heat with Walker at .378 and Musial at .374. Lanier, in a slump, was now just 7-5. Cooper was number two in wins on the staff at 8-3, just behind Munger at 10-2 who lost a heartbreaker to Bill Lee of Philadelphia, 1-0.

The Cardinals started another streak in early July and won seven in a row. Then the unbelievable happened. The vaunted Cardinal pitching staff allowed 20 runs in two days, losing both games. But Cooper, Wilks, Brecheen bounced back to pitch three consecutive shutouts.

The Cardinals headed into the All Star game with six players selected for military service: Musial, Kurowski, Marion, Lanier, Munger, and Walker Cooper. Just as easily, Mort Cooper, Wilks, and Brecheen, who had already been drafted, could have qualified for the team.

Munger, with an 11-3 record and 1.34 ERA was inducted in the Army on the day of the All Star game, July 11th. He was looking forward to pitching in that game. He looked like a cinch to win 20, and possibly 25. When he returned from the service, Munger gave the Cardinals a couple of good seasons in the late 1940s, but never fully delivered on the promise he showed in 1943-44.

One year earlier, Pollet was inducted into the Army when he was 8-4 with the league's best ERA at 1.75. For two successive years, the Cardinals lost the best pitcher in the league at All Star time to the service, but they still had the depth to go on and win it all. Schmidt took his physical on July 11th.

Lanier, now 8-5, couldn't appear in the All Star game because of an arm ailment. When he won his eighth victory, the stocky left-hander started a personal 10-game winning streak. Some teams thought there was hope for them now that Munger was in the service and Lanier was ailing. St. Louis's margin was 10 1/2 over Pittsburgh and Cincinnati, as both were 51-21. The Birds were on a pace to win 110. The chase for a new total wins record began again.

Musial forged ahead of Walker in the batting race, .373 to .372, and Hopp was now up to .327. Cooper won his seventh in a row and was 9-3, while Brecheen picked up some of the slack to reach 6-1. Wilks was 4-1 and moved into the rotation. Jurisch was the fifth starter at 5-5.

A few optimistic clubs thought the loss of Munger would slow the Cardinals, but the new front line pitching quartet of Cooper, Lanier (now sound again), Wilks, and Brecheen kept them flying high. After the loss of Munger, the team won six of seven and 12 of 15. They were now at 61-24, 13 1/2 in front of Cincinnati and 15 in front of Pittsburgh.

Pittsburgh held the major league mark for the largest winning margin ever at 27 1/2 set in 1902. That team finished 103-36, a pace that would have produced 114 wins in a 154-game schedule.

There was a possibility of an all St. Louis series as the Browns were in first, but they were having a much harder time of it then their cross-town rivals. Speculation rose again that the Cardinals could break the Cubs 116-win mark. They won nine straight and on July 30th had won 14 of 16 in their most recent surge.

The Cardinals had three doubleheaders in four days and it would take strong hitting to carry a seven-man pitching staff through it. Byerly was expected to help, but he arrived from Columbus in poor condition. Then he was hit on the knee in batting practice, and further aggravated it running in the outfield.

When Cooper shut out Philadelphia, it was his fifth shutout of the year and the team's 17th. For the 1942-44 seasons the Cardinals pitching staff would hurl 65 shutouts and Cooper would pitch 23 of them, leading the league in 1942 and 1944. Cooper was now 12-4 and well on his way to his third 20-win season in a row. Wilks was 8-1 and Brecheen was 8-2, while Lanier was 10-5. When Jurisch won raising record 7-6 by the first of August, it was thought that he would win 12 or so. As it turned out that was his last victory of the season.

The batting race was still tight with Musial ahead at .351 while Walker was hitting .348. Both were still hitting exceptionally well, but each had come down from their lofty perches earlier in the season. St. Louis had a 15 1/2 game margin on Cincinnati and 16 over Pittsburgh. The team was now 68-26, a .723 pace, but "only" good enough for 111 victories.

Lanier's story was an interesting one. He broke his right arm twice as a young boy, which forced him to become a lefthander. Initially he was not given a lot of hope to pitch in the majors, but he had been a winning pitcher ever since he became a regular in 1940. Since then he was 9-6, 10-8, 13-8 and 15-7, with only his 1940 ERA (3.34) over 3.00. In 1943 he had a 1.90 ERA, second best in the league.

In Cincinnati, Wilks was hit in the head by a line drive off the bat of Steve Mesner (utility man for St. Louis in 1941). He was rushed to the hospital, but x-rays showed no serious injury. He went back to his pitching duties. Cooper was 14-5, Lanier was 12-5, (halfway through his 10 game winning streak), and Brecheen was 10-2. St. Louis's margin stood at 16 over Cincinnati and 18 1/2 over Pittsburgh, as the Cardinals were 72-27. Hopp was the key spark in the most recent drive that raised their lead to 18 1/2 games.

In mid-August Southworth was given a two-year contract. He was the first manager since Branch Rickey to be given such a deal. Since taking over the reins in early 1940 he had been 464-221, a .677 winning percentage.

Lanier won three games in one week in mid-August to tie him with Cooper for the team lead in wins at 15 each. He had two complete game wins and picked up one in relief. When Cincinnati's Walters beat the Cardinals it marked the fifth time this season he had defeated them.

Breadon said the majors were doing an excellent job of educating the youth of America on baseball. It was being done through baseball camps and American Legion play. The Cardinals were and always have been very instrumental and heavily involved in supporting both.

On August 18th, the Cardinals achieved another milestone as they won their 80th game, the earliest any team has ever reach that figure. The negative was that the Cardinal run away was hurting night game attendance.

Walker Cooper had a big hitting weekend on August 19th and August 20th. On the 19th, he had a single, two doubles and a home run in five at bats as his brother beat the Braves, 8-4. In the first game on August 20th, he had a single, double and home run in five at bats as the Cardinals won 15-5. He hit a home run in the second game that day, but the Cardinals lost 5-3.

Pittsburgh won 11 in a row, but only gained a half game as the Cardinals went 11-1 during the same stretch. Breadon was learning the same lesson that Connie Mack learned years ago. Now matter how great a team is, fans tire of it if victories come too easily.

Fans prefer to see a hotly contested race. It brings more excitement and enthusiasm to the ball park.

Toward the end of August , the Cardinals were 84-29, 17 1/2 games ahead of Pittsburgh and 19 1/2 over Cincinnati. They were on a pace to win 114 or 115. They needed to step up the pace a little to outpace the Cubs record. It really is asking something of a team that has won almost three of four games, to improve to four of five. They were also trying to beat the 1902 Pirates record margin of 27 1/2 games.

Walker edged ahead of Musial in the batting race, .357 to .356. Hopp was playing a great centerfield and moved into the batting race with a .346 average. If Southworth had played more of a running game, Hopp's name would be at the top of the stolen base list. The Cardinals top four pitchers were a combined 53-13. Cooper was 16-5, Lanier 15-5, Wilks 11-1, and Brecheen 11-2.

In a recent series with Pittsburgh,h the Cardinals were 1-1-1, and went 16-3-1 on their recent home stand with two to go against Cincinnati.

With a 90-30 mark the Cardinals had four goals: First and foremost, win the pennant. Second, break the Chicago Cubs win record of 116. They were on a pace to go 116-38, while the Cubs were 116-36. Third, beat the 1902 Pittsburgh margin of 27 1/2 games. The Redbirds were 18 1/2 ahead, and on a pace to be 25 games ahead. Finally, have the earliest clinching date ever. The 1931 Cardinals held that record with a September 16th date.

1944 also saw the earliest date yet for three teams to be eliminated from the race. Brooklyn fell on August 20th, while Boston went by the wayside on the 22nd and Philadelphia on the 24th. If Pittsburgh had been in the American league they would be in first place by seven games, which was twice the lead of the St. Louis Browns.

The batting race continued strung as Musial and Walker were

tied at .353 each, with Hopp right behind at .344 and Cooper moving up to .331. Musial had 85 RBIs and Sanders, at .304, had 90. With 34 games to go, both players were expected to exceed 100 RBIs. The last Cardinal to have 100 RBIs was Johnny Mize in 1941 with exactly that number. Cooper moved to 18-5 and Lanier, with his 10-game winning streak,was 17-5. Both looked like sure 20-game winners. Brecheen was 13-2 and Wilks was 12-1.

Wilks was now the latest rookie find from the Cardinals farm system. Meanwhile, Litwhiler was reclassified as 1A and was expected to go into the service shortly.

The Cardinals built their lead to 20 1/2 with a 92-30 mark over second place Pittsburgh at 72-51. If the team could hold that pace they would tie the record for victories, and possibly break it if they could get even hotter, as if that were possible. All of a sudden the team got shocked as they dropped four straight at Pittsburgh and their margin was reduced to 16 1/2 games. It was their worst streak since losing six straight in July 1943.

Even though the team had lost seven of their last 11 and chances for new records seemed to be frittering away, the club was swamped with requests for World Series tickets. The slump continued and on September 9th the Cubs beat St. Louis for the first time and handed Wilks his third loss of the year. The Cubs won again the next day, 1-0, before Cooper stoped them for his 21st win.

Cooper could beat his career high of 22, as he would have four or five more starts. Meanwhile, Lanier was complaining of a sore elbow. He had lost his last four starts and was in jeopardy of not winning 20 games. Walters handed the Cardinals another defeat, making it six times he had beaten them that year, and the third time he had shut them out.

Walker crept ahead in the batting race, .360 to .353, while Hopp slid back to .336 and Cooper to .324. Musial and Sanders have had just three RBIs each in the past two weeks. One of the reasons for

Musial's decline was the serious injury he suffered in a collision on September 10th. He later said he returned to play too soon. Since the Cardinals where so far ahead he should have stayed out longer to allow his injuries to heal.

Musial was then called to Donora, Pa. because of his father's serious illness. The mental strain, added to his physical injuries, hurt his hitting in the last month of the season and undoubtedly cost him the batting title and the Cardinals several victories.

Even more alarming was the situation with Lanier. At one point, he was challenging for the league lead in wins but now was complaining of a sore arm. He had lost four in a row, a losing streak that would reach seven. Lanier would finish with a 17-12 mark. That was a fine record, but he was 17-5 at one point. It is somewhat ironic that Lanier had a sore arm in each of his losing streaks. He started the season 6-0 and was in fine physical shape. Then he lost three of next four decisions while his arm hurt him. His arm then got better and he won 10 in a row. His arm started bothering him again and he lost seven in a row.

The Cardinals' tailspin had fans gasping and worrying. Most fans didn't believe they would lose the pennant, but there was concern about how well they would play in the World Series. On September 19th the Redbirds lost a doubleheader to the Cubs and had lost eight of nine and 15 of their last 20. After having a 10-3 edge on Pittsburgh they lost the last nine to finish the season at 10-12 against them. That was the first time since 1940 the team had lost a series for the year to anyone.

Southworth was concerned that the Cardinals were backing into the pennant. He wanted to win it outright. Southworth had it planned all differently. He was thinking of new win total, record victory margin, earliest clinching date ever. None of it happened. St. Louis' lead was down to 13 1/2 and their record was 96-45. Pittsburgh was 82-58, and the team had clinched a tie.

The Cardinals finally turned it around and won nine of their last 13, playing like they did for the first three quarters of the season, for a final record of 105-49 If that 5-15 had been reversed they would have had an excellent chance of tying or breaking the total victory record. Finally, on September 21st, the Cardinals clinched the pennant, winning the first game of a doubleheader with Boston.

There was no hoopla, no wild celebration. Maybe it was taken for granted or had been delayed so long. The team just walked off the field after the game just as if it were any other game. The let down of the previous three weeks undoubtedly had a lot to do with the quiet and reserved attitude the team had.

It was the third straight pennant for the Cardinals and it showed the strength of their farm system. Because of the farm system, the Cards could still field a team superior to any club in either league. The Cardinals had an estimated $500,000 of talent in the service and had sold $100,000 of talent the past two seasons. They sold players to impoverished teams and still had young players they could develop and turn into stars. There was enough depth to allow the Cardinals to sell Gumbert to Cincinnati and Elwin (Preacher) Roe to Pittsburgh, their two chief rivals. Gumbert won 10 for Cincinnati and Roe picked up 13 for Pittsburgh.

On the 1944 team, only two players on the Cardinals, Litwhiler and Garms, did not come through the farm system. It was a typical Cardinal team.

The Cardinals believed in apprenticeship for their players. They wanted them to spend several seasons in the minors, so they could be thoroughly schooled in their craft. The 20 Cardinal regulars had 96 years of minor league experience behind them. Wilks spent six seasons in the minors before he had his chance. Cooper and Lanier each had five years in the minors.

Brecheen was considered by many to be too small to make it in the majors. He began at Greenville in 1935 and didn't arrive in the

148

majors to stay until 1943. He pitched for the Cardinals for 10 years, finishing with a 127-79 record.

Schmidt began his career in 1937 at Shelby, North Carolina, while Jurisch started at Opelousa, Louisiana in 1939 and Blix Donnelly began in 1938 at Daytona Beach, Florida. These seven hurlers had a composite of 38 years of minor league experience before getting their chance at the majors.

The same was true with the position players. Walker Cooper had seven years in the minors, while Kurowski had six. Marion, Musial, Hopp and Sanders each spent four season in the minors and Verban spent eight. Sanders had started at Paducah, Kentucky in 1938.

Not only were players groomed, polished and developed in the minors, the same process was used to develop managers and coaches as well. Southworth started managing at Rochester in 1928. Gonzales, a former catcher, started coaching young pitchers in 1931.

There were some who wanted to do away with the farm system, and use a draft type operation for securing players. They argued it would lead to more parity. The Cardinals and the Yankees were classic examples of excellent farm systems. Later on, Rickey would do the same thing with the Dodgers, who would win six pennants between 1947 and 1956.

Dixie Walker finished the season with a .357 average to win the batting title. Musial was second at .347, slowed down by his injury in early September. He had 94 RBIs, and Hopp had 72 while hitting .336. Cooper finished at .317 with 72 RBIs and tied the Cardinal team record for home runs by a catcher at 13. Kurowski tailed off to .270, but had 95 runs, 20 home runs and 87 RBIs. Sanders led the team with 102 RBIs, while hitting .295.

Cooper finished at 22-7, 2.46 ERA and seven shut outs, which led the league. Lanier was 17-12, 2.65 ERA and five shut outs. Wilks was 17-4, 2.65 ERA and four shut outs, while Brecheen was 16-5,

2.85 ERA and three shut outs. This front four won 72 and lost just 28, a .720 win percentage.

No team in baseball in 1944 could match St. Louis's top four pitchers. The Detroit Tigers' top four won 79, paced by Hal Newhouser with 29 and Dizzy Trout with 27, but they also lost 49. Rube Gentry was 12-14 and Stubby Overmire was 11-11.

The World Series

The St. Louis Browns clinched the American League pennant on the final day of the season and created the first and only all-St. Louis World Series. It would be the first time that all the games of the World Series would be played in the same park since 1922 when the New York Yankees and the New York Giants played at the Polo Grounds, in 1921 and 1922 (Yankee Stadium wasn't ready until 1923).

The Cardinals were heavy favorites to win the World Series, but the Browns were the sentimental favorites. The Cardinals had a fairly long injury list entering the World Series. Lanier complained of a sore arm and had not pitched since September 22nd. Musial had a knee injury and Marion was in bad health. Jurisch also was nursing a sore arm.

The Cardinals were confident, but not cocky. They had out-hit the Browns .278 to .253. The Cardinals made 106 errors in the season versus the Browns' 161. The Cardinals had an edge in home runs, 100-71, shutouts 26-16, complete games 89-69, and ERA with a 2.67 mark compared to the Browns' 3.17. Catching was a major weakness of the Browns as the Cardinals' Walker Cooper was considered the best in the majors. All the statistics favored the Cardinals.

The Series would turn out to be a pitchers' delight, as the Cardinals batted just .240, while the Browns hit an anemic .183. If the Browns' fielding had kept pace with their hitting the outcome might have been different. The Browns made 10 errors to the Cardinals one.

The series saw a new record for strikeouts by two teams in a six-game Series. The Browns fanned 49 times and the Cardinals had 43 go down on strikes. For the Browns, Gene Moore, Mark Christman, and Chet Laabs each fanned six times. Hopp led the Cardinals with eight whiffs.

Early in the Series, the Cardinals were lethargic and looked like the team that had slumped in early and mid-September. Starting with the fourth game, they looked like the dynamo that had swept through the National League for the first 122 games. All played well in the Series, but shortstop Marty Marion was unbelievable.

In game one, Cooper tossed a two-hitter and lost 2-1 to Denny Galehouse when Gene Moore singled and George McQuinn hit a two-run home run in the fourth. Game two saw a great relief job by Blix Donnelly to win the game for the Redbirds in 10 innings, 3-2. In the eighth inning, Donnelly relieved Lanier after Mike Kreevich had doubled. He then fanned Laabs, Vernon Stephens, and Christman. In the 11th, McQuinn opened with a double, but great fielding by Donnelly on a bunt by Christman got McQuinn out at third.

Instead of the Browns having runners on first and third with nobody out, there was a runner on first with one out. Many consider that the crucial play of the Series. If the Browns had won the game, they would have been up two games to none. The Browns made four errors as the Cardinals won 3-2. The Cardinals' first two runs were unearned, allowed by three errors (two by Nelson Potter and one by Christman).

In the third Verban singled, and Potter messed up Lanier's bunt. First he fumbled it, then he threw it into right field trying to get Verban, who wound up at third. Verban scored on a ground out by Bergamo. With one out in the fourth, Sanders walked, Kurowski singled, Marion was safe on Christman's error, and Verban brought Sanders home with a sacrifice fly.

For 6 1/3 innings, the only hit off Lanier was a bunt by Moore. Then Ray Hayworth, Moore, and Mancuso tied the game with successive hits. That's when Donnelly relieved. In the Cardinals 11th, Sanders singled, Kurowski sacrificed, Marion was intentionally passed, and O'Dea, pinch hitting for Verban, singled Sanders home with the winning run.

In game three, Jack Kramer stopped the Cardinals 6-2, as the Browns kayoed Wilks with a four-run third with five singles. Schmidt was unscored upon in 3 1/3 innings. The Browns added two in the seventh off Jurisch on a walk and doubles by McQuinn, who hit .438 for the Series, and Don Gutteridge. The Cardinals had just seven hits, as Kramer fanned 10.

In game four, Brecheen defeated the Browns 5-1. Although he allowed nine hits, all were singles. Musial was the hitting star of the game with a walk, single, double, and home run in five at bats. His two-run home run in the first got the team started. Cooper hit a triple in the ninth, but was thrown out trying for an inside the park home run.

The Series was knotted at two games each. Game five was a return match-up for Galehouse and Cooper. Again Galehouse pitched brilliantly. However, this time Cooper shutout the Browns, allowing just seven hits and fanning 12. Litwhiler and Sanders each hit solo home runs for the only scoring in the game.

With a three games to two lead, Southworth picked Lanier to try to nail it down. Lanier allowed a home run to Laabs in the second and that was all the Browns scoring for the day. In the sixth with the Cardinals ahead 3-1, Lanier walked Laabs and McQuinn with one out. Then he made a wild pitch to Christman which put runners on second and third. Wilks entered the game and got Christman ground to Kurowski, who threw home and Cooper tagged Laabs out. Hayworth then flied out to Hopp. That was the last Browns' threat of the Series. Wilks retired all 11 men he faced. The Cardinals scored all their runs in the fourth. With one out, Cooper walked, Sanders singled, and an error by Stephens on Kurowski's grounder allowed Cooper to score. Marion lined out, but Verban and Lanier each hit the first pitch for a single, scoring two runs. The Cardinals had a 3-1 lead that would carry them to their fifth World Series title in eight tries.

Verban, after going just two for his first 12 and being lifted for a pinch hitter in each of the first three games, was five for his last seven. He finished at seven for 17 and the Cardinals best average at during the Series of .412. Sanders had one hit in each game and batted .286, while Cooper hit .318 and Musial hit .304.

Marion played brilliant ball in the Series. He made no errors and many great plays. Stephens committed three errors. Stephens, the better offensive threat hit the same as Marion, .227. For the regular season Marion was voted MVP, making three consecutive seasons a Cardinal had won the MVP award. Musial was glad for Marion, and said it was a real tribute to a defensive player.

Epilogue

The 1944 Cardinals were just one of six clubs to lead their league in runs, batting, fielding, and ERA. One of the other five was the 1946 Cardinals, substantially the same club playing in a tougher league.

The Cardinals lost four more players to the service before the start of the 1945 season: Walker Cooper, Schmidt, Litwhiler, and the biggest loss of all, Musial. Still they figured they had enough talent to win a fourth straight title. The only other National League team to do that was the Giants in 1921-24.

The club still had good pitching, led by Cooper, Lanier, Wilks, and Brecheen. But that was where fate intervened. Cooper came down with an elbow injury and after a 2-0 mark and 1.50 ERA in four games, Breadon shocked St. Louis fans by trading him to Boston. He was the Cardinal meal ticket, winner of 65 games the past three years, still he was traded.

Cooper continued to have physical problems and was just 7-4 for Boston, as he could make only 11 starts. Early in the season, the Cardinals acquired 30-year old Charles "Red" Barrett, who had been bouncing around the majors since 1937. He was in 12 games with Cincinnati from 1937-40, posting a 3-0 mark. He was traded to Boston and reappeared in the majors in 1943 going 12-18 that year followed by a 9-16 record in 1944. In 1945, prior to his trade to the Cardinals, he was 2-3 with a 4.74 ERA in nine games.

St. Louis had traded the premier pitcher in the league for one that had lost 34 games the past two years, and whose career mark was 26-37. However, Barrett more than held his own, going 21-9 with a 2.73 ERA in 34 games for St. Louis in 1945. He led the league with 23 victories and 24 complete games.

Lanier was 2-2 with 1.73 ERA when he was called into service in 1945. Wilks developed a sore arm and was just 4-7. Thus, three of the four top pitchers of 1944 were of no value to the Cardinals in 1945. Only Brecheen was able to carry his weight. He only got into 24 games, 18 as a starter, but was 15-4 with a 2.52 ERA.

The Cardinals brought up Ken Burkhart and, as a rookie, he was 18-8 with a 2.90 ERA, Burkhart appeared in 42 games, 22 as a starter. He was a pleasant surprise. Unfortunately the rest of the staff produced journeyman numbers. The front three was 54-21, while the balance of the staff was 41-38.

The Cardinals finished 1945 at 95-59, three games behind the Chicago Cubs. The Cubs were greatly helped by the mid season acquisition of Hank Borowy from the Yankees. He had been 10-5 for New York. He was even better for Chicago, going 11-2, with a league best 2.14 ERA and completing 11 of 14 starts. Without him, the Cardinals would have repeated, despite all their losses to the military and other misfortunes.

Even with the loss of Musial, Litwhiler, and Cooper, the run production was only 16 runs fewer than in 1944. Kurowski had a big season, hitting .323 with 21 home runs and 102 RBIs. Al "Red" Schoendienst was a rookie in 1945 when he hit .278 and led the league in stolen bases playing left field.

The Cardinals acquired Buster Adams from the Phillies. He had been a Cardinal farm hand at one time. Adams would finish the season with 104 runs scored, 22 home runs, 109 RBIs and a .287 average. Although Kurowski was the only .300 hitter, every Cardinal batted between .276 and .292 except O'Dea, who had become the regular catcher, who hit .254.

The Cardinals defeated the Cubs 16 of 22 times during the season, but the Cubs made hay with the second division. Their main patsy was Cincinnati, who finished 61-93 after a third place finish in 1944. The Cubs defeated Cincinnati in 21 of 22 games, while the Cardinals were 13-9 against them. The Cubs also swept 20 doubleheaders.

For the first six years of the 1940s the Cardinals had three first place finishes, two second, and a third. They also had two World Series titles to their credit. The decade wasn't over and the Redbirds would cover themselves with more glory before it ended.

George Kurowski

Johnny Hopp

Ray Sanders

Max Lanier

ROW FOUR L-R   Jones, Sisler, Kluttz, Krist, Rice, Burkhart, Doc Weaver, Wilks, Garagiola, Donnelly, Brecheen, Cross,
ROW THREE L-R   Schmidt, Sessi, Beazley, Schoendienst, Walker, Endicott, Pollet, Dusak, O'Dea, Grodzicki, Barrett, Ward
ROW TWO L-R   Marion, Kurowski, Musial, Brazle, Wares, Dyer, Gonzales, Adams, Moore, Slaughter, Dickson
ROW ONE L-R   B. Scanlon, E. Dyer Jr. (Bat Boys)

1946

The Pennant Almost Went South Of The Border

Prologue

The war in the Pacific and Europe had ended and the troops were returning home. This meant major league ball could return to its pre-World War II status. While most major leaguers came back, some would never be the same. Careers were shattered for various reasons. The innocence of baseball in 1941 would not be the same in the years after the war. Many changes would take place.

A new war loomed on the horizon as Senor Don Jorge Pasquel, president and guiding genius of the Mexican League, declared war on Organized Baseball. He claimed to have a bankroll of $30,000,000 and he wanted to lure American players to Mexico with offers far beyond what they were used to playing for.

Baseball owners called foul, but at this juncture legally nothing could be done about it. Pasquel said, "Organized Baseball is just getting a dose of its own medicine." For years major league clubs had raided minor league teams, especially if in a pennant drive late in the season. Many times the teams they raided were also in a pennant fight, but the major league club didn't care.

This wasn't true of all teams, as many wanted the minor league clubs to grow and prosper. They knew that a pennant in Rochester, Newark, Omaha, or Columbia was just as important as in St. Louis, New York, or Detroit. It meant as much to the fans in those cities as it did in the majors.

Pasquel already had Luis Olmo of the Dodgers under contract for a reported three years at $40,000 tax-free plus all expenses for him and his wife. The Dodgers' final offer was $12,000 per year, which he said was too little, too late. Pasqual had signed outfielder Danny Gardella of the Giants or was trying to get Joe Medwick, even though he was now 34.

Pasquel felt he could still hit, especially in the Mexican League and would also be a great gate attraction. He was also trying to get Babe Ruth as one of the eight owners. Neither of these deals had come to fruition.

Branch Rickey asked Commissioner Albert (Happy) Chandler to issue a ban against Mexican jumpers. Major League owners awaited the commissioners' decision. He said it is to early to issue a blanket policy. For the present, each case must be decided on its own merits. The latest jumper was pitcher Alex Carrasquel of the Chicago White Sox.

Meanwhile the Cardinals had a new manager, Eddie Dyer, who had once been a southpaw in their farm system. Billy Southworth had left the team after a dispute with owner Sam Breadon. Dyer's goal was to establish another Gashouse Gang type team. He took the first step by restoring Terry Moore as team captain, as he had the guts, grit, spirit, and speed ala the 1934 team.

The Cardinals had lost a heartbreaker in 1945, which ended their three-year reign atop the National League. They wanted some revenge. The 1945 team was a good one, albeit short many of its stars. It battled hard and won 95 games, but the Cubs won 98. A mid season acquisition of Hank Borowy, who was 11-2 for them and winning 21 of 22 from Cincinnati gave them the pennant, even though they lost 16 of 22 to the Cardinals.

The Cardinals were installed as heavy favorites to win the pennant in 1946. They had reassembled most of the team that won the 1942-44 pennants. The club had Moore, Stan Musial, and Enos Slaughter in the outfield. The infield consisted of a combination of Marty Marion, Whitey Kurowski, Lou Klein, Emil Verban, and Red Schoendienst with Dick Sisler and Ray Sanders battling for first base.

Catching was the one weak spot. Ken O'Dea had back problems and Del Rice and Del Wilber hadn't measured up at this point for the starting catching position.

Verban and Klein were expected to fight it out for second base, with Schoendienst as infield or outfield reserve. Dyer has said, "if

Red hit only .278 against war time pitching, what can we expect when the real pitchers return?" At this time he wasn't impressed with the Redhead.

Kurowski would be the third baseman, assuming he got into shape and signed his contract, as he was the lone Cardinal holdout. They needed his big righthanded bat in the lineup, especially since Walker Cooper had been sold to the Giants in the off season and Danny Litwhiler was still in the Army. Jeff Cross and Erv Dusak would be reserve infielders, with Dusak also available for outfield duty. There is also Buster Adams, who had a big year in 1945, and Harry Walker ready to play in the outfield should injury befall any of the three starters.

It is the pitching where the Cardinals were expected to glow. They had Charles "Red" Barrett and Ken Burkhart, who had won 41 games the previous year, Harry Brecheen, and Ted Wilks from the 1945 team. Returning from the service were Max Lanier, Howard Pollet, Murray Dickson, Johnny Beazley, Ernie White, and Johnny Grodzicki. It is uncertain when George "Red" Munger will be out of the Army.

Dyer was on the hot spot. He had to win or else. He had replaced a highly successful and popular manager in Southworth. In four and two-thirds years, he won 480 and lost just 225. For the seasons 1942-45 he averaged 103 wins per year. He has three pennants, two World Championships, and two second place finishes.

As the veterans returned from the service, they pushed the young kids and old timers out of the lineup and, in many instances, back to the minors or out of the league completely. The Cardinals were no different. Gone from this team would be the likes of Augie Bergamo, Debs Garms, George Dockins, Jack Creel, and Bud Byerly.

Dyer's problems started in spring training. Not only did he have

162

to compete against Southworth's record, he had to worry about the Cardinals being overrated. To add to his problems, players started to have injuries and sore arms.

Breadon had sold Hopp to Boston prior to the start of the season as well as Jimmy Brown and Johnny Wyrostek to Pittsburgh and Cincinnati respectively. Moore was having leg problems and was doubtful to open in center field. If so, then Walker would get a chance to play. Grodzicki, who was a highly touted rookie before the war, had a serious shrapnel injury to his right leg and had trouble making the proper pitching delivery. It is questionable if he would be able to play and it looked like a potentially fine career was over.

Beazley, the hero of the 1942 World Series, had developed arm trouble and White was once again nursing a sore arm. Beazley was 21-6 in 1942 and White was 17-7 in 1941 and both were heavily counted on for this season, especially since Morton Cooper was no longer with the team and Munger was still in the Army. All of a sudden that rosy forecast looked a little tarnished.

In the meantime, a problem developed with Kurowski, the only Cardinal holdout. The concern was if he would be ready to play when he did agree to a contract. Dusak and Schoendienst were both working out at third, just in case. Kurowski eventually won his pay fight then had to battle for his job. He received an estimated $13,500.

Dyer was starting to have second thoughts about the Redhead. The more he saw, the more he liked. He had shown he could play the outfield, third, shortstop, and second. Little did Dyer realize at the time that he had the man who would become the premier second baseman in the league for a dozen years.

Dyer named his present big five pitching staff; Pollet, Brecheen, Lanier, Barrett, and Freddie Martin. Martin was a 30-year old rookie, who had waited 11 years for the chance to play in the majors.

He had spent seven in the minors and four in the Army.

If Beazley, Grodzicki and White came around, the Cardinals looked unbeatable. They still had Wilks, Burkhart, and Dickson in the bullpen. This could be the best Cardinal pitching staff in history. Dyer was concerned about the "super duper" rating given the Cardinals and that the pennant was theirs before a ball was pitched. Breadon sold Sanders to Boston for $40,000. Dick Sisler, son of St. Louis Browns great George Sisler, was to play first, putting a lot of pressure on the young man. He not only had to prove himself, but he had his father's reputation to live up to.

About that time, there was a movement for a players' guild or union. The organizer proposed a pay arbitration policy. If a player and owner couldn't get together, they would go to an arbitrator who would make the decision. Also proposed was that a player would get a portion of the sale price anytime he was sold to another team. Further, a minimum salary should be established.

Needless to say, the owners were opposed to these requests and many said it would destroy the game of baseball. They fell that eliminating the reserve clause would destroy the foundation on which baseball was built. The owners with the most money could then bid for, and get, the best players. Parity could not and would not exist in baseball. They must have had a crystal ball to see what would happen in the 1980s and 1990s.

This is the fourth attempt to form a players' guild or union. Robert Murphy, a Boston labor relations counselor, was the man spearheading the latest effort. The first effort was organized by John Montgomery Ward, a lawyer and shortstop in 1885. His guild had received some concessions, but when it had backed the Players League (a share-the-wealth concept) the players jumped to the league. It had collapsed within one year.

It had been revived 10 years later with Charley Zimmermann as president, but had died again in 1902. The third union, the Players

Fraternity, reached considerable power when it was formed in 1912 by Dave Fultz, lawyer and former outfielder. It lasted until 1918 when the United States got into World War I and when the War Department put in its "Work or Fight" order, it collapsed.

Regular Season Play

The 1946 baseball wars began with the Cardinals losing their opener, but then Pollet, Brecheen, and Lanier held Pittsburgh and Chicago to two runs in three games. Pollet gave up the only runs on a two-run home run by Ralph Kiner, soon to be baseball's new home run king. Schoendienst's great play spurred Kurowski to get in shape to win his job back and trade rumors circulated around the hard-hitting third baseman.

The Cardinals shining star, their pitching staff, began to flicker and dim. Barrett was unimpressive. The Cardinals were 9-2, then lost a doubleheader at home to the Chicago Cubs on April 28th. Lanier had been unbeatable in the early going, while Pollet and Brecheen were inconsistent. Beazley had pitched opening day, but had been unable to throw since. Dickson and Donnelly, counted on for bullpen duty, had not done the job. After two weeks Barrett was still winless.

Marion was out with an injury from the first game on April 28th so Schoendienst went to shortstop and Kurowski got into the lineup at third. Walker, subbing for Moore, was just 1 for 17. Despite all this, St. Louis was tied with Brooklyn for first place.

The Cardinals, in need of catching help, got involved in a three-way trade with the Phillies and Giants. The Cardinals sent Verban and Al Jurisch to the Phillies, who sent Vince DiMaggio to the Giants, who sent Clyde Klutz to the Cardinals.

The Redbird express had slowed to a walk, stymied by bad weather and hill problems. They won just one game in a week and it began to look like the race would not be a Cardinal runaway.

After winning his first two starts, Pollet was hit hard each of the last two Sunday games (April 28th and May 5th). However Lanier got his fourth consecutive complete game win and, at 4-0, was the ace of the staff.

Beazley still hadn't pitched since opening day. Brecheen also ran into problems. He was hit hard by the Pirates and Giants. In his next start he pitched eight strong innings against them before getting rocked for four runs in the ninth. Meanwhile Barrett hadn't pitched since April 28th, while Howard Krist and Wilks were hit hard in relief.

Krist was another Cardinal pitcher who never regained his form. He started and relieved during his career, with most of the emphasis on the latter. Krist was 3-1 with the Cardinals in 1937 then didn't return to stay until 1941, when he was 10-0. He followed that year with 13-3 and 11-5 seasons. After two years in the service he came back with a 37-9 career mark, but he would only appear in 15 games this year, finish at 0-2, then end his major league career.

With Verban gone, the trade rumors surrounding Kurowski subsided. He was playing third with Schoendienst at second. Walker started at three for 28, while Hopp, now with the Braves, had two home runs, two doubles, and three singles in a doubleheader against the Cardinals. The Cardinals have their own hot hitter, as Musial was 12 for his last 20, including four doubles and two triples.

After three weeks in the season St. Louis and Brooklyn were tied for first, with Boston third and Chicago fourth. Billy Herman led the league with .405, followed by Dixie Walker at .381 and Musial at .368.

Dyer believed the Cardinals had a good ball club, but forecasters giving them the pennant on a silver platter had hurt. It made some of the players think they had it made, no real competition, when that was not true. The fans thought the team would have a breeze and were disappointed to find the club not running away with it.

Dyer knew the team had more problems than the critics realized.

No one knew the depth of the arm problems with the pitching staff. He did not have a dependable righthanded starter. Neither Beazley, Barrett, or Burkhart could be counted on for that role. Munger was still in the service and Dickson and Wilks were working out of the bullpen.

Moore had been used sparingly as his legs were not in shape. Walker hadn't hit as he did in 1942-43, when he hit over .300 for the two seasons. Kurowski was a long hold out and was slow getting into shape. Marion, while fielding well, was not hitting. Only Musial, Schoendienst, and Slaughter had performed as expected.

Sunday doubleheaders at Sportsman's Park were fun in the early '40s. They were filled with hot dogs, peanuts, soda, cold beer, and Cardinal victories. So far this season the team was 1-5 in three home doubleheaders. They lost one to archrival Chicago and one to Cincinnati and split a twin-bill with Boston. The boo birds were out in strong numbers on Sunday, May 12th, after the team dropped a twin bill to Cincinnati.

With Sisler not hitting, and Sanders and Hopp gone, Dyer considered using Musial at first base. He was hitting .403, while Schoendienst was at .333, Slaughter at .304, and Kurowski was up to .310. They had good hitting, but the pitching, which was expected to be the best in baseball, hadn't performed up to its press clippings. Although Pollet was 2-1, he was winless in his last three starts. Brooklyn was 15-7 and the Cardinals were two back with a 12-8 mark, after starting 9-2.

Billy Werber, former major league infielder, said union security was not suited to game of baseball. Werber, known as a hard negotiator in his time, did not believe baseball should have a union. Seniority was the cornerstone of a union and it should not and could not apply in the game. If seniority were the rule, it could force a manager to play an over the hill veteran in place of a hot young prospect.

Werber said that ball players were highly individualistic performers and there were only 400 of them in the major leagues. No other profession had such a small cadre of personnel. In his opinion baseball would wither and dye on the vine.

In mid May, the Cardinals took five of six road games from Brooklyn, Boston, and Philadelphia. The two wins in Brooklyn put the team back in first place by a half game. They got great pitching from Pollet, Lanier, and Brecheen. Breadon told Lou Perini, owner of the Boston Braves, that Kurowski was not for sale, not for even $100,000. He also ridiculed a rumor that Pollet would be traded for veteran first baseman Babe Young of the Giants.

Musial adapted to first base and would play 75 percent of his games at that position this year. He continued to battle Dixie Walker for the batting lead, holding a slight edge at .375 to .370. Kurowski was hot and now hitting .349 with Schoendienst still at .333, while Slaughter and Moore were both at .300. Lanier was 5-0, with five complete games in five starts and an ERA less than two runs per game. He looked like he was headed for a 20-win season. He was pitching better than he did during his six or ten game winning streak in 1944.

Just when it looked like the pieces were falling into place and the team was starting to jell, a bombshell dropped. Pasquel lured Klein, Martin (2-1), and Lanier to Mexico. Lanier left with a 6-0 mark and six complete games in six starts. Even more alarming he had a 21-7 career mark against the Dodgers. Lanier signed for $30,000 a year for five years plus a $50,000 signing bonus.

While the team could probably survive the loss of Klein and Martin, although Martin had two complete games in three starts and could have been the righthanded started the team needed, the real loss was Lanier. He was pitching like a potential 25-game winner. This was a serious blow to the pennant chances. The team was left with only two dependable starters, Pollet and Brecheen.

In the meantime Moore, Slaughter, and Musial turned down big contract offers from Pasquel. He contended he would get Musial to sign. Pasquel and former major league catcher Mickey Owen visited Musial. He and his wife, Lil, were in the process of moving to Southwest St. Louis City and had rented a bungalow. This would be the first time that they had not lived in a cramped apartment or hotel.

Owen was with Pasquel to try to convince Musial of the advantages of playing baseball in Mexico. Pasquel placed five $10,000 cashiers checks on the bed, each made out to Musial and said that was his signing bonus. In addition, he would get $25,000 a year for five years. Musial said he would have to think it over. Pasquel still wanted Slaughter and Moore.

Dyer had talked to the team and explained to them what it meant to be a big league ball player in the United States. He was a convincing, eloquent speaker. The players listened. Dyer offered the clincher to Musial when he said, "Stan, you've got two children. Do you want them to hear someone say, 'there are the kids of a guy who broke his contract?'" That did it. Musial turned down the offer.

Reporters continued to hound him and when they saw him packing, they asked if he was moving. He told them yes, not to Mexico, but to Mardel Avenue. He played that night and, despite all the commotion and state of flux, got two hits. At home he asked his wife the date and when she replied, he told her he would remember that date (June 6th) forever. It was also D-Day, the Normandy Invasion.

Kurowski had also been approached by the Pasquel but turned him down. He said (in his usual blunt manner), "I believe in getting all the dough I can, but once signed, I honor that contract. Let's forget this Mexican business and try to concentrate on winning the pennant and getting into the World Series." With that, the Mexican Adventure was ended.

Back in the winter Dyer's main concern about his pitching staff was how to get enough work for all of them. He thought he had at least seven dependable starters; Barrett, Beazley, Burkhart, Krist, and White were 88-35 in their last season of work, counting White's 1941 record. With Pollet, Brecheen, Lanier, Wilks, and Dickson, added to the mix the possibilities seemed unlimited.

Now with the decimating injuries and defections, Dyer was forced to scrape the barrel for hurlers. The mound difficulties continued to multiply. Pitched had moved from number one asset, to his number one problem. He still needed a number one righthanded pitcher and adequate relief pitching. The latter had been spotty.

Beazley had pitched a complete game win, a four-hitter over the Giants, giving him the confidence that he was returning to his old self. But in his next start on May 23rd against the Cubs he was bombed. Two days later he went to Nashville, Tennessee to see his family doctor in hopes of finding a cure for his problem.

Other righthand pitchers tried and failed to fill the void. Barrett was still winless, while Burkhart was inconsistent. Wilks did a good job relieving Beazley in Chicago, then was bombed by the Giants in a start on June 2nd. The search for a dependable righthanded starter continued.

Brooklyn had forged ahead by 3 1/2 games on their 28-14 mark, while St. Louis was 24-17. It looked like a two-team race. Cincinnati had the best team ERA with 3.39, while Brooklyn was second at 3.6, and St. Louis third with 3.74.

Musial "slipped" to .340, hurt by all the turmoil over the Mexican situation. The pressure from the media and Mexico had become almost unbearable at times. His slump also hurt the Cardinals, although Schoendienst was now at .358, Kurowski .327, and Slaughter at .304 was on a pace for 100 or more RBIs. Pollet had now become the ace of the staff at 4-2.

Just when it looked like everyone could concentrate on playing baseball without any more distractions, a new one popped up. A players strike threatened by the Pirates was averted. The players arguments included a minimum wage of $5,000 per season, arbitration, a pension plan, and a percentage of the money if a player was sold. The players would eventually receive the first three, but not the fourth, as that was considered a prerogative of management.

Just when things looked the darkest a ray of sunshine finally peeped through. The Cardinals were just 4-6 at home versus New York, who would finish last, Boston, and Philadelphia. On June 8th, Barrett gained his first victory of the season with a one-hitter against Philadelphia. He retired the first 22 men before Del Ennis singled.

No one had expected the jovial Barrett to win 23 again, most figured he would win between 15 and 18 games. The way he had pitched this spring, most observers believed he would be playing somewhere else if Lanier and Martin hadn't jumped and Beazley hadn't developed arm trouble.

Litwhiler, recently released from the Army, was sold to Boston for $15,000. Just as the Cardinals trailed the Dodgers in the standings, so did Musial in his batting race with Dixie Walker. He was down by 34 points, hitting .342. Pollet, now considered the ace of the staff had lost his last two starts and was 4-3.

Not only did the team have pitching problems, the hitting had not been consistent. Musial, Slaughter, Schoendienst, and Kurowski had carried the load, but nobody else had really produced. Adams and Harry Walker were not hitting, as both were well below .200. Musial returned to first as Sisler was hitting a disappointing .260 with little power.

Their pitching continued to be the Achilles heel. Just when it looked like Barrett was going to pitch like the Barrett of 1945, he returned to the form he had displayed all spring. He was bombed by the Dodgers in relief on June 11th, then the Phillies hit him for five runs in one third of an inning. One bright spot was Joe Garagiola, the 20-year old catcher just released from the Army. Everyone was predicting a bright future for the fellow from The Hill, the Italian district in south St. Louis where Garagiola and Yogi Berra grew up together.

Another rumor surfaced concerning the Cardinals and Breadon. It was suggested that Breadon had tried to sell the Cardinals to Pasquel during his trip to Mexico. He flatly denied the story. Breadon gave Musial a $5,000 bonus after he turned down Pasquel's last offer.

Part of the GI Bill stipulated that returning veterans had to either be given their old jobs back or an equal position or, failing either one, a year's salary. When applied to major league baseball this ruling would affect 143 players. The courts had not ruled whether this provision applied to major league baseball because of the uniqueness of the skills required.

The Cardinals received some good news when Musial, Slaughter, Marion, Kurowski, Pollet, and Brecheen were chosen for the annual All Star game. Unfortunately, their fate in that game was no better than their team's as the National League lost, 12-0, in the most lopsided score in the history of the classic. Ted Williams hit two home runs for the American League.

Before the All Star break the Cardinals swept all four in Boston, then stumbled in New York and Brooklyn, losing two of three in each town. Brooklyn defeated Brazle and Brecheen, only Pollet could win. It seemed Brecheen had also developed arm trouble.

Dyer had said, "If we are no more than five games behind by July 4th, we will win." It wasn't likely that he would be five behind. They returned home on July 1st, 5 1/2 games out and proceeded to lose two games to the Reds while Brooklyn was taking two from Philadelphia. Now they were 7 1/2 out, when many thought by this time the team would be 10 or 15 games in front.

It seemed as though the team just couldn't stand prosperity or stay injury free. Schoendienst had been out with bad ankles, but was back in the lineup. Moore had to go to the sidelines again, as his legs were giving him trouble once more. Dyer now preferred having Musial at first, although the Musial preferred the outfield. But he would play wherever the team needed him.

In 1944, their last pennant winning season, the Cards had played 11 doubleheaders through July 4th and were 17-4-1. This year it looked like the team had lost its Sunday punch. In nine doubleheaders they were 6-12. They had played two Sunday single games, winning one in Chicago and losing one in Brooklyn. It was difficult to conceive that a team with six All Stars would play so poorly on Sundays. So far the Cardinals had been the big disappointment of the season.

The pitching was the main reason the Cardinals had not done as well as expected. Dyer hated to keep harping on it, but losing Lanier and Martin were crushing blows. The team might have withstood it had not other misfortunes befallen the staff. Beazley never got started, Barrett had his one brief moment, and Brecheen had been unlucky and bothered by a sore arm. Brazle and Burkhart had been inconsistent.

Only Pollet and Dickson, now a starter, had been pitching winning ball. The club had not been a powerhouse and many well pitched games were lost.

Musial, Schoendienst, Slaughter, and Kurowski had tried to carry the team. They sure could have used Hopp's .350 average then. Musial still trailed Dixie Walker, .361 to .372, while Slaughter had slumped and was down to .276. Adams was at .185, Walker at .183 and O'Dea was .123. Approaching the halfway mark, Brooklyn was 45-23 with a comfortable 7 1/2 game bulge on the 37-30 Cardinals, who were being pressed by third place Chicago.

Just before the break, the team made a couple of minor transactions. They sold O'Dea to the Braves and Blix Donnelly (1-2) to

Philadelphia. The club also got hot and whittled the lead to five games by winning seven of eight, including their first doubleheader at home when they defeated Pittsburgh. Dickson was now 5-2 as was Burkhart, while Pollet was 8-4 and the staff leader. Unfortunately, Burkhart would provide little help in the second half, whereas Dickson would be a major asset.

As the team fell further behind, they tried to find their pennant drive anthem "Pass the Biscuits, Mirandy", a World War II Spike Jones novelty hit song. The Cardinals had used that as their victory chant down the stretch drive in 1944, playing it each time the team won, which was often in those days. Unfortunately, a copy couldn't be found, so it looked like Mirandy had passed her last biscuit.

The Cardinals drew 87,047 for a three-day, four-game set against Brooklyn on July 14th, 15th, and 16th in St. Louis. The team swept all four games and momentarily were in first place by a half game. So far this year, they had taken nine of 12 from Brooklyn.

The recent surge was fueled by the improved hitting of Musial and Slaughter as well as improved pitching. Many thought Musial was playing first rather than in the outfield only because of his hitting. However, he was playing first base like George Sisler or Hal Chase. Slaughter had raised his average to over .300 again.

The Cardinals could have used Munger, but they still hadn't heard when he would be released from the Army. On July 14th Slaughter hit a two-run home run for a 5-3 Cardinal win. The next day Musial hit a home run in the 12th inning for a 2-1 victory. In that game Dickson retired the last 16 batters for a complete game win.

In the doubleheader the Cardinals won the first game 10-4. Brecheen had pitched great ball, but wilted in the ninth. Barrett came in and fanned the last two hitters to end the game. In the second game, Dusak hit a three-run home run as a pinch hitter in the bottom of the ninth for a 5-4 win, giving Pollet his 10th victory. Marion had been hit by a pitch and Klutz singled prior to Dusak's home run. After that home run he got the nickname "Four Sack" Dusak. In the first game Musial had two singles, a triple and another home run. The club was starting to make its move.

Hopp has took over the league led in batting with a .383 mark, while Walker was second at .369, and Musial was third at .365. The banner attendance for the Brooklyn series gave the Cardinals the opportunity to break their all time attendance record of 778,147 set in 1928.

Meanwhile, labor issues kept coming up. National League president Ford Frick said that annual contracts of less than $5,000 were wrong. Some clubs wanted the level at $6,000. Some of the other issues to be resolved between the players and the owners were:

- Abolish the 10-day notice of release clause
- No reduction in salary if sent to minors
- A pension plan for the players
- Improve clubhouse and dugout conditions
- Minimum pay of $5,000

The minimum pay was the number one issue. Only 29 players in the league made less than the minimum. So it did not seem to be a major sticking point in the discussions. Dismissal for cause would probably replace the 10-day notice. It looked like the pension plan would be started after the World Series.

Durocher said the Chicago Cubs were the team to beat, not the Cardinals. He said they would have to lose eight of nine in the west before anyone would hear of the Cardinals. He failed to mention that they lost four straight to the Redbirds. Durocher seemed to be setting himself up for the same thing Bill Terry, then manager of the Giants, did with his inquiry about whether the Dodgers were still in the league.

Dickson, a relief expert, was now a winning starter. He had ice water in his veins. He was the leading righthander on staff. His pitching change made it possible for the Cardinals to start on their third eastern trip tied with Pittsburgh. Dickson had beaten the Dodgers in 12 innings on July 14th. Then on the 18th he relieved Brazle against the Phillies and allowed just two hits in four innings and won 5-4.

Dickson then beat Johnny Sain, who was on his way to a 20-win season, 3-1 in 10 innings. In 26 innings, Dickson allowed just two runs, had two complete game wins, and was 3-0 overall. The Cardinals were 16-6 on their last home stand, and had swept four doubleheaders. So far they were .641 on the road, but only .583 at home. More good news; Munger was scheduled to join the team on August 7th. "It's going to be a fight to the wire", stated Dyer.

The Cardinal hitters went into a swoon, scoring just 10 runs in seven games in the east. Things looked great after an outstanding home stand. With their strong record on the road, everyone thought they would roll on this trip, but it didn't happen. They opened by losing two of three in New York and Boston and the wheels seemed to be coming off the wagon.

The team went into Brooklyn and lost the first game, 2-1 to fall behind by 3 1/2 games. On July 31st, the Cardinals broke out of their hitting slump and scored 10 runs. They had four triples and two doubles, including a triple by Marion who finally got a hit after 24 hitless at bats. On August 1st, Slaughter's home run gave them a victory bringing them to just 1 1/2 games back.

There was some encouraging news even in the losses in Boston and New York. Beazley pitched two good games, but lost them both because the team only got one run in each game. He lost to New York in the ninth on a home run by Mize. Then a few days later home runs by Tommy Holmes and Garden Gillenwater beat him 2-1.

Dixie Walker took over the batting lead at .378 with Hopp hot on his heels at .374. Musial trailed by 17 points, but had 66 RBIs.

Mize was fourth at .345, while Slaughter was hitting .287, but had 80 RBIs and led the league in his quest for his first 100 plus RBI season. Pollet, on his way to a 20-win season, was 12-5 while Dickson was not far behind at 9-3.

The strategy to prevent Pasquel from any more raiding was early sign ups for next season. As soon as the season end, teams would start mailing out contracts in attempt to get as many players as they could under contract. The new contracts would provide teams a tighter hold on players. They would have more control over discipline, off hours and the like. There was also 99 percent support among the players for the reserve clause.

There were several other changes in the offing. One possibility was 60 days severance pay when a player was released. Also there would be no railroading of a player to minors, when there was a clear need for his services in the majors. This had been one of the major grievances of the players in the past. A player would be sent to the minors, when his services could be used elsewhere.

In 1945 the Cardinals lost to the Cubs because Chicago had been 53-13 versus the Braves, Reds, and Phillies while the Cardinals were only 38-28 against the same teams, giving Chicago a 15-game edge. The Cardinals had gone 16-6 against the Cubs, but that huge deficit against the other three teams kept the Cardinals from winning their fourth consecutive pennant.

It looked like a similar pattern was forming this season. The Cards were 6-10 versus the Giants and 9-7 against Philadelphia. Brooklyn had taken the first 10 from Philadelphia. Dyer denied that the club had a tendency to let down against second division teams. The problem lay in the pitching staff. The club tried to save Pollet, Brecheen, and Dickson for Brooklyn and took their chances against the other teams.

On August 15th, the Cardinals would return home for a three-week home stand. They hoped Munger would be ready to pitch by then. That would be their chance to make a serious move. They were playing like the 1926, 1928, 1930, 1934, and 1942 teams that tore the knickers off their opponents in August and September.

From July 20th to August 14th, the Cardinals had 17 complete games in 23 starts. Several pitchers were lifted for pinch hitters, but not ko'd. Brecheen was getting more rest between starts and was now winning. Brazle pitched a two-hit shutout against Boston and a three-hit shutout against Chicago on the trip. Brazle had been a savior of late, starting and relieving. Even Beazley pitched some good games. The aces remained Pollet at 14-6 and Dickson with an 11-3 mark.

The hitting also came alive, led by Musial and Slaughter. Musial went on a 20 for 30 stretch to take the league lead at .374 over Hopp's .366 and Dixie Walker at .365. Slaughter continued to lead the league in RBIs, while hitting .300. Kurowski and Schoendienst were at .281 and .289 were the other two main hitters on the team.

There was some bad news as Moore would be limited to pinch hitting duty the rest of the season because of torn cartilage in his right knee. This was a lost year for the team captain. After three years in the Army, he was looking forward to playing in the same outfield with Musial and Slaughter and for a repeat of 1942. Being the competitor he was, he was disappointed he hadn't been able to contribute more.

Munger didn't return until September 4th, a month later than expected. Dyer said the team would have to fight down to the wire. There was no let up as the tension continued to grow. As each day passed the pressure mounted, but no one cracked. The fans felt the pressure, as their eyes scanned the newspapers for scores and their ears were glued to the radio.

Dyer hoped that the Cardinals would be in first after the home stand, but realized they had a tough eastern trip. They had to play the Cubs six times in the last nine days of the season while Brooklyn played Philadelphia and Boston, who had been their patsies all season. Up until August 13th, the Cardinals had been shut out only twice, but in a four day span they equal that mark.

The Cubs and Johnny Schmitz defeated Brecheen 1-0 and Ken Heintzelman and the Pirates beat Dickson 2-0. Brecheen had been 31-9 the last two years and with the best ERA of the three years, he would finish 15-15. He had lost a lot of tough games, like the one to Schmitz. It didn't help that, about the same time, Musial went into a two for 16 tailspin and Kurowski had to go out of the line up with arm trouble. St. Louis and Brooklyn were now deadlocked at 71-45, with the Cubs 9 1/2 back at 61-54.

The owners wanted a 168-game schedule, which would mean 24 games against each team. The players were opposed. They realized that after the labor negotiations, that the new policies would cost the owners some money. Therefore, the owners wanted to tack on some more games to make the players pay for it. The owners complained there were too many open dates, which could be reduced by increasing the number of scheduled games. After much objection from the players over 168-game schedule, the owners decided to abandon the idea.

The proposed pension plan would require each player to pay $250 into the plan. The owners would match that amount for each of the 25 players on the team. A player with 10 year service would draw $100 per month in retirement. Those with shorter service would get proportionately smaller payments.

The Cardinals had a chance to take over first place when they played the Dodgers four games over August 25th-27th, but the best they could do was to manage a split. However, on August 28th the Cardinals defeated New York twice while the Cubs beat Brooklyn so the Redbirds had a 1 1/2 game lead.

The Dodgers took game one, defeating Pollet 3-2. The Cardinals won game two, but almost blew a 10-0 lead. In game three, Dickson defeated the Dodgers 3-1, but Brooklyn beat Brecheen in the finale.

The Brooklyn series allowed the Cardinals to set a new season attendance record of 782, 943.

The press was really surprised that a team of veterans like the Cardinals could be so excited over a pennant race. The media felt that most of these guys had been through this, so they should be in a more relaxed mood. Instead, the players were like young, hungry ball players, fighting for their first pennant ever, not a team trying to win its fourth title in five years. Although the team is heavy with veterans, 12 of the players were not on any of the Cardinals pennant winners of the early '40s.

Walt Sessi, a promising outfielder who never delivered on the promise, did deliver a key home run in the pennant drive. He hit a two-out homer in the bottom of the ninth to turn defeat into victory. Sessi was used exclusively as a pinch hitter and had batted just 14 times with two hits, but this one was a big one. The team went wild, filled with exuberance after his game-winning homer. Sessi was 0 for 13 in 1941 then spent four years in the service. The lost time certainly didn't help his baseball skills. But for one shining moment, he was a hero.

The Cardinals were 13-6 versus the Dodgers on the season. They were 8-3 at home and 5-3 in Brooklyn. They figured they would have to take two of three from Brooklyn during the September 12th-14th series to win the pennant. Dodger manager Durocher's philosophy was win today, let tomorrow take care of itself. It might rain tomorrow. So if he had to use the entire pitching staff to win today, he'd do it.

Slaughter hit three home runs in a Labor Day doubleheader win over the Pirates. The Cardinals took three of five from Pittsburgh and Cincinnati in their own backyards. Meanwhile Brazle won both games of the Labor Day doubleheader. Unfortunately, Dyer had to use 15 pitchers in the five games. Pollet, now the meal ticket, couldn't pitch on September 4th against the Cubs, as he had a heavy cold. Munger took his spot and won. The Cardinals were now 73-49 and Brooklyn was 71-51, a two-game edge for St. Louis. Pollet was closing in on 20 wins with an 18-7 mark, while Dickson was 12-5, the second highest winner on the staff. Musial was opening a wide lead down the stretch hitting .367. Hopp stood at .351 and Dixie Walker was all but out of it at .331. Mize was forced out at .337 when his hand was broken by a pitch. Slaughter was now at .298 with a league high 106 RBIs.

Durocher saw the final week of the season as the flag settler. Brecheen and Brazle both finally reached .500. Brecheen should be crowding 20 victories, but the team had trouble scoring when he pitched. His ERA has been around 2.50 all season. Pollet had pitched 12 consecutive complete games until he was racked by the Pirates on September 7th for six runs, giving up six hits and two home runs in 4 1/3 innings. He was running a temperature of 102 and the effects of the illness showed in his performance.

The team had almost identical records at home as on the road; 46-26 at home and 42-25 on the road. St. Louis had built a 2 1/2 game lead on the Dodgers. The Cards were 88-51 while Brooklyn was 84-52. It looked like Musial would win the batting title as he was at.368, while Hopp was .338 and Dixie Walker had fallen to .328. Slaughter continued to lead the league with 116 RBIs.

The television clause in the contracts caused another disagreement between the owners and the players. Both sides saw a bonanza in the new medium and each wanted to be sure they got their fair share. The club owners made one more concession. They agreed to a maximum 25 percent pay cut in any one season, which seemed to satisfy the players.

The Cardinals were in their 10th hot race to the wire. They had been involved in just three romps. In 1934 and 1942 the race were decided on the last day of the season. In other years, the title was clinched or lost the Saturday before the final game.

It looked like the Cardinals were home free when they defeated Brooklyn on September 12th. However, Durocher's fighting crew bounced back to take the next two and tighten the race. Friday, September 13th, proved to be unlucky for the Redbirds as they lost to Brooklyn 4-3. Cross was out stealing to end the game with Kurowski at bat and Slaughter on deck. To many, it seemed like bad baseball on the Cardinals part.

The next day Ralph Branca shut out Brecheen and the Cardinals 5-0. Munger and Brecheen were both hit freely in Brooklyn. And to add to the woes, Dickson seemed to have lost his magic and stopped winning. Pollet picked up win number 20 on September 17th when he defeated New York, 10-2. The Cardinals finished with a 12-10 edge on last place New York by sweeping the last six games.

Pollet became the first southpaw in the National League to win 20 games since 1937 and the first Cardinal lefthander to turn the trick since Bill Sherdel won 21 in 1928. Pollet was now the Cardinals money pitcher, the one used to win the big games. On the other end of the spectrum was Beazley, so discouraged by his problems that he vowed to retire at the end of the season, at just 28 years old.

With just over one week to play St. Louis was 92-54 and Brooklyn was 90-53. The Cardinals finished with a 4-4 mark while the Dodgers were 6-5. Each had several chances to win it, but kept waiting for the other team to grab the lead. Going into the final day of the season they were tied at 96-57. The Cubs whipped St. Louis 8-3, while an old friend Mort Cooper and the Braves shut out the Dodgers, 4-0. Mort had pitched many a big game and shutout for St. Louis and now he gave them one more to help the team into the first playoff ever in baseball history, a best of three series.

The First Playoffs Ever

The playoff had been forced because the Cardinals had been in a hitting slump for the last two weeks and lost several well pitched games. Commissioner Chandler ruled that all records in the three playoff games would count in final seasons figures.

In game one, Pollet defeated Brooklyn, 4-2, for his 21st victory of the season to give him the league lead in that category.

Game two looked like a breeze with Dickson pitching and leading 8-1 going into the bottom of the ninth. He seemed to have regained his old magic. All of a sudden, the Dodger bats came alive and the score was 8-4, with one out and the bases loaded. Dickson was now out of the game and Brecheen was on the mound. He proceeded to fan Eddie Stanky and Howard Schultz to end the game.

Back in St. Louis, it was pandemonium as the Redbirds had brought home another pennant, their ninth in 21 seasons. During that time they had finished second six times. They had truly become the team of destiny in the National League. What had started out in spring as an expected romp had turned into one of the most exciting seasons the team has ever played, deadlocked on the final day and requiring a playoff. Then they won the first two to clinch the pennant.

Dickson finished with a 15-6, 2.89 ERA, while Brecheen also won 15, but lost 15 despite an excellent 2.49 ERA. He too could have been a 20-game winner, given proper support. Brazle was the only other hurler in double digits, with an 11-10 mark and 3.29 ERA. Musial wrapped up his second batting title with a .365 mark, while Slaughter captured the RBI crown with 130. Musial also led in hits (228), runs (124), doubles (50), triples (20) and had 16 home runs and 103 RBIs. Those stats assured him of his second MVP award. Kurowski finished at .301 and 89 RBIs, while Slaughter finished exactly at .300.

183

The World Series

The coming World Series pitted two teams that had won five times each in the fall classic, Boston and St. Louis. Boston had never lost, while St. Louis had been defeated three times. This would be Boston's first appearance in post season since 1918 and they were installed as heavy favorites to win the title.

The heavy hitting Red Sox had three .300 hitters in Ted Williams at .342, Johnny Pesky at .335, and Dom DiMaggio at .316. They also had three hitters with 100 or more RBIs, again led by Williams with 123, followed by Rudy York with 119 and Bobby Doerr with 116. Pesky led the league with 208 hits and scored 115 runs, while Williams led the majors in runs scored with 142, greatly helped by his 156 walks. His 38 home runs were second to Hank Greenberg's 44, in his last season in the American League.

The first game was played in St. Louis on October 6th and a York home run in the 10th inning defeated Pollet and the Cardinals 3-2. Pollet allowed nine hits, but six came in the last three innings as he weakened, handicapped by a torn muscle in his side. He carried a 2-1 lead into the ninth inning but Boston tied it, to set up the 10th for York's game winning smash.

Game two saw Brecheen pitch a four-hit shutout to even the series against the hard hitting Red Sox before 35,815. The Cardinals scored in the third on a double by Rice and Brecheen's single. The Cardinals got their final two runs in the fifth when Rice singled and Brecheen sacrificed. When Higgins threw wild, the runners ended up on second and third. Schoendienst grounded out, but Moore singled scoring Rice. Then Musial hit into a force play scoring Brecheen. After two games Musial and Williams were each one for nine.

The scene shifted to Boston for the next three games. On October 9th, before a crowd of 34,500 packed Fenway Park, Dave "Boo" Ferris, 25-6 in the regular season, blanked the Cardinals 4-0 on six hits. York was the hitting hero again for Boston as he had two hits, including a three-run homer, scored two runs, and had three RBIs. The major damage was done in the first. Pesky singled and DiMaggio grounded out to Musial. Williams was intentionally passed and York hit a home run off Dickson. Musial and Williams were now each 2 for 12.

The next day, before 35,645, the Cardinals evened the Series tying the record for most hits in a game at 20. Kurowski, Slaughter and Garagiola each had four hits in a 12-3 romp behind Munger, who defeated first game starter Tex Hughson. Musial had two hits and two RBIs, while Marion broke out of his slump with three hits and three RBIs. Slaughter hit the team's only home run in the Series.

Game five went to Boston as Joe Dobson defeated Pollet and the Cardinals 6-3. This time Pollet was hit hard. Much of the reason was the bad back that bothered him and would make him unavailable for the rest of the Series. Slaughter was hit on the elbow by a pitch and had to leave the game. The Redbirds managed just four hits off Joe Dobson. York was given three intentional passes.

The Cardinals returned to St. Louis with their backs to the wall. They had been down three games to two before and had come back to win in 1926 and 1934. In 1944 they were down two games to one and came back to take it all. They saw no reason they couldn't repeat that performance. Nor did their fans, as 35,678 showed up on October 13th for game number six.

The Cardinals didn't disappoint them, up-ending Boston 4-1 behind the brilliant pitching of Brecheen. He allowed just seven hits, and in two games the powerful hitting Red Sox had scored just one run in 18 innings against the little lefthander. The Cardinals defeated Mickey Harris for the second time in the series.

Slaughter played despite his painful injury, as nothing was going to keep the old war-horse out of the lineup. In the third, Rice singled and Brecheen attempted to sacrifice, but Rice was out at second. Schoendienst doubled and Moore's fly out scored Brecheen.

185

Musial and Kurowski singled to score Schoendienst. Then Slaughter followed with a base hit to score Musial and knock out 17-game winner Harris. Hughson relieved, pitching scoreless ball for four innings.

No game was played on October 14th which was in the Cardinals favor, as the rest made Brecheen available to relieve in game seven. Attendance was 36,143 for the final game, which, like the rest of Series, was a see-saw affair. Boston scored first in the first inning, but the Cardinals tied it in the second. They forged ahead in the fifth on three hits for a 3-1 lead.

However, in the eighth, the Red Sox rallied, to tie the game. With no outs, third baseman Rip Russell singled and George Metkovich doubled with Russell stopping at third. Brecheen came in to relieve and he quickly retired Wally Moses and Pinky Higgins, but DiMaggio doubled to tie the score.

In the bottom of the eighth, Slaughter led off with a single, but two outs later he was still on first when Walker hit a line drive over Pesky's head for a single. Slaughter was off at the crack of the bat, never pausing. When Pesky momentarily held the ball, he beat the relay to the plate. This "mad dash" has become one of the classic moments in baseball history, Slaughter's all out, daring dash from first, scoring on a single. Some later books credit Walker with a double because he took second on the throw home, which slightly cheapens Slaughter's effort. However, it was a single and he scored because of his all out hustle, which is the way he played the game for 19 years. This was also the trademark of Cardinal ball clubs.

Brecheen now took a 4-3 lead in the ninth inning, but the game wasn't over. York and Doerr singled with no outs, putting men on first and second. Once again Brecheen was master of the situation, retiring Higgins, Roy Partee and Tom McBride to end the game and give the Cardinals their sixth World Championship.

The celebration in St. Louis rivaled those of the pre-war days.

St. Louis fans saw another dynasty in the making. They had dreams of pennants and World Series titles the rest of the decade, but these would soon fade away.

Meanwhile, the Red Sox have not won a World Series since 1918. Some say a curse was placed on the team when they sold Babe Ruth to the Yankees for the 1919 season. They have been in several more classics, but have come away a loser each time, some of them real heartbreakers. They dropped a seven game set to the Cardinals in 1967.

Epilogue

Rumors had it that Moore would be sold or traded to Boston, where he could eventually become manager, although nothing came of this. The Cardinals decided to keep Moore and his off season operation enabled him to respond and play quite well in 1947. The Cardinals were the favorites, having basically the same team.

Moore, at 35, seemed to be the only real question mark and he would respond with a .283 season and play his usual brilliant center field. Young players such as Schoendienst and Garagiola only figured to get better. They would have Munger for the entire season and who can forget his memorable first half of 1944 before he had to leave for the service. Once again fate would step in and deal the Cards a bad hand, preventing a repeat.

The Cardinal farm system, which had brought so many fine players to the majors, was drying up. They were not getting the talent they had for the past 25 seasons. And other teams were catching up in this area, especially the Brooklyn Dodgers. The Cardinals would also be late in signing black players. Their first didn't come until Tom Alston was signed in 1954. The team had sold or traded away a starting lineup and pitching staff over the past half dozen seasons and this would also come back to haunt them.

The Cardinals traded Harry Walker early in 1947 to the Phillies for power hitting outfield Ron Northey, who in 311 at bats had 15 home runs and 63 RBIs while batting .293. On the other side was Walker, who would hit .372 for the Phillies, and when combined with his St. Louis stats would lead the league with a .363 mark. However, the biggest disappointment had to be pitching. Pollet and Dickson were a combined 36-15 in 1946, but fell to a composite 22-37 in 1947, with Pollet's ERA skyrocketing from 2.10 to 4.35. This was a fall of 18 games in the standings. The Cardinals won 89 games to finish five behind Brooklyn, but nothing could make up this deficit.

Brecheen was 16-11, Munger had a fine 16-5 won-loss record, Brazle was 14-8 and rookie Jim Hearn was 12-7. Unfortunately those marks weren't good enough to offset the decline in the fortunes of Dickson and Pollet. Added to that was the ERAs of Wilks and Burkhart, the former at 5.04 and the latter at 5.21. They were figured to be the bulwark of the bull pen and were a combined 7-6.

Although the team scored almost a half run per game more than in 1946, the hitting suffered from declines in Musial and Slaughter's performance. Slaughter dropped to 86 RBIs with a .294 average. Musial hit "only" .312 with 19 home runs, 95 RBIs and 113 runs scored. He was bothered by appendicitis for much of the year and at one point was down to .140. It took a heavy hitting surge in August and September to lift him over the .300 mark. Kurowski had his premier season at .304 with 27 home runs and 104 RBIs.

No one realized when the Cardinals won the 1946 championship, but it would be 18 more seasons before they would be in another World Series. The team had enough talent to finish second for the next three seasons, including a heartbreaking loss in 1949.

For the three years they averaged over 90 wins a season. Most of the 1950s, except for runs in 1952 and 1957, were dismal for St. Louis fans. The only real thing that had to cheer was the hitting of Musial. Much like the late 1990s fans had with Mark McGwire.

Red Schoendienst

Murry Dickson

Enos Slaughter

Stan Musial

ROW FOUR L-R   Sadecki, Uecker, Spiezio, Maxvill, McCarver, Shannon, Taylor, James, Buchek
ROW THREE L-R   Richardson, Washburn, Simmons, Gibson, Skinner, Cuellar, Craig, Brock, Milliken, Warwick, Humphreys
ROW TWO L-R   Flood, Boyer, Groat, Pollet, Schultz, Keane, Benson, Schoendienst, White, Schultz, Javier
ROW ONE L-R   Baker (Bat Boy)

1964

At Long Last

Prologue

The last time the Cardinals won the pennant, there were 16 major league teams with St. Louis being the farthest west. By 1964, there were 20 teams from the west coast to the east coast.

There had been six franchise moves and four new teams installed since the Cardinals last won a pennant. The St. Louis Browns were now the Baltimore Orioles, while the Philadelphia Athletics became the Kansas City Athletics. The Boston Braves became the Milwaukee Braves, and the Brooklyn Dodgers were now the Los Angeles Dodgers. The New York Giants moved to San Francisco Giants and the Washington Senators were now the Minnesota Twins. Two new teams had been added in the American League, the Los Angeles Angels and the Washington Senators. The National League added a team in Houston, the Colt 45's, and one back in New York, the Mets.

When St. Louis last won a pennant, teams traveled by train. Now they traveled by air. Some teams chartered flights, others owned their r own planes. The 1946 season was the last year that baseball was all white. It had become integrated, but the Cardinals were slow to change. They didn't sign their first black player until 1954, when the signed first baseman Tom Alston. The first black player of any consequence was "Sad" Sam Jones, who pitched in 1957-58 and was 12-9 and 14-13 for the two years.

The Cardinals and their fans entered the 1964 season with high hopes. The team had come close to winning it all in 1963. A spirited drive which saw them win 19 of 20 in September to put them within one game of the Los Angeles Dodgers, but they were swept in a three-game showdown. Still the team finished second with 93 victories, their best season since the near miss season of 1949.

The strength of the team lay in its iron man infield of Kenny Boyer at third, Dick Groat at shortstop, Julian Javier at second and Bill White at first. That foursome averaged 160 games per person in 1963 and each had been an All Star.

The pitching staff looked sound and deep. Returning were 18-game winners Bob Gibson and Ernie Broglio. The latter had led the league in wins in 1960 with 21. Curt Simmons won 15 in 1963 and Ray Sadecki gave the club 10 wins, pitching great baseball in the second half. He had won 14 in 1961.

The bullpen was anchored by Rod Taylor and Bobby Shantz, as the pair won 15 and saved 22 in 1963. Veterans Lew Burdette and Barney Schultz were available for relief work and the former was a spot starter. The Cardinals had acquired Roger Craig from New York in the off season and were expecting 12 wins from him. His goal was 18. Craig was only 15-46 the past two seasons, and the Mets 93-229.

Catching did not appear to be a problem, as the Cardinals had Tim McCarver, who had won his wings in the 1963 battle. Supporting him were Carl Sawatski and Bob Uecker.

The problem potentially could be in the outfield. For the first time since 1941, (except 1945 when he was in the Navy,) the Cardinals would feature a line-up without their all time great, Stan Musial. He had retired at the end of the 1963 season. Charley James seemed to be the heir apparent, as he hit .276 with 59 RBIs in 388 at bats in 1963. If he faltered, waiting in the wings were rookies Johnny Lewis, Gary Kolb, Doug Clemens, and veteran Carl Warwick.

Centerfield would be manned by Curt Flood and it was in good hands. He had established himself as one of the premier center fielders in the league, the equal of Willie Mays. He could go get them with Mays, though he lacked Mays' powerful arm. However, Flood was more accurate. Flood had developed into a .300 hitter and a top notch lead-off man, but didn't have Mays' power.

General Manager Bing Devine declared the pennant race would be a free-for-all, with six teams having a chance at the title, including Los Angeles, San Francisco, Milwaukee, Philadelphia, Cincinnati, and St. Louis. All six had won at least 84 games in 1963.

The Cardinals faced some problems. Sadecki was an "iffy" project, but, at age 22, the team had to work with him. Simmons wanted to improve on his 0-3 record versus the Dodgers, but it really wasn't his fault. In 36 innings, the club had scored only one run for him.

Al Dark, the Giants' manager, thought the Cardinals were on an eclipse. He didn't think they could replace Musial. The outfield was crowded with lots of names, but the talent was questionable. He questioned whether, at 34, Simmons could put together back to back strong seasons. He also wondered if the iron man Cardinal infield of 1963 could duplicate their previous effort.

The truth of the matter was that the infield would again average 160 games, led by their All Star third baseman, Boyer. He was recognized as the best third baseman in the league, offensively and defensively. He was among the all time leading run producers in Cardinal history. This quartet was the real strength of the Redbirds ball club.

Manager Johnny Keane wanted the team to bear down in spring training so they could make a fast start. The field was going to be crowded he wanted to get out in front. It was going to be a year-long struggle. Keane planed on giving a long hard look to rookie Jeoffery Long as a potential home run hitter. The problem was he plays first base and a knee injury prohibited him from outfield duty.

The former Cardinal executive and now Dodger General Manager Branch Rickey said if Washburn's arm was okay the Cardinals could win the pennant. He pointed to Simmons, Gibson, Broglio, and Washburn as a powerful starting quartet. Not only did Broglio win 18 games, but he left leading in five other games that the bullpen couldn't save for him. Rickey believed this staff had the potential to match that of the 1942 club, which was his baseball gem.

As spring training drew to a close, the probable opening day line-up looked like Flood, Javier, Groat, White, Boyer, James, Warwick, and McCarver. Keane quickly pointed out that no outfielder had taken charge, so James and Warwick could be replaced. He would like a lefthanded bat in the outfield, meaning Kolb, Clemens, or Lewis.

There had been some concern of racial friction on the St. Louis team, but it was handled pretty well by Flood, Gibson, and White on the black side and Boyer, McCarver, and Mike Shannon on the white side. If there was a problem, it was brought out into the open and discussed frankly. It was not left to fester and create a major issue. Gibson believed this was what promoted the racial harmony on the team.

The Cardinals finished spring training at 17-10. Despite that record and finishing second in 1963, most scribes picked the team sixth. A few said they could finish as high as fourth. They didn't believe that the Cardinals could get good years from so many ball players. The fourth place rating was given because of their outstanding infield.

Keane envisioned a six-team race and was pinning the teams' pennant hopes on the arms of Gibson, Broglio, and Simmons. He planned to start the first two in 40 games each this season. So far, Sadecki had been unimpressive in spring and Washburn was slow rounding into shape.

Regular Season Play

The Cardinals opened the season on the west coast and Broglio lost on opening day, April 14th, to Sandy Koufax and the Dodgers 4-0. Gibson evened matters the next day with a 6-2 victory. The team moved on to San Francisco, where Simmons pitched a two-hit, 2-0 shutout over the Giants. They lost 4-3 in 10 innings the next day when Taylor walked in the winning run. The club outhit the Giants 12 to 4, but left 13 men on base. Broglio came back to win the finale, 3-2, for his first victory of the season.

Gibson then took Houston's measure 6-1 and, at the end of the first week, the team was in sixth place with a 4-3 record. Boyer had hit two home runs in the early going, serving notice he was going to have another big season.

One note of tragedy in all of this. Eddie Dyer, manager of the last Cardinal World Series winner in 1946, died on April 20th. Dyer had managed the Cardinals from 1946-50, winning one pennant and finishing second three times. When his 1950 team slipped to fifth, at 78-75, Dyer was released. The ballclub had become old and several of the pitchers had lost the zip on their pitches, but, as usual, the manager took the heat.

After the first two weeks of the 1964 season, the team was 8-6 and in fifth place, but only two games out. The hitting, other than McCarver and Boyer, was lacking. The Cards were batting just .230 as a team. This was basically the same team that led the league in hitting at .271 last year. Their talented infield was off to a slow start, batting just a composite .230. Shantz and Taylor had failed to display the same form that brought 15 wins and 22 saves to the party last season.

McCarver was a real bright spot for the Cardinals in the early going. His catching was a decided improvement over the tandem of Gene Oliver and Sawatski from the early stages of 1963. McCarver caught 126 games that year, most of them after the first month of the season.

The first bean ball war of the season erupted on May 4th at Busch Stadium between the Cardinals and the Philadelphia Phillies. First, Javier was decked by pitcher Dennis Bennett, after Flood hit a home run off him. The next inning, Bennett was the first batter and drew two high hard ones from Gibson. Umpire Doug Harvey gave Gibson a warning and an automatic $50 fine.

In the home half of the fourth, reliever Jack Baldschun plunked Gibson in the left thigh. Enraged, Gibson flung his bat at the mound, which was caught by the glove hand of Baldschun. Rhubarbs immediately flared up all over the stadium and Gibson was ejected. The Cardinals protested because Baldschun had not been read the riot act after his first pitch made Gibson do the cha-cha.

The Cardinals thought they had been treated unfairly, as neither Bennett nor Baldschun had been banished, but Gibson who had allowed just three hits and one run in four innings was ejected. When Keane looked for a pitcher to replace Gibson, who left leading 5-1, six pitchers reached for their gloves. Craig was selected and received credit for the victory in a 9-2 win. Gibson didn't realize it at the time, but this fracas would cost him a 20-win season, as he finished the year with 19 wins.

The Cardinals team batting had fallen to .208 when the hitters got hot and batted over .300 on their recent home stand. Boyer was at .371, Groat had raised his average to .284, and White climbed to .293. Even Lewis and James joined in the hitting act, but the team could only go 3-3 for the week.

It seemed now that the hitting had returned, but the pitching was deserting them. On successive Saturday nights (April 25th and May 4th), the bullpen blew leads in the ninth inning. The Cards had just one save in the first 18 games.

On May 3rd, the pitching, both starting and relieving, reached its worse. Broglio blew a 7-3 lead, and relievers Taylor, Sadecki, and Burdette handed a 12-8 game to the Pittsburgh Pirates.

The Cardinal batters played Jekyll and Hyde at home and on the road when it came to hitting. In the first 11 home games the team scored 61 runs, but only 22 in the first seven road games. In 1963, only the Minnesota Twins scored more runs then the Cardinals.

In 1963, Washburn won his first five starts, hurt his shoulder, then lost three in a row. He spent the rest of the season nursing his shoulder back to normal. His career would be dotted with injuries and in only one of eight seasons as a full time starter would he be able to start 30 games. A lot of his talent was lost with repeated arm and shoulder ailments and other injuries.

He had started off the 1964 season 2-0 with 2-1 victories over Philadelphia and pitched seven innings in a 10-1 win over New York. Meanwhile Sadecki was beginning to justify Keane's confidence in him. He lost a tough one, 1-0, to Pittsburgh then got a 3-2 win over Philadelphia.

After three weeks, the Cardinals, 11-9, were tied with Cincinnati for fifth place, 2 1/2 games behind first place San Francisco. Gibson was now 3-0 with a 5-1 victory over the Mets. He had to wait three weeks for win number three. He had pitched well, but the Cardinals were not providing him hitting support, so he left several games trailing or tied, and the decisions went to another pitcher. The bullpen remained shaky as Shantz was a disappointment and Taylor was inconsistent.

Craig did good relief work in saving a game for Simmons on May 8th against Pittsburgh and Taylor pitched well in relief of Washburn in the 10-1 victory. Gibson enjoyed a 1.96 ERA and Washburn had a 1.23 ERA. Broglio was 2-1, but with a 4.15 ERA, while Sadecki was just 1-3. Boyer continued his fine hitting, with .347 average, four home runs and 18 RBIs in the first 26 games. His bat was carrying the team. They team had moved up to third with a 14-11 record, but they were still 2 1/2 behind the pace setting Giants.

Because of his poor spring showing and early kayo in his first start, Sadecki was bypassed in the rotation in favor of Gibson, Broglio, Washburn, Simmons, and Craig. In 1963 he had also started slowly. After the first six weeks he was 0-4, then went on a 10-4 run. He lost his last two starts, but had pitched effectively. His team was shut out in both games. Based on his performance of the last four months of last season, the Cardinals had high hopes for Sadecki this year.

When Craig relieved Gibson in the game in which he was ejected, that opened the opportunity for Sadecki to start. If he could pitch effectively, that would allow Craig to return to the bullpen, where the Cardinals needed help. On May 16th, Sadecki won 6-5, allowing six hits and three runs to the Braves in the ninth inning. His relief allowed two runs in the ninth.

One of the encouraging features of Sadecki's pitching was that he had not allowed a home run this year. Last season he gave up 25, one more than the 24 allowed by Broglio. Simmons was 13-2 against the Phillies since they released him.

The Cardinal hitting attack continued to be spotty. Boyer was at .344 with 22 RBIs for the first 32 games, but White was hitting just .248 with 10 RBIs. Last season White had hit .304 with 27 home runs and 109 RBIs. Javier went on a 12 for 21 spree that raised his average from .173 to .260. Keane continued platooning James, Warwick, Clemens, and Lewis. None had shown that he could hit consistently to play everyday. James was hitting .280, but had just eight RBIs in 93 at bats.

As May drew to a close, Boyer was hitting .348 with 32 RBIs in 39 games, but had just 14 extra base hits. There was some concern about his lack of power hitting, but Keane figured it would all come in time. On the downside, the Cardinals had fanned 228 times, which was ahead of last year's pace, and they had grounded into more double plays than at the same time one year ago.

There was encouraging news from the starting staff. Since May 7th, Gibson, Simmons, and Sadecki were a combined 9-0. On May 20th, Gibson had a stiff shoulder. To loosen it he polished his car then shut out the Cubs on four hits, 1-0, fanning 12 men. On May 23rd, Simmons pitched a three-hitter against the Braves. Hank Aaron was just 2 for 23 against Simmons since the start of 1963. He said Simmons was the toughest pitcher for him in the league.

In his 10th pitching appearance, Craig was bombed as Rico Carty of the Braves had two home runs and five RBIs. Philadelphia had now forged into the lead by a half game over the Giants. The

Cardinals were tied with Pittsburgh at 22-18 for third, three games out.

The team's two weak spots seemed to be the outfield and inconsistent pitching. Simmons was 6-2 with a 2.39 ERA, while Gibson was 4-0 with 2.17 ERA. Gibson had pitched in nine games, but because of lack of support, had just four decisions, fortunately all victories. Craig was 3-2 and 2.88 ERA. From there the story wasn't pretty. Sadecki was 3-4 with 4.15 ERA, Shantz was 1-3, and Taylor was 0-1 with 7.96 ERA.

Washburn was day-to-day and no one was sure when he would be able to start again. The Cardinals, in need of another starter, traded Burdette to the Cubs for Glen Hobbie, who was 0-3 with 8.00 ERA. On the surface it didn't look as if Hobbie would be of great help as he was 51-70 for the past five seasons, only one of which was a winning year. When he started would depend on the condition of Washburn.

The Cardinals were in third place, trailing Philadelphia by 3 1/2 games. Much of their decent start could be attributed to Gibson and Flood. Gibson was 5-1 with 2.04 ERA, while Flood was hitting .317. Last year Flood had hit .278 in the first half, but .328 in the second to finish at .302 with 200 hits.

Dizzy Dean said Gibson reminded him of himself and his brother Paul the way he just wound up and fogged the ball in there. He predicted big things for Gibson in the coming years.

The Cardinals went into a tailspin in late May, losing five in a row. Two were back-to-back 2-1 defeats to the Giants, suffered by Gibson and Simmons. Sadecki stopped the skid with a 4-3 win while Broglio defeated Cincinnati 7-1 on May 30th. Washburn continued to have his problems, as he was wild and taken out in the first inning of a 6-0 loss to Cincinnati.

For the past couple of seasons, Cardinal teams have had problems winning on Sunday. They were just 15-21 in 1963, a factor that played heavily in their second place finish to Los Angeles. So far this season, they were just 4-7.

The Cardinals were tottering in June, as the team wasted good pitching and the hitters swooned. They also hit a stretch of poor relief work. White was hitting just .107 against Cincinnati and Javier went into an 0 for 16 slump. Except for Flood, little production was received from the outfield.

Hobbie made his debut as a starter on June fifth. He was given the chance when Broglio came down with a groin injury. He was ahead 4-1 when relieved in the eighth inning. The bullpen failed and a Boyer error in the ninth spelled defeat.

When the Cardinals lost on Sunday, June 17th to the Reds, it made their Sunday record just 4-8. Simmons gave up two home runs in the game, bringing his total to 12 for the year. That was one fewer than he gave up in all of 1963.

Boyer, Flood, and McCarver were all over .300, but White continued to struggle, hitting just .232 with 18 RBIs in the first 50 games. Only Gibson had a winning record and an ERA below 3.00 for starts, as he was 5-2 with 2.06 ERA. Simmons had slumped, losing three straight and was now 6-5 with 3.25 ERA. Sadecki had a winning record, 5-4, but a 4.18 ERA. Craig, Shantz, Taylor, Broglio, and Washburn were a combined 9-15.

In the first six weeks, St. Louis was 22-14 and right in thick of the pennant race. Then came a long slump, during which the team was just 6-17 to push their record to 28-31, good for eighth place, 7 1/2 games out of first. During the first two weeks of June, the club was just 3-11, as the hitters went into another slump, scoring just 29 runs. The malignancy was so bad it even affected Boyer, who went hitless in a six-game series on the west coast. Through the middle of June, Cardinal pinch hitters had only one hit in 26 trips to the plate.

Devine was aware that changes had to be made if the team was to make a run at the pennant. He began by bringing pitcher Mike

Cuellar up from the minors and, on the same date, traded a minor league catcher and $35,000 for outfielder Bob Skinner from Cincinnati. This was Skinner's 10th season in the majors and, while his name wasn't sounded in the same vein as Aaron or Mays, he was a capable ballplayer. During his career for Pittsburgh and Cincinnati he had hit over .300 three times with a high of .321 for Pittsburgh in 1958, where he played until traded in mid-season 1963 to Cincinnati. He also had hit as many as 20 home runs, scored 93 runs and had 86 RBIs in different seasons. Devine and Keane felt Skinner could bring some lefthanded pop to the lineup as Kolb, Clemens, and Lewis hadn't delivered.

But the big news would come two days later on June 15th when the Cardinals traded Broglio and Shantz to the Cubs for an unknown and unproven outfielder named Lou Brock. Gibson, who later said the acquisition of Brock was the key to winning the pennant, was very much opposed to the trade. He said, "as bad as we need pitching how can we trade an 18-game winner for a .250 hitter." Broglio had led the league with 21 wins in 1960.

Devine said the trade was for the future. The Cardinals also received journeyman pitchers Jack Spring and Paul Toth, both shipped to the minors. Many questioned Devine's move, as Brock was batting just .251 this season. He was considered a better than average outfielder with a strong arm, plus he had great speed. He had stolen 10 bases this season and the entire Cardinal team had 14.

Devine hated to give up the 28-year old Broglio, whom he figured was just coming into his peak years, but the Cardinals needed a lefthanded bat with speed in the lineup. He still figured Broglio, who left the team with a 3-5 record, would win 15 games this season and have many more successful years.

Of course, it turned out that the Cardinals made the steal of the century. While Brock had more than 3,000 career hits and held the single season stolen base record (118) and career record (928) at one point, Broglio only lasted through 1966, going 7-19. Brock also led the league in stolen bases eight of nine times from 1966 through 1974.

The team sent Lewis to Jacksonville and Keane installed Brock in the lead-off spot. He and Flood served as great table setters for the Cardinals three, four, and five hitters.

But pitching continued to be spotty. Craig was hit hard in four straight relief appearances, yielding 12 runs over that time frame. Gibson's ERA was well below three runs per game, but he was just 5-4 due to lack of hitting. Sadecki had trimmed his ERA to 3.68, but was just 6-5.

Cardinal hitters, other than Flood or Boyer, were still not producing. Groat was at .269 while McCarver was hitting .277. The rest dropped precipitously. White was .241 with 21 RBIs in 61 games, James was hitting .238, and Javier just .220.

Flying feet had been the trademark of most of the Cardinal pennant winners. They may not have led the league in stolen bases, but they used speed on the base paths to take that extra base. So fans became excited as they hailed Brock as a nice compliment to speedy Javier and Flood. Brock's first appearance at home coincided with Taylor's resurgence and the hot hitting of Javier.

In Brock's first game on June 16th he had a triple, single, and two walks in five plate appearances as Simmons grabbed the victory. The next day he drove in the winning run in Washburn's 2-1 victory. With Brock on board, the team reeled off four straight wins, two over Houston to complete the road trip and the first two over San Francisco to start the home stand.

Nobody realized it at the time, but that was Washburn's last victory of the season. Calcium deposits prohibited him from pitching for the rest of the season. Washburn finished at 3-4, pitching only 57 innings. He had been counted on for 200 innings and 15 to 18 victories.

Meanwhile in the San Francisco series Javier hit a home run in each of the first two games. Brock was stopped in the first game against San Francisco but came back with two hits in each of the next three games, including a double, triple, and a home run. He also had two steals in his first three games and was hitting .348 since joining the team.

While the news was bad about Washburn, the Cardinals received good news from Taylor's performance in June. After a miserable April and May, he had nine flawless appearances in June, adding three straight victories. On June 17th, with the tying run at third ,he fanned Joe Gaines. The next night he protected a one run lead with runners at second and third and only one out. He fanned Mays and got Orlando Cepeda to ground out.

On June 19th, he relieved Gibson, who had a 3-1 lead. After the first two pitches to Tom Haller were balls, he got him and Jim Davenport to ground out and then retired Chuck Hiller on a pop up to end the game. His secret was keeping the ball low and in the first two months of the season his pitches had been up.

White went 11 for 24 to raise his average to .248, while Sadecki had seven wins, three short of his 1963 total. Dark said the Cardinals needed Washburn to win the pennant. He claimed without him, they are doomed. In their recent spurt the Cards had moved into fourth place and trimmed Philadelphia's lead over them to six games.

Sadecki now has eight wins and the Cardinals thought the addition of Cuellar and Hobbie would improve the bullpen but they were still in ninth place for a couple reasons. First was the inability to hold leads in the late innings. Other than Taylor's mid-June performance, the bullpen had blown leads. Secondly, until June 25th the Cardinals had not been able to come from behind late in the game to win.

On that day, for the first time this season, they did it. Down 2-1 to the Cubs, they scored three runs in the eighth for a 4-2 victory. However, the next day the old pattern set in. The Cardinals took a 5-4 lead into the ninth against Philadelphia and Clay Dalrymple hit a two-run home run off Taylor to win the game, 6-5.

Pitching, which had been the Cardinals strong suit, left them. Over a 12-game stretch they allowed 65 runs. In only three games did the opposition score fewer than three runs. They played a doubleheader with the Phillies on June 27th and gained a split behind Sadecki, but Cuellar lost 5-0, despite Richie Allen fanning five times. Even Gibson got into the act of not holding leads. Against the Braves he blew a 4-3 lead in the ninth as the team lost 7-4.

The Cardinals gave up on Long and sold him to the Chicago White Sox and called up Mike Shannon. Shannon was a strong-throwing, excellent defensive outfielder, who could hit for power. The addition of him and Brock would make a big difference in the Cardinal team in the second half.

At this point the team was 39-40, in sixth place, and nine games out. Devine examined the feeble Cardinals and said, "Only a hot streak can save you. It's a long shot. There is a steep hill to climb. There are several good clubs ahead of use and they're not all going to get beat everyday."

There were several reasons for the team's collapse, besides the bullpen failure. In the early part of the season when the starting pitching was strong, they had no timely hitting. The veteran ball players were not hitting, putting undue pressure on the younger players. The defense had been bad all season and the team lacked long-ball power, especially at home, where the Cardinals usually hit well. On the last home stand they had been out-homered 16-5.

A comparison of three players showed the Cardinals plight. White was hitting .328 with 13 home runs and 58 RBIs at this time a year ago versus .265, seven home runs and 30 RBIs. James had a .301 average and 30 RBIs last year as compared to .227 and 15

RBIs this year. Groat was at .325 with five home runs and 40 RBIs and is hitting .291, but no home runs and just 28 RBIs. Also missing were Musial's eight home runs and 35 RBIs at the halfway point.

On the plus side was Javier with 10 home runs and 39 RBIs, while Sadecki and Simmons are each 9-6. The Cardinals had fallen 10 games back by the All Star break. When Gibson beat New York 3-1 on July 10th, it was his first win since June 19th.

When the Cardinals swept a doubleheader from the Pirates on July 13th, it is the first time since September 13, 1963 the team had won a twinbill. White, Brock, and Shannon were the hitting stars. White and Brock had a home run in both games and for White that was his first since June 5th. Brock was on base 10 times in the doubleheader, while Shannon had two RBIs in the second game and added three more the next day. One of Brock's home runs was inside-the-park.

One situation that plagued the team was an internal problem that had to do with Keane and Groat, but it was affecting the entire team's performance. Keane had given Groat the hit-and-run privilege at his discretion, but when he tried it three times in a game in Los Angeles and it backfired, Keane revoked the privilege. Groat rebelled and the two of them stopped talking.

Gibson said he took nothing away from Groat, he was a good hitter and shortstop, but his personality didn't seem to blend with the rest of the club. He was a hush-hush guy and if he had something to say, he almost whispered it. This was on a club noted for its frankness and outspokenness.

Just after the All Star game, Keane called a club house meeting at Shea Stadium. He said, "You guys might get me fired, God damn it, but if you do, you can bet your asses that I'm taking some of you bastards with me." He also let the players know what he thought about second guessing and talking behind his back.

This shocked newcomers like Brock and Shannon, but the veterans were use to such frank meetings. Afterwards Groat apologized to Keane and admitted he had been one of the chief offenders. The two were finally together.

This seemed to fire up the team and they won eight of their next 11 to climb from 13 out on the loss side to six. Skinner had proven to be a valuable pinch-hitter. On July 14th, after being down 6-0 to Koufax, the Cardinals rallied to win 8-7 on Skinner's two-run RBI single. A few days later, Skinner got a double to put the team on top 7-6. In another game, he drew a walk to prolong an inning in which the Cardinals scored 11 runs on their way to a 15-7 romp.

During a seven-game span the only complete game was by Gibson in a 7-6 win on July 19th over the Mets. Gibson and Sadecki had also been used in relief to help save games. The team still lacked a reliever to shut down the opposition late in the game and protect a lead. Shannon had become the best rightfielder the team had since the days of Enos Slaughter.

The Cardinals offense was strong during a 10-game home stand in late July, scoring 57 runs. Unfortunately the pitching allowed 83 and they finished with a 4-6 record. In the first two games at Philadelphia in late July the Cardinals pitchers gave up nine runs in each game, but salvaged a split.

Cardinal president August Busch Jr. was not pleased with the Cardinals' performance. Busch indicated there was a limit to his patience after three straight losses to the Pirates. He said on July 23rd, "I'm not happy with the morale of the club. The players look listless on the field. You have to condemn the pitching and then you can go on from there."

Busch praised Keane and thought he was a good manager. As for some of the other personnel, Busch added, "A lot of things could happen at the end of the season. I've got my fingers crossed that we'll do better, but I don't know."

On July 25th, Simmons had a 10-2 lead going into the bottom of the ninth when he tired. He allowed a single, two walks and two more singles, which brought Glen Hobbie to the mound. Hobbie walked the first batter and had two balls on Allen, when he was replaced by Taylor, who completed the pass and then served up a two-run single to Alex Johnson. He was replaced by Cuellar, as the score was now 10-8. John Herrnstein pinch hit and a long smash to deep center, which the wind held up and allowed Flood to catch for a sacrifice fly. Johnson, who broke at the crack of the bat had to return to first, tagged up too late and was thrown out at second for a double play. Gus Triandos then popped out to end the game.

Over a 12-game stretch, the Cardinals used 44 pitchers. During the month of July the starting corps, an early season strength, had just four complete games.

The Cardinals were finally able to get some decent pitching and took the next two from Philadelphia, 6-1 on a five-hitter behind rookie Gordon Richardson and another five-hitter by Sadecki in a 4-1 win. This gave the Cardinals three out of four against the Phillies and enabled them to cut the lead to seven games.

Boyer, White, Flood, and McCarver were the heavy hitters in the Philadelphia series. Boyer led the league with 73 RBIs. The Cardinals had more hits than any team in the major leagues except the Boston Red Sox. However, five National League teams and seven American League teams have outscored them, pointing out the Cardinals failure to get timely hitting. In 1963 they outscored the opposition 4.6 to 3.9 runs per game, whereas this year they trail 4.4 to 4.1.

The mercury in St. Louis hit 100 on August 2nd, but some of the Cardinals' bats were just as hot. White had raised his average to .296, after an 0 for 18 drought in June. He hit .362 in July, while Brock has been hitting .351 since joining the Cardinals. Flood and Boyer continued their steady hitting all season. For the month of

July the Cardinals tied Milwaukee for the best record in the league at 17-11, despite all the defense, pitching and lack of timely hitting problems.

Early in the season, Gibson's ERA was down in the low twos, but the team couldn't score when he was pitching and as a result he had a low total of victories. When Mel Queen hit a three-run homer off Gibson on August 1st it marked the fifth straight game he gave up six earned runs. Gibson's record had fallen to 8-9 and his ERA had climbed to 3.55. While it was a very respectable figure, it was going the wrong way.

Sometimes the moves you don't make that are the best ones. Over the winter months the Cardinals had offered Sadecki for sale, but there were no serious takers, at least not at the Cardinals' asking price. This turned out to be a blessing, for since May he had won four games each month and now led the team with 12 wins, while Simmons was right behind with 11.

Just when it seemed like there was harmony in the clubhouse and maybe the team could still make a stretch drive, though 8 1/2 games out, another bombshell hit. Busch fired Devine as general manager. Bob Howsam was named business manager of the team as a stepping stone to being named general manager at the end of the season.

Rumors were rampant that Branch Rickey, the senior consultant of the Cardinals, maneuvered the changes. Busch flatly denied it. "Rickey had nothing to do with it. I did not consult him until I'd made up my mind." For some time Busch had been disappointed with the Cardinals play and wanted to shake up the team.

Busch had not been impressed with Devine's trades and was disappointed at the caliber of talent coming out of the farm system. In retrospect his trades looked pretty good, as he acquired Groat, Brock, Flood, and Javier. The players for whom they were traded would all be gone by 1967. On balance, his trades worked out well to the Cardinals advantage. Devine said, "I hope they win soon. If so they will win with my players."

Devine was well-liked and respected by the players. This was before the days of agents and he did the negotiating with the players one-on-one. To a man they always said he was fair. After Devine's firing the team could have just rolled over and played dead. Instead they decided to make a spirited run for the pennant. This was Devine's team and if they could win it all, it would be his vindication.

By early August the team was showing the spark and drive of a pennant winner like the great Cardinal teams of the past. The bullpen and the delegation from Jacksonville was doing a good job. Richardson and Cuellar had pitched winning ball as spot starters, and were also used in the bullpen. Bob Humphries had been brought up and posted a 2-0, 2.51 ERA record in 28 relief appearances, .

However, the real saviour out of the bullpen was Barney Schultz, who had been with the team in early spring, but had been sent down to the Jacksonville AAA farm club, then managed by former Cards great Harry Walker. Schultz was recalled in late July and appeared in 30 games, saving 14, and posting a 1.65 ERA. The four aforementioned pitchers became known as the delegation from Jacksonville, where all four had been playing.

This was Schultz's third tour of duty with the Cardinals. He had pitched for the team in 1955 and again in 1963. In his first eight appearances, covering 12 innings, he had five saves and gave up no runs. He had helped in victories over San Francisco on August 10th and August 12th, and over Houston on August 17th and 18th.

Through August 16th, Humphries was in 16 games and had a 1.80 ERA. Cuellar had appeared in 20 games and compiled a 4-2 record. Meanwhile, Sadecki picked up wins 14 and 15 against Los Angeles on August 14th and Houston on August 18th. Simmons got his 13th win in Los Angeles on August 16th.

From July 25th to August 18th the team was 17-7, but gained lit-

210

tle ground on Philadelphia, who was 15-9 during the same period. Nevertheless the boys just kept plugging away, looking for a chink in the Phillies' armor. The Cardinals eight-game win streak ended in Los Angeles when a bad hop ground ball beat Gibson, 4-3.

The team seemed to have two problems. First was the inability to win at home, as the team was just 32-28. Last season they had been 53-28 at home. Thus, with 20 games to play, they had lost as many as they did all last season at home. On the road, the team was 31-27 and headed for their first road record over .500 since 1957.

Their second problem was the lack of a power-hitting lefthanded batter to take advantage of the right field pavilion in the old Sportsman's Park which had been recently renamed Busch Stadium. They had White, but that is where it stopped. Brock had shown some flashes of power, but wasn't considered a true home run hitter. The disappointments of Kolb, Clemens, and Lewis stood out glaringly.

The Redbirds could fly, but their home run total was puny. In 1960 and 1963 they had the home run edge on opponents at home. Since 1950 the home run shortage has hurt the team in numerous years. This season they are 42-81 in their own ball park. In 1960 the club out homered the enemy at home 78-64 and last the 1963 season it was 79-70.

The first 18 days of August, the bullpen allowed no earned runs in 33 innings. It looked like the team had gotten its pitching problem straightened out. Sadecki and Simmons were pushing toward 18 to 20 wins each while Gibson had come out of his slump. He was 9-10 with an ERA of around 3.60 at the end of July. Since then, he had six straight complete game victories in which he allowed a total of just six runs.

However, despite all this, the team was still nine games out with 36 to play. The pennant hungry fans in St. Louis were hoping for a patented Cardinal stretch drive. The fans were also hoping for a repeat of the 19-of-20 win streak the Cardinals had in 1963. When their stretch drive started the team was 47-48, and they would go 46-21 the rest of the way.

Despite playing well, the club still wasn't gaining much ground on the Phillies. However, the team was playing so well they started to believe the predictions of Fifi Latour.

The Fifi thing started innocuously with a few notes mailed to the club house. They were written in red ink and encouraged the team to hang in there, that they would win it all. They were always signed, "Fifi Latour, an Old Stripper". Some thought she was actually Bob Bauman, team trainer. Bauman later confessed "she" was actually a male physician from Venice, Florida.

No matter who or what he/she was, it seemed to have a positive effect on the team. It was almost an uncanny prediction for Cardinal victories and pretty soon the team believed it could overtake the Phillies.

The pennant fever had all the players caught up in the spirit and none wanted to miss a game. On September 4th, Boyer was sick and was going to ask for the day off, but decided to play. He hit a three-run home run and became the first National League player to have 100 RBIs. His home run gave the club an 8-5 victory over the Cubs. A week later the team was just five games out, the closest they have been since early in the season. However, there were only 23 games to go.

In the midst of the pennant drive another ugly rumor popped up, distracting the team in the middle of the peenant fight. A story came out that administrative changes in St. Louis would cost Keane his job. Now that Devine was gone, Keane could be on his way out. He carried the label of "Devine" man.

Groat said that without Boyer, the Cardinals would be in the second division. He had been the league's best third basemen five of the last six years. He was an inspirational and star team leader.

Boyer won five Gold Gloves in 1958-61 and 1963.

He was involved in an unusual daredevil play in a rundown where he tagged out two runners on the same play. Del Crandall was on second base for the Braves when Johnny Logan hit the ball to Groat, who fired to Boyer at third. Boyer chased Crandall back toward second, hoping that Logan could reach there before he was tagged out. Boyer tagged Crandall, then made a desperation dive and tagged Logan before the sliding player hit the bag. Boyer said he never heard of anyone else making the same type of play. Boyer said, "Maybe it wasn't the smartest thing to do," as he could have had an ear sheared by Logan's spikes.

Speaking of rare feats the Cardinals accomplished one on September 13th against the Cubs at Wrigley Field. They scored in every inning to become only the second team to score in all nine innings. The New York Giants accomplished the feat against the Phillies in 1923. It had been done four times in the American League, but each time it was by the home team and they only had to play eight innings, as they won the game.

The Cardinals victory drive was the story of a new hero each day. It was not a one man show, but a true team effort. Brock has batted .351 since the trade and Shannon, in addition to his fine defensive play in right field, hit at a pace of 20 home runs and 100 RBIs. Fans couldn't help but wonder what the standings would be like if these two had been with the team all season.

Cincinnati proved to be a snake pit for the Cardinals in 1964. On September 18th, Simmons had a 4-0 lead after four innings and the game was rained out. It was rescheduled for the next day as part of a twilight doubleheader. Gibson was staked to a 6-0 lead, as he hit three doubles in the game, only to lose in the ninth inning, 7-6, on a three run-home run by Frank Robinson.

The next day they had another 6-0 lead, but blew this one, too. The key play was when Flood lost a fly ball in the sun. The bull-

213

pen, which had performed so brilliantly of late, let them down this time. The team salvaged the final game with Sadecki the winner and a save recorded by Schultz. However, time was running out, as they were 6 1/2 games out of first. Groat got his first home run of the season at Cincinnati on September 20th.

Busch was still sidestepping the question of Keane's fate, although he was clearly not happy with the Cardinals' performance. While they had played pennant-winning ball for the past two months, he believed it was "too little, too late".

There were many heroes down the stretch. Gibson was 10-2 for the last two and one half months. Sadecki got his 20th win against the Phillies on September 29th, 4-2 with relief help from Schultz. From September 25th-29th Schultz appeared in each game and was credited with three saves. The Cardinals went on a 26-9 spree and Schultz got one win and 11 saves during that stretch.

The hitters came in for their share of glory also. After slow starts, both White and Groat got hot. Boyer was having another big year at the plate and in the field. Shannon had 42 RBIs in just 233 at bats, one of the best ratios in the majors. Brock, McCarver, Flood, and Javier had all been big contributors down the stretch drive.

The Cardinals entered the final weekend of the season with a 92-67 record, one half game ahead of Cincinnati (92-68) and 2 1/2 games ahead of the Phillies (90-70). Cincinnati would play the Phillies twice (Friday and Sunday) while the Cardinals had the lowly Mets, loser of 109 games that season.

The odds and fate seemed to be with the Cardinals. While Cincinnati and Philadelphia were trying to knock each other off, they had the weakest team in baseball. However, for the season the Mets had been tough for the Cardinals in St. Louis winning four of six. Al Jackson beat Gibson, 1-0 in the opener, but Philadelphia won, 4-3 over Cincinnati. The Cardinals held onto their one-half game lead and Philadelphia was 1 1/2 games outs.

The next day Sadecki was gunning for his 21st victory, but instead suffered his 11th defeat, as the Mets pounded him and an array of relievers for an 15-5 victory. Cincinnati and Philadelphia didn't play, so now after 161 games, the Cardinals and Cincinnati were tied for first with Philadelphia one game back.

The possibility of a playoff loomed largely. If Cincinnati won, the Cardinals had to win to force a playoff. If Philadelphia won and the Cardinals lost, then there was a three-way playoff. Philadelphia shut out the Reds, 10-0 to set up the possibility of a three team play-off.

Simmons started for the Cardinals and struggled early, but carried a 2-1 lead into the fifth. The Mets scored two on a wind blown double and took the lead 3-2. That brought Gibson into the game. Keane said to Gibson, "Go as hard as you can for as long as you can. We have Barney ready in case you need him." Simmons added, "Good luck, Hoot" as he slapped him on the rear and walked off the mound.

The Cards scored three in the bottom of the fifth to go ahead 5-3. At the same time the score was posted on the Phillies game and they were ahead, 4-0. The Cardinals built their lead to 8-4, while Philadelphia was up 9-0. The fans were cheering with every pitch, the players were walking nervously in the dugout, waiting to unleash the joy that had been building in them for months.

The final score of the Philadelphia-Cincinnati game was posted and it was a 10-0 victory for Philadelphia. Everyone thought the team was now home free as they carried an 11-4 lead into the ninth inning. Gibson was just completely worn out. This was his second game in three days and fourth in nine days. The Mets scored a run and there was just one out. He wanted to finish, but knew Keane was right to bring in Schultz. He got the last two outs and bedlam broke loose.

The Cardinals had won the pennant for the first time since 1946.

An 18-year drought was over. The corridor to the clubhouse was filled with several thousand cheering people. The clubhouse was like a madhouse, filled with reporters, TV people, and city and county officials. The clubhouse celebration lasted for more than three hours as everyone, players and fans alike wanted to savor this moment.

A reporter said to Musial, "Too bad you didn't play one more year, Stan, so that you could be part of this." Musial answered, "If I had played one more year, we wouldn't have won the pennant, because we wouldn't have traded for Lou Brock."

Now all that was left was to face the Yankees in the World Series, with whom they were tied two series wins each in head-to-head competition. The Yankees didn't have an easy job winning either. They finished one game ahead of the Chicago White Sox and two up on the Baltimore Orioles.

The World Series

The Yankees were installed as the pre-series favorites, but that was nothing new for St. Louis. They had been picked as the underdog many times and come back to take it all.

The first game, played in St. Louis, pitted Sadecki against Whitey Ford, the winner of 10 World Series games, the most by any pitcher in the history of the game. It turned out to be a slugfest with the Cardinals winning 9-5.

The Cardinals were down, 4-2, when Shannon hit a home run off Ford to tie the game. McCarver followed with a double and that ended Ford's work for the day, as well as the Series. He would not appear in another game. Al Downing came in and faced pinch hitter Carl Warwick, batting for Dal Maxvill (who was playing in place of the injured Javier). Warwick singled and Flood tripled to make the score 6-4. The Cardinals added three insurance runs in the eighth and Sadecki got the victory with the save going to Schultz.

This was only the second time in their World Series history that the Cardinals had won the first game. The 1934 team was the only other one to do it.

Game two featured Gibson against Mel Stottlemyre and the latter had the better of the day. The bullpen which had been performing so admirably let the team down, as the Yankees scored four runs off Schultz, Gordon Richardson, and Craig in the ninth inning.

The Yankees had taken the lead in the sixth when Mantle walked on a disputed 3-2 call. Joe Pepitone was hit by a pitch, hotly disputed by Gibson and McCarver. Groat had to grab Gibson to keep him from being ejected. After tempers settled, the game resumed and Tom Tresh singled Mantle home. The Yankees then added two more runs off Gibson in the seventh, for a 4-1 lead.

Attendance was identical, 30,805 at each game. With the Series tied, it moved to New York and the Yankees had visions of sweeping in their home town and not having to go back to St. Louis.

Game three was a pitchers' duel between Simmons and Jim Bouton, with the Yankees winning. 2-1. It was a major disappointment for Simmons. He had waited 14 years to pitch in a World Series and then couldn't get the victory. In 1950, when a member of the Philadelphia Whiz Kids, he was drafted into the military and missed the last three weeks of the season, as well as the Series.

Schultz replaced Simmons in the bottom of the ninth and, on the first pitch, Mantle hit his 16th World Series home run, breaking a tie with Babe Ruth as the all-time home run king in World Series play. That home run was also the margin of victory for the Yankees.

The fourth game featured a pairing of Sadecki and Downing, but the former couldn't get out of the first inning. Things looked pretty grim for the Redbirds, already down two games to one, and now trailing, 3-0, after one inning of play. But this time the bullpen held. Craig allowed just two hits in 4 2/3 scoreless innings of relief. Boyer then hit a grand slam home run in the fifth and St. Louis was up, 4-3.

Taylor came in and shut the door, pitching four innings of hitless relief. Not only was the Series tied at two games each, Craig, loser of 46 games for the Mets in 1962-63, had won a World Series game.

Game five was a rematch of Stottlemyre and Gibson, and the Cards had a 2-0 lead going into the bottom of the ninth. Tresh then hit a home run of Gibson to tie the game, but in the 10th inning, McCarver hit a three-run shot to give the Cardinals a 5-2 victory and Gibson his first World Series win. He fanned 13, giving him a total of 22 for the first two games. Total attendance was just under 200,000 for the three games at Yankee Stadium.

The scene now shifted back to St. Louis and the momentum was with the home town boys and their 3-2 lead. More than 10,000 cheering fans met the team and put on a celebration reminiscent of those of the '20s, '30s, and '40s. It was a cheering mob, replete with a band and huge cake. A victory in game six and the title would be theirs, but the Yankees weren't going to go down without a fight.

It was Bouton versus Simmons, and the latter was going to get a chance for a World Series win. He had been highly effective in game three, allowing just one run in eight innings. He left this game trailing 3-1 in the seventh, so in his two starts he didn't pitch bad ball, but the club just didn't score for him.

Schultz came in and although he had been brilliant down the stretch, he lost his magic in the Series. He and reliever Richardson were bombed for five runs in the eight inning, including a grand slam by Pepitone Earlier in the game Mantle and Maris had also hit home runs.

The Cardinals had one player tie a record and another come close. Shannon fanned five consecutive times, the last two times he was up in game five and the first three in game six. He matched a record set by John Devore of the Giants in 1911, later tied by George Mogridge of the Senators in 1924 and again by George Pipgras of the Yankees in 1932. Mantle had duplicated the feat in

1953, but Mogridge and Pipgras were pitchers.

McCarver had five consecutive hits, one short of the record. He had two singles before his game winning home run in the game five then he had two singles his first two times up in game six. On his chance to tie the record, McCarver flew out to Maris. The Yankees ended up winning game six, 8-3.

For game seven, both Stottlemyre and Gibson were coming back with just two days rest. The Cardinals broke on top in the fourth when Boyer singled, Groat walked, and McCarver hit into a force play. But when Phil Linz threw wild, Boyer scored. Shannon singled putting runners at first and third. They then pulled the double steal with McCarver scoring and Shannon going to second. Maxvill singled and Shannon beat Mantle's throw home. Cardinal speed had done the trick.

Downing took over in the fifth and Brock hit a home run, White singled, and Boyer doubled. In came Rollie Sheldon and he got Groat to ground out as White scored. McCarver hit a short fly to right field, but Boyer beat Mantle's throw home. Once again Cardinal speed spelled the difference.

The Yankees got back into the game in the sixth when Richardson and Maris singled in front of Mantle's 17th career World Series home run. Boyer hit a home run for the Cardinals in the seventh to make it 7-3, which was the score entering the ninth. Tresh opened by fanning, but Clete Boyer, Ken's brother, hit a home run. Johnny Blanchard as a pinch hitter became Gibson's ninth strikeout victim of the day and 31st of the Series. Linz followed with a home run, but Bobby Richardson popped out to end the game.

The celebration that the victory touched off was just as wild as the one following the clinching of the pennant. It lasted for hours and the fans and players alike savored every moment of the beautiful victory. Gibson was voted MVP of the Series and given a new Corvette, while Boyer was chosen MVP of the National League.

There were several new Series records set: Most hits (13) by Richardson and most strikeouts (31) by Gibson. Mantle set two. He now had 17 career World Series home runs and 42 runs scored. Although Mantle played another four seasons the Yankees never made it back to another World Series with him.

Epilogue

A few days after the World Series win, players and fans alike were shocked when Keane resigned as Cardinal manager and replaced Yogi Berra, who had been axed as manager of the Yankees. It was a real disappointment, as Keane had spurred this team on to victory. The two men, Devine and Keane, so responsible for the Cardinal triumph, were gone. At least the World Series win was vindication for Devine. He was voted executive of the year for the second straight season.

The Cardinals should have been the team to dominate the league the rest of the decade, as only Groat, White and Boyer among the regulars were over 30. Of the starting pitchers Simmons was 36, but the rest were all under 30. But as often happens, fate played mean tricks.

In 1965, the Cardinals gold plated iron man infield ran into difficulties. White fell to .289 with 24 home runs, but just 73 RBIs, while Boyer had recurring back problems and hit just .260 with 13 home runs and 75 RBIs. Javier had a broken finger and appeared in just 77 games, hitting .227. His keystone partner, Groat batted just .254. They dropped from an average of 160 games per person the last two seasons to 130.

Shannon played in 124 games, but batted just 244 times as he was used for defensive purposes in many games. His average fell to .221 with just 25 RBIs. Only Flood, Brock, and McCarver turned in respectable years, hitting .310, .298, and .276, respectively. Flood led the team with 83 RBIs.

The pitching also proved a disappointment. Gibson was able to become a 20 game winner for the first time, but it ended there. Simmons and Sadecki went from a combined 38-20 to 15-30, a 16 1/2 game swing which is exactly what the Cardinals finished behind Los Angeles. Simmons was 9-15 and would be out of baseball after the 1967 season. Sadecki would remain in the big leagues through 1977, but would win in double digits only two more seasons. He won 12 in 1967 and 1968, pitching for San Francisco.

The 1965 team finished one game under .500 at 80-81. It would be a couple more seasons and a virtually new pitching staff, plus several changes in the regulars, before St. Louis was back on top again.

Bill White

Dick Groat

Ken Boyer

Curt Flood

ROW FOUR L-R   Maxville, Woodeshick, Jaster, Ricketts, Gagliano, Romano, Bressoud, Spiezio, Brock, Washburn
ROW THREE L-R   Gibson, Hoerner, Willis, McCarver, Hughs, Carlton, Cosman, Tolan, Javier, Shannon, Johnson, Bauman
ROW TWO L-R   Flood, Cepeda, Schultz, Muffett, Schoendienst, Sisler, Milliken, Briles, Jackson, Maris
ROW ONE L-R   Deason, J. Gibson (Bat Boys)

1967

El Birdos

Prologue

Since winning the World Series in 1964, the Cardinals had fallen on hard times. They were 80-81 in 1965 and finished seventh, and 83-79 in 1966, finishing sixth. This necessitated changes and Stan Musial replaced Bob Howsam as general manager. Many did not think Musial would make a good general manager, but it turned out they were wrong. He understood the players and their problems, as he had been one for 22 years.

The Cardinals had received bad publicity with the firing of Bing Devine in 1964 and Johnny Keane's resignation right after the World Series victory. They made Red Schoendienst manager, partly as a goodwill gesture with the public. He too turned out to be a good manager and the longest serving Redbird manager of all time (1965-76).

The front office felt that having Schoendienst as manager and Musial as general manager would bring a lot of fans to the ball park. They were two of the most popular Cardinal players of all time.

In 1966, the Cardinals offense generated only 571 runs and as a result a lot of games were lost. Gibson won 21 and lost 12 despite a 2.44 ERA. He could have won several more with better run support. Al Jackson, whom the Cardinals acquired from the Mets for Ken Boyer in 1965, had a fine 2.51 ERA but a 13-15 record, another victim of poor hitting support.

Ray Washburn rebounded from a 9-11 mark in 1965 to 11-9 in 1966. Young Larry Jaster also won 11, dropped five, and posted a 3.26 ERA. His real feat was hurling five shutouts against the pennant winning Los Angeles Dodgers. Nelson Briles had a good ERA, 3.21, but was just 4-15.

The Cardinals batted just .251 with Orlando Cepeda leading the way at .303 with 17 home runs and 73 RBIs in 123 games. However, the keystone combination of Julian Javier and Dal Maxvill hit just .228 and .244 respectively. Curt Flood fell to .278, but led the team with 78 RBI. Mike Shannon, besides playing a great right field, hit .288 with 16 home runs and 64 RBIs.

Tim McCarver hit .274 with 12 home runs and 68 RBIs. He led the league with 13 triples to become the first catcher to accomplish that feat. Lou Brock hit .285 and led the league with 74 stolen bases, but fanned 134 times.

So what the Cardinals needed was more power in the lineup. They figured if they could get Roger Maris from the Yankees they would try Shannon at third base. The team realized the latter was a risky move, taking an excellent outfielder with a strong throwing arm and trying to convert him into a third baseman. But the team was willing to take the chance and Shannon was willing to gamble if it would help the club.

The Cardinals had the opportunity to get Maris for Charley Smith, who had replaced Ken Boyer at third, and had been a major disappointment. There was some concern about getting Maris, the single season home run king as he had a reputation for being a non-conformist, blunt, frank, arrogant, and outspoken. He had been jarred by the national spotlight and had trouble handling it. The media had made his life unbearable in that now famous 1961 season, when he broke Babe Ruth's hallowed home run record. Basically, people didn't want him to do it. He received threatening calls, nasty letters, and the like. It went on all season until he became a recluse and withdrew from the media as much as possible, which didn't endear him to the press corps.

All Maris ever wanted was the opportunity to play baseball. He said he didn't need or want a season like 61 in '61. He would be perfectly content to play a good rightfield, bat .280, hit 25-35 home runs, and drive in 100 runs. The headlines could go to someone else. He wanted his privacy.

There was some skepticism when the Cardinals acquired Maris, but in time he turned out to be completely different from his image. He readily signed autographs, and he was cordial with the press, fans, and players alike. The players lauded the addition of Maris, believing he would be a major asset not only with his bat, but his spirit and quiet leadership.

In 1966, the Cardinals had the worst strikeout to walk ratio in the league. They fanned 977 times and walked just 345. Maxvill had the best ratio with 61 whiffs and 37 walks. Schoendienst was determined his team would improve on this phase of the game in 1967. During his career Schoendienst walked 606 times and fanned just 346 times in 8,479 official at bats.

While the forecasters didn't pick the Cardinals very high in standings, anywhere from fourth to sixth, the team had other thoughts. They believed the addition of Maris and Shannon succeeding at third would make a much more solid ball club. Also, the Cardinals had a wealth of young pitchers. Twenty-nine year old Dick Hughes (10 years in the minors), Briles, and Steve Carlton all pitched in the Puerto Rican Winter League and distinguished themselves. Hughes was 11-2, 1.79 ERA, Briles was 12-3, 2.46 ERA, and Carlton was 9-5, 2.08 ERA. All three were counted on for prominent positions on the pitching staff in the coming season.

Schoendienst said for the first month of the season he would use four starters: Gibson, Washburn, Jackson, and Jaster. Hughes was a leading candidate for number five and Carlton for the sixth or spot starter. Briles looked to be the long man in relief. Gibson wanted four full days between starts and Schoendienst said he could have that after the first month of the season.

The bullpen, in addition to Briles, would be manned by Joe Hoerner, Hal Woodeshick, and Ron Willis. Hoerner was brilliant in '66, going 5-1 with a 1.54 ERA and 13 saves. Woodeshick was 2-1 with a 1.92 ERA and four saves. Willis came up in September and was not scored on in four appearances.

While the Cardinals wanted Shannon to be the third baseman, there were many challengers for the job including Ed Spezio, Jerry

Buchek, Phil Gagliano, and Ted Savage. The first three were all infielders, but Savage believed he could play third, even though he was an outfielder.

Maris had experienced disappointing seasons back-to-back, hitting .239 in '64 and and .233 in '65 with just 21 home runs total. He had a number of injuries, but believed he could come back and become a key factor for the Cardinals. Cepeda was poised for a big season. He would be with the team for the entire year and hoped to improve on his numbers very dramatically.

George Kissell had been around baseball for a long time and was the Cardinals' "Mr. Fix-it." He was called a "roving coach". If a player had a problem it was Kissell's job to help him over the situation and get him back on the right track. He worked with both the major league and minor league players.

He had to figure out each individual so he could develop the right approach and get the player in the right frame of mind to succeed. His number one rule was never copy another player, whether you are a hitter or pitcher. He worked with the fielders on pivot plays, throwing, charging ground balls in the outfield, and hitting for more power and the with pitchers on using the tools they had.

Pitching figured to be the Cardinals' strong suit, although the scribes didn't see it that way. Too many young and unproven pitchers they said. Gibson said this was the best Cardinals staff he has ever been on, including the 1964 pennant winning team. His goal was third place or higher and he would like to win 20 or more. He had progressed each of the last four seasons. He had won 18, 19, 20, and 21.

Brock stole more bases than six National League teams, but he wanted to improve on his success rate. He seemed stuck at a 70 percent success rate until last season, when he improved to 80 percent. He was 74 of 92 in 1966. Most baseball men contended that anything less than 67 was detrimental to the team.

In the Grapefruit League, the Cardinals finished fourth with a 16-12 mark and a 3.11 team ERA. The team had four pitchers that could start or relieve, Carlton, Briles, Hughes, and Jackson, which gave the team a tremendous amount of flexibility.

Regular Season Play

The Cardinals came out of the gate flying, winning their first five games, during which Brock hit five home runs. He started off like he wanted to break Maris' record. On April 11th, the Cardinals drew the largest opening day crowd ever at 38,117. They saw Gibson fan 13 men and beat Juan Marichal and the Giants 6-0. Gibson tied a major league record by fanning the first five batters in the game. The Cardinals were the only club with an edge over the high-kicking Marichal.

In the opening game, Maris had a double and bunt single. He would go eight for 17 on the home stand. He was friendly and cheerful, signing autographs and cooperating with everyone. He was just the opposite of his image.

On April 14th, Jaster's scoreless streak against the Dodgers came to an end at 52 innings, as the Cardinals beat the Dodgers 8-4. He left the game in the ninth inning after yielding a triple to Jim Lefebrve and a single to Ron Fairly.

In Gibson's victory, Brock had a three-run home run. Then on April 15th, Brock hit two home runs in a 13-4 rout. The next day he hit the first pitch from Mike Cuellar for a home run, giving him three home runs on three pitches. Brock got a single next time up, missing his bid for four straight home runs. He hit another one off Cuellar later in the game to give him seven consecutive hits. His goal this year was to add more power and to cut down on strikeouts.

On April 16th, Carlton relieved Gibson in the seventh with an 8-7 lead over Houston. He got Joe Morgan to fly out then fanned Jim

Wynn and Eddie Mathews. The next inning, he opened by fanning Bob Aspromonte and Aaron Pointer for four strikeouts in a row. Javier, who hit just .227 and .228 the last two seasons, was off to a great start, hitting .407 after 12 days. He hit a home run off Gaylord Perry on April 18th and hit a winning home run the next night. He also had a two run single that night. The Cardinals won those games by scores of 2-1 and 7-5 and became the dark horse of the National League.

As of April 22nd, Gibson and Jaster were both 2-0, while Brock, Maris, Cepeda, and Javier were all off to a fast start. Shannon was sidelined in the season opener with a pulled muscle. Gagliano replaced him and had a hit in every game, until stopped by Don Drysdale on April 22nd. Shannon returned to lineup and was hit on the thumb by a pitch from Don Sutton. So he was out again.

Carlton looked like a sure winner. He saved Gibson's 11-8 win and then beat Houston 7-2 with ninth inning relief help from Dick Hughes. On April 27th, Gibson was miffed about being lifted in the seventh at Houston with three on and no outs. Woodeshick came in and gave up a bases loaded triple and Gibson lost his first game of the season.

As of May 2nd, the team was tied for fourth at 9-7, while Cincinnati was off and running at 15-5. Gibson was 3-1 with a 3.30 ERA, while Jaster was 2-1, but had a sky high ERA of 5.85. Briles had no decisions, but had been brilliant in relief, posting a 1.13 ERA for six games. Brock had six home runs and 18 RBIs and was batting .400 to lead the team in all three categories. McCarver and Shannon were both batting .330, Flood was at .325 and Cepeda was hitting .319 with 10 RBIs, but had just one home run.

Cepeda gave the nickname of El Birdos to the Cardinals. This was his way of cheering the team on, as he was one of the cheerleaders of the club. His nickname was "Cha Cha". Other nicknames included "Hoot" for Gibson, "Bones" for Maxvill, and "Creeper" for Jaster.

Javier was the "Phantom", Maris was "Rajah", McCarver was "Doggie", Washburn was "Dead Body", and Shannon was "Moon Man". This had become a well-knit cohesive group of guys who wanted to challenge for the flag. It was reminiscent of earlier Cardinal pennant winning teams.

Flood played 1966 without making an error. On May 7th, he set a new National League mark for errorless games by an outfielder at 206. The Cardinal pitching continued to confound the league as Gibson and Washburn, both suffering from colds pitched back-to-back two hit shut outs over Cincinnati. The pieces were starting to come together as Maris hit his first home run on May 9th against the Pirates.

Cepeda and Shannon both broke out of their long-ball slumps as the former hit four home runs in Chicago in early May while Shannon hit two. That was the kind of power they had and it was just a matter of time before the two broke loose. The Cardinals have five players at or above .300 with a sixth, Javier, at .299. The hitting seemed to be well distributed. As of May 9th, Cincinnati was still leading with 17-8 record, Pittsburgh (which had a lot of its games rained out) was 12-7, while the Cardinals were 13-9.

Dave Ricketts took over as the back-up catcher, pushing Johnny Romano to third string. Ricketts also starred as a pinch hitter. In 1966, the Cardinals were anemic as pinch hitters going just 35 for 200, for a .175 average. Pinch hitting is one of the toughest roles in baseball. The batter comes off the bench cold to face the pitcher for the first time. So far Ricketts had been three for five, with each hit figuring in a scoring inning.

Gibson had a 15-2 mark against the New York Mets entering this season. On Saturday night, May 16th, he started at Busch against them and was really firing the ball in the first inning when the rain came and the game was postponed. The next day, Gibson started again, but said he never really got loose. They ko'd him in the third inning and won 3-1.

So far the get-away game on the road had been a jinx for the Cardinals, as they had lost each of those games in the five series they had played. Meanwhile, they continued to tread water, staying in fourth place at 15-11, four games behind first place Cincinnati. The team felt that it was just a matter of time before they went on a tear. The spirit was there, they just hadn't put all the pieces together.

The Cardinals had delivered excellent hitting, averaging five runs per game. With their pitching they could easily win over 60 percent of their games. Cepeda was at .373, Brock was .331 with eight home runs, 24 RBIs, and 14 stolen bases. Shannon, McCarver, Flood, and Maris were all over .300, with the first two having 19 RBIs each.

The pitching continued to see changes in the rotation. One of the great things Schoendienst had going was flexibility in his staff. Jackson was now in the bullpen and Jaster was back in the rotation, despite a 5.32 ERA. Carlton was a full time starter while Hughes relieved and started.

The Cardinals had a mixture of white, black, and Hispanic players. Gibson called the Cardinals the "Rainbow Coalition" long before Jesse Jackson ever coined the phrase. Unlike many teams, where each group went off on its own, it was not uncommon to see two black and three whites out together, or a Hispanic, a black, and couple of white players having dinner. This made for cohesiveness and unity on the club, something that was lacking from many other teams. The Cardinals were a team, on and off the field.

The Cardinals' hospital list included Shannon and Javier. Shannon had lost 10 pounds and was run down. He was sent back home to St. John's Mercy Hospital in St. Louis and he missed eight games on the nine-game road trip. Javier was out with a groin injury and was day-to-day.

When Brock was asked where he got his new found power and

hitting strength, he replied, "from eating a milk shake a day." Whether or not it really does the trick, he has a milk shake before every game and thus far this season it paid big dividends. On the recent trip where the Cardinals were 6-3, Brock was 17 for 42 with eight stolen bases and 10 RBIs. Always known as a speedster, he now added power to his repertoire.

The Cardinal pitching overall had been good, although some of the records didn't match their ERAs. Gibson had a 3.22 ERA, but was just 5-4, while Jaster was 3-1 with a 5.28 ERA. The Cards seemed to hit when Jaster was pitching. It should also be noted Gibson usually drew the tougher mound opponents.

Not only did the Cardinals have to battle for the pennant, they also had to contend with the fomenting problem of union attempts by Marvin Miller, executive director of the Major League Players Association. He wanted to raise the minimum salary from $7,000 a year to $12,000. Miller said since the minimum was established 20 years ago at $5,000, cost of living had gone up 70 percent, so the salary hadn't kept pace with the inflation rate.

The owners countered that a lower starting salary made the athlete work that much harder to prove himself and get into a higher bracket. Take away the incentive and you destroy the drive and desire that makes sports what it is, the owners argued. They also said the reserve clause was good for baseball, as it was the foundation on which the game was built. Miller countered it is a one-way street which favors the owners, not the players.

Another proposal was to organize the black athletes of the baseball, basketball, and football teams. (There were no black hockey players.) Bill White, the former Cardinal first baseman and now with the Phillies, was opposed to either type of union. He said if they have a union of just black players, they will isolate themselves from the mainstream and will suffer in the long run. There would be fewer opportunities and ever fewer financial rewards.

Behind this was another movement involving baseball, football, basketball, and hockey players to form into one union for negotiating purposes. Such a general union was also opposed. You couldn't have one encompassing all sports, as each was different from the others. Their needs and demands were not the same.

About this time, the Cardinals ran into famous trumpeter and band leader Harry James at the Sheraton Hotel in Philadelphia on May 26th. Harry was a long time Cardinal fan going back to the 1940s. He was a frustrated shortstop who played semi-pro ball out of his home town, Beaumont, Texas. He was set to sign with the Tigers, because their top farm club was at Beaumont. But his dad said to stick with the trumpet, as he would have to spend several years in the minors before reaching the majors, which was the situation in those days.

James was a good friend of Billy Southworth, Schoendienst, and the Cooper Brothers, Mort and Walker. James would put on a spare uniform that belonged to pitcher Blix Donnelly and drill with the Redbirds. He still had the uniform and a glove Marty Marion used. "I remember a young outfielder breaking in back in the early '40s too." said Harry, "I think his name was Musial."

James missed the 1964 World Series as it slipped up on him and he couldn't change his plans. This time he told the Redbirds he was ready. "I'll be in Lake Tahoe at that time, but time is arranged for me to take off if the Cardinals win the pennant. I'll have my band out in center field playing before the opening game in St. Louis," said James.

Willis was given a nice raise as he has done an excellent job out of the bullpen. He had appeared in 18 of the team's first 41 games. Willis had been and continued to be a valuable asset in the bullpen, which was already headed by Hoerner.

Despite their fine play, the Cardinals were only in second place with a 27-18 mark to Cincinnati's 34-18. (Remembrances of 1942 of the Cardinal-Brooklyn race were brought to life.) The Cardinals had five hitters over .300 at the time with Cepeda leading at .351 with six home runs and 29 RBIs, while Brock was at .348 with 13 home runs, 37 RBIs, and 22 stolen bases. Five pitchers had won at least three games each, with Gibson leading the way with six. The others were Hughes and Jaster with three each, while Carlton and Jackson had four apiece.

June 9th was memorable for Cepeda for three reason. First, he hit his 250th career home run. Secondly, it was an inside the park home run. Thirdly, it helped defeat the Dodgers and Claude Osteen, 3-2. The next night was another banner night for a Redbird. Maris hit his first Cardinal home run at home as he hit a three-run shot in the 11th inning to defeat Los Angeles and Bob Miller, 5-2.

Washburn's mark of 2-3 was not very impressive. But he had started 11 times and had just one bad game. That was the second start of the season against Los Angeles, when he was lifted in the fourth inning. In all his other games, he had pitched at least 6 2/3 innings. The Cardinals were 5-1 in his no decision games, which means he had kept his team in the game for them to have a chance to win. Plus he had been the stabilizer and allowed the bullpen to rest until late innings.

While the Cardinals were having problems on the baseball diamond, fireworks were going off between Marvin Miller, executive director of the Major League Baseball Players Association, and Joe Cronin, president of the American League. The latter denied baseball was dragging its feet on the issue of minimum salary.

Commissioner Bowie Kuhn also pointed out the owners unilaterally offered in August 1966 to put $4,000,000 annually in the pension fund and eliminate players contributions. Kuhn still held that a union would be to the detriment of baseball players, as their income was tied to performance.

Ernie Banks of the Cubs seemed to voice the consensus of the black players when he said they should shun a union, but he would support placing them in administrative jobs for which they were qualified when their playing days are over. While some wanted to become managers, many would prefer more secure jobs, such as traveling secretary, office assistant or other administrative positions.

As mid June approached, the Cardinals found themselves second once again at 32-21, still trailing Cincinnati by three games. The team boasted seven .300 hitters, with just Maxvill not part of the charmed circle. Brock was at .332, but his average had been falling. The team was still looking for a hot streak to put them into first place.

On June 14th, McCarver hit his third career grand slam, this time off Billy O'Dell to beat Pittsburgh 7-4. This marked the Redbirds 26th win in 32 games with the Pirates. McCarver also hit a grand slam off O'Dell in St. Louis in 1965 when O'Dell was with the Braves. His first grand slam came against the Mets in the Polo Grounds in 1963 and was an inside the park one.

The way Bobby Tolan played, he looked like a super star. He was fast, a good base runner, and could field and hit. As a pinch hitter, he was five for 15 with two doubles. He only hit .185 in September 1965 with the team and just .172 in early 1966 and then was sent back to the minors. He returned as a much improved and more confident player.

The Cardinals finally broke through and landed in first on June 20th with a 37-22 mark while Cincinnati is 40-26. Gibson picked up his seventh win against Pittsburgh in a 7-4 game and improved his career mark against them to 17-4. Maxvill, although in a slump, continued to field brilliantly. Gibson, Hughes, and Jackson had accounted for 19 of the Cardinals first 37 wins, almost like the Deans of the '30s.

After the Dodger's Don Drysdale lost to the Cardinals 2-0 on June 21st, he said they were the team to beat. They had pitching, hitting, speed, and defense. The Cardinals' climb to the top was made despite allowing a half run per game more than they had in 1966. The difference was they have scored one and a half more runs per game. Timely hitting was the difference this year.

The Cardinals continued their torrid pace as they defeated the Pirates and Giants two of three each. Then they swept two each from Los Angeles and Houston, giving them an 8-2 mark for the trip and a stretch of 13 out of 15.

Offensively, Cepeda and McCarver led the way on the trip. Cepeda had 13 RBIs, giving him 48 for the season. He had missed four games when he was ill and played five games when he was sub-par. At the time, he led the league with 18 doubles and was in a groove when he was hitting to right center. He had also been more patient at the plate, walking 31 times versus 38 all of last season. McCarver had three home runs and hit .441 on the trip.

The Redbird's spirited play was packing in the fans. On June 25th, they drew a record crowd for a doubleheader with the Phillies, as 47,014 wild, cheering Cardinals fans flowed into the ball park.

The Cardinals' injury list started to grow. This was where the depth would tell and separate the men from the boys. Washburn received credit for a 2-0 victory over the Dodgers on June 21st, but would be out for four weeks after his thumb was injured by a line drive off the bat of John Roseboro. Hoerner and Briles saved the game for him.

McCarver and Maris were both forced to miss the Philadelphia doubleheader. McCarver split a fingernail on his right hand when he was hit by a foul tip. He did get into one game as a pinch hitter. Maris was hit by pitch on the right elbow. He had hit a game-winning home run the night before in a 3-2 victory.

Slowly the team was starting to widen the margin between them and the rest of the field. As of June 27th, The El Birdos were now 43-24 while Cincinnati was 3 1/2 back at 42-30. In the past two weeks, St. Louis was 11-3, while Cincinnati was 4-9.

The Cardinals had six hitters at .300 or better, but there was concern about Brock. After that great early start, he had cooled considerably and his average dropped to .309. He also had not hit a home run in several weeks. The pitching continued to impress as Gibson was 9-5, 3.00 ERA, Hughes was 7-2, 2.48 ERA and Carlton was 5-4, 3.63 ERA. Jackson was 5-3, but had a horrendous 5.14 ERA and was working out of the bullpen.

The Cardinals had been beating righthanders as they were 30-12 against them, but were just 13-14 versus lefthanders. With only two lefthanded hitters (Brock and McCarver) in the lineup they were uncharacteristically vulnerable to lefthanded pitching.

Young players and reserves had also come in for their share of glory. When Shannon went into a slump, he was benched and Spezio replaced him. He did a good job fielding and hitting, especially against lefthanded pitching. On the night rookie Jim Cosman beat the Giants 3-1, Spezio got two hits.

Hughes, after pitching at least eight innings in seven consecutive games, was bombed on June 28th. He was knocked out in the fourth as the team's five game winning streak was broken. It was his worst outing of the year. Meanwhile, Briles had eight straight good relief appearances through June 28th, and picked up two victories in the process.

Only Cepeda and McCarver remained above .300 as Brock had now fallen to .294, without a home run in more than a month. Even though the hitting had fallen off some, the team continued a winning pace because the pitching was outstanding. Hughes, Gibson, Washburn and Carlton had done the job as starters, while Willis, Hoerner, and Briles were excellent out of the bullpen.

McCarver was becoming recognized as the best catcher in the National League, both offensively and defensively. He had a low strikeout total because he didn't swing at bad pitches. In 1966, he was the fifth toughest to fan in the league. McCarver reminded people of Mickey Cochrane with his aggressiveness and speed.

The Cardinals were setting the pace in the National League and sent Gibson, McCarver, Cepeda, and Brock to the All Star game. There is a tradition in baseball that the team in first place on July 4th will win the pennant more often than not. Up to this season, the team in first place had won the pennant 54 percent of the time. This was the first time the Cardinals had been in first place on July 4th since 1950. In mid July, the Memphis, Tennessee fans invaded St. Louis. More than 450 came to St. Louis to honor three Cardinals from Memphis, Willis, McCarver, and Gagliano.

If you walked into the Cardinal clubhouse on the afternoon of July 15th, you wouldn't know the team was in first place. It was a room full of "gloom and doom". On that day, in the fourth inning, Gibson was hit by a line drive on the lower part of his right leg, cracking the fibula. He faced three more batters. One flied out and two walked. Then he collapsed to the ground.

Gibson was expected to be out about six weeks. Shannon said, "this means the monkey is on somebody's back. Somebody has to pick it up." This was a severe jolt to the pennant hopes. Gone was a pitcher who had won 60 games the past three years and was headed for another 20 plus win season.

The Cardinals not only lost Gibson, but the game as well. Then they were swept in a doubleheader by the Mets the next day. Things were at a low ebb for the Redbirds. Their margin had been cut to two games, but worse, the spirit seemed gone.

One bright spot was that Washburn was returning to the starting rotation. Schoendienst had planned on three days rest for Gibson starting in Cincinnati due to the shaky bullpen. There had been inconsistency from some of the relievers.

The troubles continued as Flood went on the disabled list with a sore shoulder, which will give Johnson and Tolan more playing time. Rickets was also temporarily sidelined with a pulled muscle in the rib cage area. That meant the only backup to McCarver was Romano.

There was a feeling among the Cardinals, especially the pitchers, that they had enough talent to carry on and keep the team at or near the top until Gibson returned. Everyone realized Gibson could not be replaced, but they didn't think the race was over for them just because he went down. Each pitcher would just have to do a little more.

The Cardinals added Jack Lamabe, veteran right hand relief pitcher. In his initial outing he was a better hitter than pitcher. He hit a single to drive in the tying run. When he took the mound was rocked for five runs and the loss. Not a very good start or pickup for Gibson.

One bright thought was that Gibson had an amazing body and had come back quickly from other injuries. He broke the same leg when swinging in the batting cage in 1962. It was near the end of the season so he wasn't available until the next spring. He started 1963 slowly with a 1-3 mark, but finished at 18-9 in that spirited late season drive. However, the concern was time will be short and if he started back slowly, it might be too late for this season.

Briles was assigned the role of taking Gibson's place in the rotation. When Gibson went down he was 10-6 with a 3.52 ERA. Briles was 4-3 with 3.60 ERA. As of July 18th, St. Louis (52-36) held a two game lead on Chicago (50-38). Cepeda continued hitting around the .350 mark and led the league in RBIs, while McCarver and Flood gave strong support. Brock continued his slide and was now down to .287 and hadn't had a home run in almost two months.

Prior to July 23rd, St. Louis was 40-22 versus righthanders, but continued to struggle against lefthanders, going 14-17. That day they played a doubleheader against Atlanta. In game one, they beat lefty Denny Lemaster 3-1. In game two, they beat another left-hander, relief specialist Ramon Hernandez, 8-3. Willis got a save in each game as well as a two-run double in the nightcap. A former outfielder, he was not an easy out at the plate.

In seven appearances, after floundering for several weeks, he had allowed no runs, four hits, and fanned 13 in 10 2/3 innings. It looked like his part of the bullpen was back on track. Shannon had a two-run home run in the doubleheader, breaking up Ed Rakow's bid for a no-hitter in the fifth inning of game two. He also made two fine plays in the outfield, as he was there in Flood's absence.

It was hoped that Lamabe would help shore up the bullpen, but his initial performances had left much to be desired. He lost three games in his first six days with the Cardinals and the fans were wanting his scalp or to have him shipped out of town. So the Cardinals lost a young prospect and got a pitcher who lost three games in the first six days he was with the team.

The Cardinals had widened their lead over the Cubs to 3 1/2 games, mainly because they played better on the road than at home. They were 29-22 at home and 32-18 on the road. The three top contenders, Chicago, Cincinnati, and Atlanta, all had excellent home records, but losing road records, especially Atlanta. The Cardinals were the only National League team with a winning road record, which was why they were in first place.

The situation didn't look all that bright for the Cardinals after Gibson broke his leg. They were then 3-3 in their next six games. Many of the skeptics believed the Cardinals would crack, but the Redbirds righted their ship and flew off. They won seven of eight and regained their 3 1/2 game margin.

Washburn had come off the disabled list when Gibson went on and pitched three straight strong games by July 30th, winning two of them. Carlton pitched in with two victories. Hughes shook his slump and got a victory, giving the Cardinals their first complete game in 20 starts.

Briles picked up a 4-2 victory over the Cubs and Willis had two wins in relief. Meanwhile, Hoerner, Woodeshick and Lamabe all pitched well in relief. After his initial problems, Lamabe pitched creditable baseball and the fans no longer hunted for his scalp or wanted to run him out of town.

The hitting also became revitalized as Cepeda raised his home run total to 18 by hitting three homers in two games at Atlanta. Javier had three RBIs in the Briles victory over the Cubs and Brock seemed to be coming out of his long swoon with a seven for 12 series.

More good news continued to come the Redbirds' way, as Flood played in his first game in three weeks, got two hits, and scored two runs in the Cardinals' 9-1 win over Atlanta on July 28th. Shannon, McCarver, and Maris all had timely hits as they were new heroes every day.

The Cardinals also found their long ball punch as they out homered Atlanta 6-0. The team picked up five wins against left-handers to improve to 17-19, still far below their 44-21 mark against righthanders.

Hoerner was a loosey-goosey guy on a loosey-goosey ball club. He was a number one prankster. His jokes included banging heavy bats on metal chairs next to unsuspecting ballplayers. But he would have a tough time topping his latest performance: Driving the wayward bus.

It happened after the July 28th night game in Atlanta. The bus company neglected to send a driver for the chartered bus. After the grumbling players cooled their heels for about an hour, Hoerner decided to make his first start after years in the bullpen. Several teammates jumped overboard, including Flood.

When the bus pulled out, Flood yelled, "Hey, all our money is on that thing." He was thinking about the World Series cash the players represented.

Hoerner said, "I flicked a few switches and we were off." The noisy band of riders included Cepeda, who kept yelling, "Go, go, go." Whenever a police car approached the bus got quiet. Then once it was out of sight it all started again.

Hoerner gave the teammates a scare when he chose a lane under a bridge which had a clearance reading of 10 feet, 10 inches. One player said, "I don't think busses take that lane, but Joe did." Joe told his teammates that had nothing to worry about, the bus is only 10 feet high, so he had 10 inches to spare. No problem. When he pulled into the hotel driveway he smashed into an "Exit Only" sign. The players scattered like a bunch of kids, breaking a window in the process.

The Cardinals were on a roll by early August. By the end of the first week, they had increased their lead to 8 1/2 games, with everyone taking their turn at being the hero. They swept the Reds in three games to push them further back. McCarver was called for two weeks army reserves and Ricketts subbed for him. He got a bases loaded pinch hit on August 5th to beat the Reds.

Gagliano filled in for Javier in Chicago when he had a muscle pull in his thigh. Gagliano fielded and hit well. One player kidded Gibson, "We're going to vote you just a half share, Hoot," referring to potential past season bonuses. Gibson, as fast with a quip as a pitch, countered with, "Yeah, and I'll take back my 10 wins, and you're out of first place."

Just as the Redbirds were soaring, both Cincinnati and Chicago were floundering. The Cardinals went 11-2, while the other two were 5-8 and 3-11, respectively. San Francisco took the opportunity to move into second place. Actually, the Cardinal drive was 13-2, with most of it against first division teams. They were 5-0 versus Atlanta, 3-0 versus Cincinnati, and 5-2 versus Chicago.

Much of the Cardinal success could be attributed to its pitching staff, especially the young pitchers. Once again this harkened back to the similarity to the Cardinal teams of the early 1940s. Five of the Cardinal pitchers spent all or part of 1966 in the minors.

Carlton was there for most of the season. Hoerner, Willis, and Jaster each spent at least a month there and Hughes the entire season.

Yet these five were key in carrying this team, especially with Gibson on the disabled list. Briles was only in his second season, giving the team six of their 10 pitchers with less than two years major league experience. This sextet had a combined 40-24 record, a certain pennant winning pace.

There was also great flexibility in this staff, as several members could start or relieve. Briles, Hughes, Carlton, and Jaster had demonstrated this capability and that they could perform equally well in either role. This was another feature similar to the Cardinal staffs of the 1940s.

Willis had started well, then ran into a slump and, for much of May and June, was of little benefit to the team. Then he righted himself and had been red hot for the past month. During that time, he made 12 appearances, pitching 18 2/3 scoreless innings. The bullpen, anchored by him, Hoerner, and Lamabe, had become virtually unhittable or unbeatable.

Pennant fever was running high, gripping the fans of St. Louis. Although it had only been three years since the last winner, they were ready for another. On August 5th, a record crowd of 48,019 screaming, whooping Cardinal fans jammed Busch Stadium for a night game against the Cincinnati Reds. They were not disappointed, as they got more than their money's worth. The game went 12 innings and the Cardinals won 5-4.

McCarver owned a restaurant in Memphis, so on August 5th, when the team was to play the Cubs in a doubleheader, he called his restaurant and said if they swept the doubleheader, the drinks were on the house. Happily, McCarver popped for the crowd at his restaurant as the Cards took the pair.

The Redbirds seemed to like to fly more at night than day. During the day the team was just 21-18, but at night they were a torrid 46-23.

Willis's turn around continued as he pitched two hitless innings of relief to gain a win on August 5th then the next day pitched 3 2/3 innings of shut out relief for the save.

Another reclamation project was Brock. He started a 13-game hitting streak on July 24th during which he raised his average from .276 to .295, scored 16 runs, had five doubles, two triples, and his first home run in almost two months.

In two successive series against Chicago, Brock hit .519 (15 for 29). It seemed the sight of a Chicago uniform brought out the thumper in Brock. Flood had also raised his average to .328 since coming off the disabled list, buoyed by a 10-game streak of 19 for 40. With these two healthy and hot, the team appeared ready for whoever the American League opponent would be in the World Series.

The Cardinal pennant fever gripped St. Louis and the town was a sea of red. During the first 10 games of a long August home stand the Cardinals drew 353,272. That was more than the famous 1934 Gashouse Gang drew. Their attendance was just 334,863. However, one must remember that was the depth of the depression with 25 percent unemployment and another 25 percent underemployed. If people didn't have money for bread and milk, they certainly didn't have it for baseball games. Also, Busch Stadium held more than Sportsman's Park.

The Redbirds continued to fly high, as they stretched their lead over second place San Francisco to 11 games. The main reason for the big lead was the team's ability to win close games. During one stretch, they won six games in a row, all by one run. Three of those were against San Francisco, who was 15-25 in such affairs. The Cardinals were 25-13, which was the difference in the standings.

The return of Flood had also been key in the recent Redbird winning streak. In his first 17 games back, Flood hit .433, while the team was 13-4. During this time they allowed just 54 runs, with the opposition scoring more than three runs in a game only four times. Since Flood became a regular in 1961 he had batted .322, .296, .302, .311, .310, but slumped to .267 in 1966.

The Cardinals hit a mild slump in the middle of August when they lost two out of three to Los Angeles. Part of those defeats can be chalked to Cepeda being suspended for two games. Cepeda was kicked out of a game for using a taboo phrase. He said he said it to himself, but umpire Stan Landis contended that Cepeda referred to him. The other two umpires, Augie Donatelli and Al Barlick, supported Landis.

The El Birdos used the same method for success as past Cardinal winners, and beating the first division teams had given them a big margin. From July 3rd to August 17th, the Redbirds were 21-6 versus first division teams. They were 5-1 versus Cincinnati, 5-2 against Atlanta, 8-2 with Chicago, and had a 3-1 edge over San Francisco.

As the middle of August approached, Cepeda was at .340 with 21 home runs and 89 RBIs. Fans were projecting a 30-home run and 125-RBI season for the spirited first baseman. Flood and McCarver both continued at well over the .300 pace and Brock had climbed to .294 with 15 home runs, 57 doubles, and 37 stolen bases. Lost in the shuffle was Shannon, hitting just .256 but with 56 RBIs.

By late August, the Cardinals had swept 12 series and been swept just once. For the season they have a commanding 24-9-6 mark in series records. After the team had fallen into a first place tie with the Cubs, they went on a 20-4 tear to build an 11 1/2 game bulge.

All the pieces had come together for this team. The hitting had been exceptional and the pitching outstanding, both the bullpen and the starters. Javier had been hitting as he did in 1963-64 and Flood hit .443 since off the disabled list, raising his average to .337.

The team did go two weeks without a complete game until Carlton went nine innings on August 18th. However, the bullpen had done yeoman work. Hughes was now the team leader at 12-4, while Carlton was second at 11-6. Washburn had won eight and Jaster and Briles seven each to round out the starting rotation.

The team was on a verge of a new attendance record. With 15 home games to go, the Cardinals needed just 30,000 fans to break last year's record attendance of 1,712,980. The club looks like a cinch to break the 2,000,000 mark for the first time in their history.

Meanwhile, second place was playing musical chairs with a new occupant almost every day. It kept bouncing back between San Francisco, Chicago, Atlanta, and Cincinnati. The question was no longer who would win the pennant, but who would finish second to St. Louis and by how much.

On August 25th, in a two-night double header against the Mets, the Cardinals drew 35,025 fans to set a new attendance record of 1,715,088.

Cepeda got his 100th RBI in a 6-1 win at Los Angeles. Against San Francisco he had the winning RBI in five of the games. For the year, he hit .419 against his old team. This was his way of getting revenge on the club that hadn't wanted him and thought him washed up.

There were a number of reasons why the Cardinals were in first. Maris's ability to handle the job in right. While he hadn't hit like the Maris of old, at least for power, he was the leading clutch hitter in the league. He had more game winning hits than any other player. He was also a team leader and a role model for the younger players.

Another reason was the successful switch of Shannon to third base. While he would be the first to admit he was no Ken Boyer or Ron Santo at third base, he did a better than average job. Also his ability to make the switch allowed Maris to play in right field, especially against righthanded pitching.

Certainly great seasons from Cepeda, Flood, Javier, Brock, and McCarver were also instrumental in this triumphant year. The team couldn't have made it without all these guys putting together the kind of year they did. Added to this was the experience in a pennant race of the entire starting line up. They had been through the grind before and knew the pressures that were there.

Heading into the last month of the season, Hughes was 13-4, Carlton was 11-7, Briles was 9-5, and Willis was 5-3 with seven saves. Briles stepped in for Gibson and had gone 5-2 in his absence. He had a personal four-game winning streak.

Then of course, there were the deals that weren't made. The Cardinals turned down a deal from Chicago which would have given them Billy Williams, an eventual Hall of Fame outfielder, for Briles, Carlton, Tolan, and Alex Johnson. They also turned down a deal that would have sent Briles, Carton, Shannon, and Gagliano to Cincinnati for Cardenas, Gordie Coleman, and Joey Jay.

It seemed everyone wanted Briles and Carlton. Both would go on to have successful major league careers. Carlton would become the second winningest lefthander of all time with 329 wins and be elected to the Hall of Fame. Briles, while not achieving that same level, certainly did not have to apologize for his career. He finished with 129 career wins, including five seasons between 14 and 19.

This team also had to overcame its share of injuries. In addition to Gibson's injury, the team had at one time or another, Washburn, Flood, Spezio, Hoerner, Shannon, Javier, and Ricketts out of the lineup for extended periods. Shannon, who would finish with 77 RBIs in just 130 games, missed his chance for 100 because of various illness and injuries.

Finally, and maybe most important, was the manager Schoendienst. His patience with the handling of the players, veterans and young alike, molded them into a cohesive playing unit.

He was patient with the pitchers, especially the young one, as they struggled at various times. But as they saw his confidence in them, it grew in themselves and they became winners. There were no prima donnas, just 25 men melded together with one common goal to win the pennant and then the World Series.

Schoendienst had missed the pennant winners of the early '40s as he was too young. He was a rookie in 1946 and played second base on that team. He would have to wait until he was a member of the Milwaukee Braves in 1957-'58 to be in another World Series. He returned to the Cardinals and finished his career in St. Louis. He was a coach on the 1964 World Series Champions.

There is an old superstition that you don't have a team photo taken on Labor Day. If you do, bad luck will befall you. Well, the Redbirds didn't believe that, and even if it were true, they could overcome it. So they had their picture taken and proceeded to lose a doubleheader to Pittsburgh, 10-8 and 9-3. The Cardinals were just 2-7 versus Pittsburgh at home this year.

The hitting stopped and the team went into a slight swoon and played 6-6 ball. Then someone reminded them of the 1964 Phillies and the Redbirds begin to fly again. They sweep Houston and scored 31 runs in four games and opened the lead to 12 games, their largest of the season. No over-confidence or possible collapse was seen here.

During a 13-game stretch prior to Labor Day, Cardinal pitchers were virtually unhittable, allowing just 13 runs. Unfortunately, they lost four of those games because their hitters also misplaced their bats. Lamabe, after a terrible start, had pitched well. In August he pitched 25 scoreless innings.

From July 24th, the team was 30-11. This was nine days after Gibson broke his leg and the club was 3-6 for that period. Hughes and Briles each won six games in that stretch to lead the way on the pitching mound. However, they weren't alone. Washburn and

Carlton had four victories each, while Willis and Lamabe won three apiece and Jaster and Jackson took two wins each.

Cepeda was hitting .347 with 24 home runs and 107 RBIs with about three weeks to go and then went into a tailspin. He would finish at .325 with 25 home runs and 111 RBIs. Still a very fine season, one that would earn him the MVP for the National League. McCarver finished second in the balloting.

Hitting in the clutch is considered critical in baseball and separates the real performers from the average. Anyone hitting .400 or more with runners in scoring position is considered to be doing an excellent job. Cepeda led the club with a .587 OBR (opportunity to bat in runs). He had the opportunity to drive in 184 runners and drove home 108. That meant that all but three of his RBIs came in clutch situations.

Brock was also highly effective, hitting .543, followed by Shannon at .439 and Marris at .403. Maris also led the league in game winning hits with 18. Although he hit just .200 against left-hand pitching and only had hits in 12 games against them, the Cardinals won 11 of those games. In other words, when Maris hit the Cardinals had a good chance of winning.

Maxvill has always been noted for his defense, not for his hitting. He played in the majors from 1962-75 and was on five World Series teams, three with St. Louis and two with Oakland. He knew how to win. In the first 15 games of September, when some had slumped, Maxvill had 14 RBIs. Just another piece to the puzzle that was this championship team.

The Cardinals clinched the pennant on September 19th on a three-hitter by Gibson. Certainly no one else deserved the honor anymore than the man who had been the bellwether of this staff for so long. It was a joyous celebration by players and fans alike.

Even though the Cardinals had just won a title three years earlier, the fans acted like it hadn't happened in 20 years. They were as exuberant, jubilant, and wild as they had been in 1964. Nothing destructive happened, however, as occurred during those times in some cities when championships were won. They just wanted to celebrate and savor the victory and that they did. The players, too, had their own celebrations, because for many, this was their first.

The season ended on a grand note as the Cardinals exceeded the 100-win mark for the fifth time in their history. Briles, in Gibson's place, did a hero's job, winning his last nine decisions to finish at 14-5. Hughes was the big winner at 16-6, while Carlton was 14-9, giving the young trio a composite 46-20 mark and, even more importantly, a bright future to look forward to.

Gibson went 3-1 after his return to finish at 13-7, while Washburn was the fifth hurler in double digits with a 10-7 record. Jaster and Jackson each won nine, while Willis and Hoerner had 10 wins and 25 saves. Lamabe, after his 0-3 start, finished at 3-4.

Brock had his biggest season to date at .299 with 206 hits, 32 doubles, 12 triples, 21 home runs, 76 RBIs, 52 stolen bases, and a league high 113 runs. His stolen bases fell because of increased hitting power. McCarver just missed .300, finishing at .295 with 14 home runs, 68 runs, and 69 RBIs. But his greatest contribution was in the handling of the young pitching staff.

Musial and Schoendienst were the spirit of St. Louis. Schoendienst was a poor coal miner's son who overcame a boyhood eye injury, a serious arm injury, and tuberculosis in manhood to rank as one of the best second baseman in National League history. Musial was the son of a poor immigrant from Donora, Pennsylvania in coal-mining country. He overcame a dead arm as a pitcher to become one of the greatest hitters in the history of the game. Look at the batting records and he ranks high in every category, being in the top five or so in many several of the most critical.

They spent 14 years together as roommates and are still the best of friends. Schoendienst almost won the batting title in 1953, hitting .342. Musial finished third at .337. Carl Furillo won at .344, when a broken hand set him down for the last three weeks. Musial was pulling for Schoendienst to win the batting title He had six titles to his name already. He was that kind of guy. "I don't care who wins the title," Stan said, "just so it stays in our room." Red's rejoinder was, "All we're interested in is winning games and filling our room with hits."

Thus, when the Cardinals won the pennant in 1967, neither Schoendienst as manager nor Musial as general manager took credit or began taking bows. They were content to do their jobs quietly, with the relaxed good humor that marked their approach to their profession, and let the ball club speak for itself.

That was the spirit of the Cardinals. That was what they were made of. They were a solid club with good hitting, great pitching, and excellent defense. A Cardinal tradition and shades of the Gashouse Gang. They played hard, but had fun while winning.

Game winning hits were a sign of hitting in the clutch. In 1967, Maris led with 18. On the Cardinals, he was followed by Javier with 15, Cepeda with 14, Shannon with 13 and Brock with 10.

The night after the Cardinals clinched the pennant, Carlton lost a real heartbreaker to the Phillies, 3-1. In that game he fanned 16 men. Schoendienst let him bat in the eighth inning, but he couldn't get any strikeouts in the ninth to tie or set a new record. He had fanned the first four hitters, seven in the first three innings, and 15 after seven innings. He fanned the first batter in the eighth, but couldn't strike out Billy Cowan or Bobby Wine or anybody in the ninth to tie the record of 18 then held by Bobby Feller and Sandy Koufax.

The club finished at 101-60, 10 1/2 games in front of second place San Francisco (91-71) and 14 ahead of third place Chicago (87-74). This marked the fifth time the Cardinals had won 100 or more games in a season. Only the New York Yankees had done it more often. The Cardinals were in a pretty elite class.

The World Series

The Cardinals were the favorites to win the World Series over the Red Sox, mainly because of their pitching. This would be a rematch for the two teams. The Cardinals had won in 1946 in a thrilling seven game adventure. Boston was looking for its first World Series title since 1918.

Game one opened at Boston on October 4th in front of 34,796 in Fenway Park. St. Louis took it 2-1 as Gibson fanned 10 batters. In the third Brock singled, Flood doubled, and Brock scored as Maris grounded out. The Cardinals got their second run in the seventh when Brock singled, stole second, took third on an infield out, and scored on another ground out by Maris. Thus, Brock had two runs scored and Maris two RBIs.

The second game was played the next day before 35,188 screaming Red Sox fans and they didn't go home disappointed. Jim Lonborg pitched a one-hitter and Carl Yastrzemski hit three home runs, accounting for four of the runs in the 5-0 shutout. Yaz had just won the AL triple crown.

The scene shifted to St. Louis and game three was played on October 7th before a sell-out crowd of 54,575. Briles was the winner in a 5-2 ball game. He saved the Cardinals once again, just as he had in mid-season. In the first inning, Brock tripled and Flood singled for the first run. In the second, McCarver singled in front of Shannon's home run. In the sixth, Brock led off with a single and Lee Stange threw wild trying to pick him off and Brock ended up at third. Maris scored him with a single. In the eight, Maris got another hit and scored on Cepeda's first hit of the series, a double. Briles held Yaz hitless.

Gibson returned in game four to the delight of another capacity crowd. He only fanned six this time, but shutout Boston 6-0. The

Cardinals tallied all the runs they would need in the first when Brock and Flood singled and both scored on Maris' double, who later scored on a hit by McCarver. Javier and Maxvill followed with hits and McCarver scored to make it 4-0. In the third Cepeda doubled, took third on a wild pitch and scored on McCarver's fly ball. Shannon walked and scored on Javier's double.

It looked like it was all over as the Cardinals now had a commanding three games to one lead. A third sell-out crowd attended game five anticipating the final victory bell to ring. The Cardinals had their great young lefthander Carlton ready to pitch. He was opposed by Lonborg. Carlton pitched a great game, but left after six innings, trailing 1-0.

Boston had scored the only run in the third when Joe Foy singled, and Mike Andrews sacrificed. Shannon errored trying to field it and Carlton also mishandled it. Both runners were safe and Ken Harrelson's single plated Foy. The game stood that way until the ninth, when George Scott walked Willis , Reggie Smith doubled and Rico Petrocelli was given an intentional pass.

When the first pitch was a ball to Elston Howard, Lamabe relieved Willis. Howard then singled to drive in two runs. Maris hit a home run with two out in the ninth inning to avert a second shut out. Lonborg had now won both Boston victories, by holding the Cardinals to one run and four hits in two games. Except for the strikeouts, his performance exceeded Gibson's, who had allowed one run and 11 hits.

The series returned to Boston and the Red Sox fans were hoping for a repeat of 1946, only in reverse. The Cardinals had gone home, down three games to two, and came back to win. They hoped their beloved Red Sox would do the same. This game opened on October 11th before 35,188 anxious fans who had come to cheer their Red Sox on.

The Cardinals started Hughes again and, for the second time, he failed. Before the day was out the Cardinals would use eight pitchers. The Red Sox started Gary Waslewski, who had a 2-2 record with no complete games in the majors. He hadn't won since July 2nd and hadn't started a game since July 29th. Waslewski would leave in the sixth with a 4-2 lead, surprising everyone.

Boston took a 1-0 lead on Petrocelli's home run in the second. In the third Javier doubled and scored on Brock's single. Brock then stole second and scored on a hit by Flood, putting the Cardinals up 2-1. In the fourth inning, the Red Sox exploded for three home runs. Yaz opened with a home run then, with two outs, Smith and Petrocelli also homered, making the score 4-2.

Brock tied it in the Cardinals' seventh with a two-run home run off eventual winner John Wyatt. However, in their half the Red Sox tallied four more times. Lamabe gave up a one-out hit to pinch hitter Dalton Jones. Brock missed a Foy fly ball that went for a double and he took third when Brock's throw home failed to get Jones. Hoerner replaced Lamabe and Andrews and Yaz singled. In came Jaster and Jerry Adair hit a sacrifice fly. Scott and Smith both got bloop hits to score Yaz for the final count of 8-4.

Once again, it came down to a seventh game to determine the winner. The game would match St. Louis ace Gibson, with three days rest, against Boston star pitcher, Lonborg, with two days rest. It was scoreless until the third when Maxvill tripled and Flood and Maris singled and a wild pitch brought in Flood.

In the fifth, Gibson hit a home run then Brock singled, stole second and third, and scored on a Maris sacrifice fly. The Cardinals wrapped it up in the sixth when McCarver doubled and Shannon was safe on an error by Foy. The ball was hard hit, and could have been called a hit. Javier hit a home run. Lonborg had tried valiantly, but with two days rest he wasn't the Lonborg of games two and five.

This final day crowd of 35,188 saw Gibson again fan 10 men and allow just three hits and two runs. For the series Gibson fanned 26 men in three complete game wins, allowing just three earned runs. He was voted the MVP of the World Series, but a couple others deserved accolades. Brock hit .414, scored eight runs, and stole seven bases, while Maris hit .385 and led the team with seven RBIs. Briles picked up a complete game win and a couple of scoreless relief innings. Carlton, even though losing his only appearance, allowed just three hits and no earned runs in six innings of work. Javier hit .360 and Shannon had a key home run.

Disappointments in the classic included Cepeda, who hit .103, McCarver at .125, and Flood at .179. Hughes was knocked out in both starts and charged with a loss. The Cardinal bullpen of Hoerner, Lamabe, and Willis did not impress.

St. Louis was once again the scene of a wild and jubilant celebration as their Cardinals had become World Champions for the eighth time. Only the Yankees had more titles. The players, veterans and young alike, basked in the glory of the triumph. Here was a team that seemed destined to win several more pennants. It looked like what Musial had said was true, a dynasty was starting.

Epilogue

The 1930 season had been the greatest hitting season of all times with nine teams in the majors hitting .300 or better. The National League had batted .303, with only two teams failing to hit .300. The Cardinals finished third at .314. The 1968 season would see a reversal, as their would be only seven .300 hitters in the major leagues.

The Cardinals would repeat as pennant winners in 1968, winning 97 games. They were on a pace to have back-to-back 100 plus win seasons for the first time since the 1942-44, but a second half slump stopped the team. Only Flood hit over .300, finishing at .301. Cepeda fell to .248 and Brock to .279. Shannon led the team with 79 RBIs.

It was the pitching which carried the ball club. Gibson was 22-

9 with the unbelievable (and record) ERA of 1.12 and 28 complete games. That ERA mark, much like Joe DiMaggio's 56 game-hitting streak, seemed destined to stand for a long time. He pitched 13 shut outs and had a 15-game winning streak, during which he pitched 10 shut outs.

Briles won 19 and Carlton 13 and Washburn 14, all with ERAs below 3.00. Hoerner was a standout in the bullpen at 8-2, 1.47 ERA and 17 saves. There were a couple of major disappointments, as Hughes developed arm trouble, was just 2-2, and would never return to the majors. A career that, although started late in the big time, looked very promising was snuffed out.

Jaster after being 23-12 for his first two plus seasons, started at 3-1 with an ERA below two. He soon faltered and finished at 9-13. That would be his last Cardinal season. He would win three more games and be finished by 1972.

The 1968 team would play the Tigers in the World Series. So for the second consecutive year, it was a re-match of two former foes. The Cardinals had defeated Detroit in 1934 when the Dean brothers each won two games. It looked like a repeat again, as the Cardinals went up three games to one.

Then a base running error in game five stopped the Cardinals who had a 3-2 lead at that point. Brock failed to slide at home and was out, thus killing a rally. They went on to lose that game and the next two and the Cardinals had lost their first seven game World Series. The city would have to wait another 14 more years before a championship flag would once again fly high at Busch Stadium

Orlando Cepeda

Lou Brock

Roger Maris

Bob Gibson

The Glory Years

ROW FOUR L-R   Forsch, Stuper, Littell, Rincon, Citarella, Olmsted, Hernandez, Kaat, Tenace, Hendrick, Oberkfell, Herr, Iorg, Sutter

ROW THREE L-R   Calise, LaPoint, Brummer, Roof, Fulgham, Green, Mura, Santana, Romo, Rasmssen

ROW TWO L-R   Gieselmann, Andujar, Kennedy, Kinnunen, Martin, Shirley, O. Smith, Landrum, L. Smith, Gonzales, Sanchez, Bjorkman, Bair, McGee, Paris

ROW ONE L-R   DeSa, Gonzales, Braun, Porter, Ricketts, Kittle, Herzog, Hiller, Lanier, Schoendienst, Tettelbach, Ramsey, Yatkeman, Bauman

1982

Whitey Ball

Prologue

It had been 14 years since a pennant flag had been hoisted at Busch Stadium. Players, management and fans alike were anxious for another Cardinal title. The dynasty that had seemed possible in the 1960s died with the Cardinals' World Series loss in 1968. Some of the young players never developed. Some of the pitchers, like Dick Hughes, developed sore arms or others, like Larry Jaster, faded out of sight.

Still others gained their greatest fame pitching elsewhere. The loss of Mike Torrez was a terrible blow. He won 174 major league games, but only 21 as a Cardinal. Jerry Reuss won 161 games, but just 22 as a Cardinal. But the greatest loss was the trade of Steve Carlton to Philadelphia. He won a career total of 329 games. Only Warren Spahn won more as a lefthander. He had 77 Cardinal wins when traded.

He had been offered $60,000 after winning 20 games in 1971. Carlton countered, he felt he was worth $75,000 or at least half as much as Bob Gibson. One word led to another and he riled president Gussie Busch, who ordered Carlton traded. When Carlton found out he was going to Philadelphia, he relented, but Busch wouldn't. Net result - it probably cost the Cardinals three or four division titles in the 1970s.

For most of the decade of the '70s, the team was not that strong. Although it finished second three times, the most games they won was 90 in 1971. In 1973 and 1974 they were 1 1/2 games out of first, but the division was not that strong. They and the fans would have to wait until the 1980s and a rebuilding process before St. Louis could claim another title.

The Cardinals had hired Whitey Herzog as manager and general manager for the 1981 season. Busch was getting on in years and wanted another championship, so he gave Whitey a free hand. There had been a lot of talent on the 1980 ball club, including five .300 hitters, but the club finished at 74-88, 17 games out.

Herzog knew changes had to be made. The club was filled with internal problems that required a wholesale house cleaning. During the week of December 7-12, 1980 Herzog made the following trades:

- Signed free agent catcher Darrell Porter;
- Received Rollie Fingers, Bob Shirley, and Gene Tenace from San Diego for Terry Kennedy, Steve Swisher, Mike Phillips, John Littlefield, John Urrea, Kim Seaman, and Al Olmstead;
- Acquired closer Bruce Sutter from the Chicago Cubs for Leon Durham, Ty Waller and Ken Reitz;
- Got Sixto Lezcanto, David Green, Lary Sorensen and Dave LaPoint from Milwaukee for Rollie Fingers, Pete Vukovich, and Ted Simmons.

These trades shook the baseball world in general and the Cardinal fans in particular. Some of the players traded had been very popular, especially Simmons. He had been one of the great favorites of the Cardinal fans and considered by many the best catcher they ever had. Herzog said he only wanted players instilled with the winning Cardinal tradition on his team.

The fans decided to take a wait and see attitude. St. Louis fans had always been fair and were willing to give Herzog, who had a good track record in the American League, a fair chance. They didn't have to wait long. While all the acquired players didn't produce, enough did to give the Cardinals a highly competitive team in 1981.

Unfortunately this was the year of the first major strike in baseball. There had been a couple of previous minor incidents, but this one had major repercussions. It began on June 12th and would wipe 50 to 55 games off each team's schedule before play was resumed. Commissioner Bowie Kuhn then decided it would be in the best interest of baseball to have a split season, so as to retain fan interest.

It was a disastrous mistake as it put four teams in a playoff system in the National League that did not have the best records. St. Louis with the best overall record in the Eastern Division, finished second each half, therefore was eliminated from the play-offs. The Reds found themselves in the same position. The owner of the best overall record in the Western Division, they, too, were prohibited from the playoffs as they were second each half.

While certainly there is no guarantee the Cardinals would have been in the World Series, at least they would have had the opportunity to play if the usual season format had been followed. Fans and players alike detested the decision, believing the split season had diluted the tradition of the national pastime.

At least the 1981 season gave the Cardinal fans hope for 1982. They had a solid infield in place, although the Garry Templeton incident in the summer of 1981 would lead to his trade. A talented individual, offensively and defensively, he had become upset with the St. Louis fans. In one game he made an, obscene gesture, which gave Cardinal management no choice but to trade him. They wouldn't give him away, but wanted a first class shortstop in his place.

Herzog began his search in earnest for a new shortstop and offered Templeton to San Diego for their young fielding whiz, Ozzie Smith. While Smith was superior to Templeton in the field, he could not hit with him. Smith's career mark was .230 with one home run for four seasons in the majors. The switch-hitting Templeton had a career .300 average with 25 home runs for five seasons. He hit .300 or better three times and he led the league in triples 1977-79, hitting a total of 50. He was one of the few batters in history to get more than 100 hits from both sides of the plate in a single season.

Herzog knew he would be giving up considerable offense, but he believed that Smith's better defense would offset that, plus he had little choice. By his actions, Templeton had made himself dispensable in St. Louis. He had to go. Second baseman Tommy Herr said he would miss him as a double play partner and pitcher Bob Forsch said he had been with him since his first day in the majors. He thought Templeton would be better off in a new environment such as San Diego.

The rest of the infield was set with Gold Glove and former MVP and batting champion Keith Hernandez at first, Herr at second, and Ken Oberkfell at third. The outfield would require some help. Lezcano had been a bust, but they had George Hendrick and his 109 RBIs. Herzog would have to do some shopping for the outfield, although he had Dane Iorg, who batted .327 in 217 at bats.

Darrell Porter lacked Simmons bat, but he was a highly efficient catcher. He would never regain the glory of his Kansas City days. Nor would he ever be taken into the hearts of the St. Louis fans like Simmons.

The pitching needed some shoring up and late in the 1981 season, Herzog had acquired in Joaquin Andujar from Houston, who was 6-1 for the Astros. He already had Forsch, who, in a shortened '81 season, was 10-5 with 3.19 ERA. Sutter was splendid with a league high 25 saves. Herzog was also hopeful that young Andy Rincon could recover from his injury to be a big winner in 1982. He had been 3-1, 1.75 ERA in five games prior to the strike.

There was a problem in Smith's contract as he had a no-trade clause. He had taken $300,000 per season rather than $500,000 to get it. If Smith went to arbitration, it could jeopardize his no-trade clause and then he could be traded. This was a dilemma for both Smith and the Cardinals.

Smith had two options facing him. Renew his contract with a trade clause and he could get a 20 percent pay cut, the maximum allowed under the first year renewal. His second option was to reject the contract offered him and submit to arbitration.

Herzog had other contract problems facing him. He needed

Andujar, but the free agent hadn't signed. Herzog still expected him to sign with the Cardinals. Herr made $45,000 in 1981 last season, but after a good season, which included 23 stolen bases and leading the league in fielding, he wanted a raise to $180,000.

Herzog finally signed Andujar to a three-year contract, the terms of which were not disclosed. In a search for pitching help, Herzog sent Lezcano to San Diego for righthander Steve Mur, but Herzog's main concern was still Smith.

Herzog was willing to offer Smith $425,000 to $450,000 with incentives that could reach $500,000, but not a no-trade clause. Smith countered that he wanted a no-trade clause unless he got $750,000. Templeton got $660,000 with four years to go. The question soon became why Smith would risk going to arbitration and playing for $240,000 when he could sign for a guaranteed $425,000 to $450,000 and play for a team that wanted him. Finally, after 62 days of hectic haggling, bargaining, and maneuvering Smith was in the Cardinal fold and Templeton became a Padre. The Cardinals had other good news on the payroll front. Outfielder Lonnie Smith signed for $225,000, while Oberkfell avoided arbitration and settled for $350,000. Pitcher Bob Shirley agreed to $260,000. Herr was the only St. Louis player now scheduled for arbitration.

In the meantime, Herzog was castigated by some for referring to Templeton as "that boy". Herzog's response was quite simple. He said, "I'm 50 and my players are 25 or so. Therefore I can call them boys."

Herzog expected Herr, Oberkfell, and recently acquired Lonnie Smith from Philadelphia to file for arbitration. However, they and the team weren't more $50,000 apart on any of them. Herzog didn't see a major problem

Herzog was planning on Lonnie Smith to be a solution to his outfield problem. He had been in the majors for most of four years, but had only 500 at bats. During that time he had averaged .315 with 60 stolen bases. He could hit and had speed, although there were questions about his defense. He wasn't always as sure of himself in the field as he was at the plate. In fact, he had led the minors in errors for five seasons.

Herzog said there was salary insanity and it was going unchecked. Owners were opening wallets and giving free agents unlimited checks. This loomed for potential disaster in the future. How right he was. A good example was California Angel owner Gene Autry, who gave a four-year $2,000,000 contract to reserve catcher Ed Ott. No one could blame the player for accepting the money. It was the owners' fault for offering it.

Another change in the sporting world was the overlapping of sports seasons. The other major sports (football, hockey and basketball) now overlapped into the baseball season. Up until 1950, the major sports tended to stay within their own season. Now everything had gone haywire. Hockey and basketball didn't end until May and soon it will be later. Football began their practice in late July and the schedule was ready to open in early September.

Salaries continued to escalate as baseball saw its first $2,000,000 per year men. When Gary Carter, George Foster, and Mike Schmidt received these contracts, a new level was established. Perhaps these three deserved this figure, but some felt it would push salaries into the upper stratosphere.

Herzog, in reviewing his team, believed he had the pieces falling into place. Forsch was the key to the Cardinal pitching success. He was the veteran and was expecting him to lead the way. He was also counting heavily on Andujar, Shirley, and Rincon. Of the latter Herzog said he could win 18 or three. Rincon broke his right arm and had shoulder injury last year and was of no value after the strike ended. Some of the players were still put out with Rincon because he hadn't stayed in condition to help them in the second half. Some blamed him for their failure to make the playoffs, not the decision by the Commissioner.

The Cardinal infield of Hernandez, Herr, Smith, and Oberkfell was the best in the league, if not in baseball. The outfield looked like it would open with Smith, Iorg and, Hendrick. Tito Landrum would be a defensive replacement for Lonnie Smith and could also platoon with Iorg. Other candidates included Gene Roof, Steve Braun, Green, and rookie Willie McGee, who could be the sleeper in the whole group.

Porter, who injured his shoulder last season, still hadn't fully recovered. Gene Tenace, the veteran back up, had a decent bat, but was not strong defensively behind the plate. The hope was that Porter would recover to assume his job, as he was needed to steady the pitching staff.

The staff would include Jim Kaat, now in his 24th season. He had 278 career wins and 16 consecutive Gold Gloves. He also had 14 winning seasons and 15 years of 10 or more victories. Eric Rasmussen was trying a comeback with the team. He, John Denny and Forsch started with the Cardinals in the mid '70s. They were thought to be the future of the Redbirds, but that never quite happened. Only Forsch was left and he had 93 wins entering this year, including six years in double digits and only one losing season in eight.

Herr avoided arbitration by signing for $165,000 and with incentives could increase that another $10,000. In arbitration cases decided to date, the owners won 14 and the players eight. There were 83 players that settled before arbitration. Losing players got an average of an 83 percent increase. Thus, even in losing the players did quite well.

Another concern in baseball had been the use of long-term contracts. It was felt that once a player was locked into a long term contract, he would or could take it easy and coast. In the majority of instances this did not prove to be true. More than 60 percent of players who had long term contracts equalled or improved on prior performance.

The early prognosticators picked Montreal first and St. Louis second. Herzog said the team could steal 200 bases. He figured 50 for Lonnie Smith with Herr and Ozzie getting 40 each. He also planed to use Tenace at first base against lefthanded pitching and switch Hernandez to left field in those games. He had played some left field last year and did satisfactorily. The main concern was moving the Gold Glove first baseman into the outfield.

However, in early spring training those plans got shelved as Tenace broke his right thumb. A few days later, Oberkfell joined him on the sick list, as he broke his left thumb. Herzog did some more house cleaning, as Shirley was traded to Cincinnati and Rasmussen was shipped to Yucatan in the Mexican League.

Herzog squelched a the trade rumor that he would send Sutter to the Mets for pitcher Neil Allen and catcher John Stearns. The Cardinals catching situation didn't look good with Porter's arm problem and Tenace's broken thumb, but trading Sutter was not the answer.

About this time, Herzog decided to step down as general manager, saying that the demands of both jobs just became too great. He said he could not do equal justice to both and properly run the team on the field. He got a new three-year contract as manager, while Joe McDonald was named as general manager.

Regular Season Play

The Cardinals opened the season with a 14-3 win over Houston behind Forsch, but then dropped the next two by scores of 3-2 and 1-0. The latter loss was charged to Andujar, who would suffer this fate all year. He would pitch great ball and have either a loss or receive a no decision due to low run production. The Cardinal

269

pitching staff allowed only six runs in three games, but the team had only one victory to show for their efforts.

The Cardinals opened at home against Pittsburgh, but the Pirates spoiled the opener beating Mark Littell in relief 11-7. The Redbirds took the second game 7-6.

On April 14th, Rincon got the Cardinals' first complete game with a 3-1 victory over the Cubs. This gave rise to hope that Rincon would pitch the way the he had been expected and make Herzog's forecast of 18 wins come true. The day before, Ozzie had hit his first home run in 1,778 at bats. His only previous homer had come against Atlanta's Larry MacWilliams on September 4, 1978.

Roof was sent to the minors as the Cardinals got down to the player limit. Tenace was off the disabled list. After a 1-3 start, the Cardinals surprised the National league with a 12 game winning streak to take over first place. The team was 13-3. Hernandez was hitting .379 and Lonnie Smith .340 with 11 stolen bases to lead the attack. The starting pitchers went at least six innings in 15 of the 16 games.

Herzog didn't need five starters in the early going, as the team had many open dates, but he used them anyway. He wanted to give all his pitchers a fair opportunity and plenty of rest.

In his first three starts, Andujar was 2-1 with a 1.08 ERA. His only loss was 1-0 on an unearned run. Eleven teams picked Andujar in the reentry draft, but he elected to sign with St. Louis. Previously, much controversy had surrounded Andujar, but not in St. Louis. He was one of the most popular players in the club house. He called himself "One Tough Dominican". He also got three hits in back-to-back starts, which was three more than he had all of last season.

McGee started the season at Louisville, but the feeling was he would be returning soon. Reserve catcher Glenn Brummer was optioned to Louisville as Tenace was available for duty again.

After the Cardinals won 12 in a row, they lost three straight as Hernandez went into a 0 for 18 slide. His average dropped to .319. Templeton was hitting .306 and he checked his and Ozzie's average daily. Ozzie was hitting .233. Templeton said sarcastically, "I'm glad he's off to such a good start."

May began with the Cardinals in first with a 15-9 mark, followed by Montreal at 11-8, and New York at 11-12. Hernandez led the Cardinal charge. If Lonnie Smith was the catalyst, Sutter the savior, then Hernandez was the adhesion of the team. A tongue lashing by Herzog had sent him into high gear.

Hernandez was the only player in the National League to hit .300 or better and finish in the top 10 for the last three seasons. Herzog knew that he was an extremely talented individual, but had a tendency to lie back, despite having won four Gold Gloves. There was good talent on the 1980 team that Herzog inherited, but it was filled with players that had attitude problems, including Hernandez. He used the tongue lashing to whip Hernandez into shape and to inspire him to become the driving force on the team. Now the veteran first baseman was the new leader by example.

In the first 18 games Hendrick played, the Cardinals were 16-2, while in the nine games he missed with inflammation and swelling of the elbow, the team was just 2-7. He was the Cardinals' trump card. Hendrick was the one real home run threat in the line up. In the 18 games he had played, Hendrick had seven home runs.

The hitting became sporadic. Hernandez went into an 0 for 24 spin, then went seven for 15. Lonnie Smith had gone 0 for 16, before getting eight hits in a three game Chicago series. Ozzie was moved to the second spot and has been hitting .341 since. Herr was dropped from his customary number two spot to eighth because he was in a five for 39 slump.

The Cardinals had four regulars, (Hernandez, Lonnie Smith, Hendrick, and Oberkfell) and three reserves (Iorg, Green, and Tenace) hitting .300 or better. Green and Iorg had been platooning in right field. Tenace was particularly impressive in spot roles. He was 6 for 14 with two doubles and two home runs.

The pitching continued to be strong with Forsch leading the way among the starters at 4-0 while Andujar was 3-2. Sutter had converted 10 of 11 save opportunities and Doug Bair was 3-0 and had allowed just one earned run in 17 2/3 innings. Sutter praised Bair's work, saying one man couldn't do it all.

Due to the team effort, the Cardinals had an early 4 1/2 game lead and were the only team in the division over .500. The Cardinals were 19-11, while New York was 14-15 and Montreal 12-13.

Hernandez and Hendrick had been the key RBI men on the team while Lonnie Smith led the league in runs scored and stolen bases. He particularly enjoyed having big games against his old team the Phillies, where he believed he was given a bad rap.

The team was averaging close to 4.5 runs per game, but it was the manner in which they were doing it that concerned Herzog. He said, "we should be getting four or five runs every night, but instead we get seven or eight tonight, and then one or two the next night. As a result we have a split for the two games. " In nine of the first 12 defeats, the Cardinals scored two runs or fewer. They were shut out three times.

At one point, the Cardinals were 15-2 versus teams in their own division, but just 4-10 against teams in the western division. While this was a pennant winning pace, Herzog knew they would have to do better against the West if they were going to get to the World Series.

Injuries altered the Cardinal line up as Green injured a hamstring and was placed on the disabled list. This gave the Cardinals the opportunity to call up McGee from Louisville. A few days later, Porter suffered a broken right finger and would be out three weeks. He had missed 38 games in 1981 due to a torn rotator cuff.

Tenace then was back on the disabled list after breaking a bone in his hand diving into first base on a pick-off play. His injury occurred after Porter broke his finger on a foul tip on May 14th. These injuries necessitated the recall of Brummer, who was now number one catcher.

Tenace was hitting .414 on 12 for 29, but slugging .931 with three doubles and four home runs. When his 10 walks and one hit by pitch were added, Tenace's on base percentage was .600. Porter was hitting just .243, but had four home runs and 16 RBIs, but his defense and handling of pitchers would be missed more than his offense. In his start against San Diego, Brummer got two doubles and helped the team to a 6-4 win.

At one point, Forsch's ERA was around four and one half runs per game, even though he was undefeated. He now had it down to 3.86 with a 5-0 record. La Point, was 2-0 and 3.18 ERA. Andujar continued to pitch great ball, but had trouble winning. He had a 2.88 ERA, but is just 3-3.

The other starters had mixed results. Mura was 3-2 with a 3.02 ERA, while John Martin was 3-4 with a ballooned 5.92 ERA. Rincon was 2-2 and 4.76 ERA. His only real good game was an early season win over the Cubs. LaPoint was now a starter and Rincon and Martin have been banished to the bullpen.

The play of the other teams in the division had improved and the Cardinal lead narrowed. Philadelphia was now third at 21-19, three games out, while New York was second with a 23-18 mark, just 1 1/2 half games behind. St. Louis continued to hold the lead with a 25-17 record.

The Cardinals, needing pitching help, recall John Stuper from Louisville. He had a 7-1 record there as a starter and would be worked into the starting rotation. Rincon would stay in the bullpen having walked 25 men while fanning just 11 in 40 innings. Contrast that with Andujar who had fanned 37 and walked just eight in 69 2/3 innings.

After six weeks of the season, the Cardinal infield had made just 11 errors, while Templeton himself made six in San Diego. The Cardinals reserves also played a key role in their drive for first place. Mike Ramsey was batting .349, subbing for Herr and Oberkfell. Green hit .338 and Landrum .325 in spot roles and pinch hitting duty.

It began to look like a four team race in the east. The Cardinals continued to lead at 30-18, but they were closely trailed by New York at 26-21, Montreal, the pre-season favorite at 24-20, and Philadelphia right behind at 24-21. Just 4 1/2 games separated the four clubs. A slump or hot streak by any of the teams could quickly jumble the standings.

McGee had been a key spark in the Cardinals attack. However, the trade to acquire him from the Yankees last October had merited little attention. The Cardinals had traded the 10th man on a 10-man pitching staff for a AA outfielder. By June, McGee was playing a great center field and hitting .348. He was platooning with Green who replaced Hendrick. This alignment allowed Smith to move to left field, where his defensive shortcomings were less obvious.

Herzog had a dilemma. Whom would he send back to the minors when Porter and Tenace returned? McGee figured it would be he. When McGee, Green, and Lonnie Smith were in the outfield together, Smith, despite his 25 stolen bases, was the slowest of the three. McGee felt much more at home with the Cardinals. He said he never felt he had a chance with the Yankees. There were too many players ahead of him.

It was doubtful that Templeton were smiling now, as his batting average had fallen to .249, while Ozzie was hitting .280. Templeton would play another 10 seasons, but the highest he would ever hit would be .282. The promise he had shown in the first five years as a Cardinal seemed to dissolve. Meanwhile, Smith would become an accomplished number two hitter, batting over .300 once and hitting above .280 on several occasions. This, of course, was in addition to all the Gold Gloves he would win.

The other Smith continued to lead the league in runs scored and was third in stolen bases. Iorg almost had become he forgotten man, but delivered whenever he had the opportunity. He had believed after the fine season he had in 1981 he would be an everyday player, but it didn't happen. He was a valuable reserve and role player, hitting .286.

The concern over Hernandez was twofold. Although he had a very respectable total of 33 RBIs, his average had slipped to .289. Of greater concern was his lack of power. He had just one home run and only 14 extra base hits. The question was, where had all the power gone? The last two full seasons (1979 and 1980) Hernandez had 133 extra base hits.

Injuries had hurt the Cardinals, but they gamely battled on. Herr was out for three weeks with a pulled muscle and Ramsey did an excellent job replacing him. The Cardinals thought about trading him, so he was given the opportunity to play regularly. Forsch picked up his coveted win number 100 by beating the Dodgers.

The batting doldrums seemed to be a growing as both Smiths and Oberkfell fell into a hitting slump. Finally, Hendrick returned to the lineup to supply some power. Due to the hitting slump, Herzog used four sacrifices (two of them squeeze plays) to win a 5-4 decision in Montreal.

Herzog's Cardinal ball clubs didn't have a lot of power hitters in the line up. Hendrick with 19 homers and Porter with 12 would be the only double digit home run hitters on the 1982 Cardinals. The entire club would hit just 67 for the year. Mark McGwire would hit more than that in his record breaking season of 1998 when he hit 70.

Herzog's teams were built on speed, defense and tight pitching. In Sutter he had the premier closer in baseball. He had a better than average pitching staff that could pitch complete games or at least deep into the game. This would be the feature of each of his pennant winners of the eighties, although the addition of Jack Clark would add a power dimension theretofore missing. The team would lead the league in stolen bases from 1982-88.

That style of play, and most of the Cardinal teams in the '80s, came to be known as Whitey Ball. It is characterized by manufactured runs and strong defense.

In 1981 Herr had started every game, but injuries plagued him in 1982. On May 13th, he injured his quadriceps muscle in Atlanta and would be out for five games. He returned on May 18th in San Diego. He re-injured it on a hit-and-run that went awry and was unable to return until June 7th, but he still was not himself. Herr admitted he had returned too early after the first injury.

The Cardinals' main problem was a lack of consistent scoring. Overall they were sixth in scoring, but it had been sporadic. In their first 60 games, the team scored two or fewer runs 21 times, posting a 3-18 record. Lack of power continued to haunt the team, as Hernandez, despite hitting .297 with 35 RBIs, still had only one home run. The Cardinals lacked someone who could come up and win a game with one swing. Hendrick and Porter were the best the team had.

Hendrick's average had fallen to .258 with 11 home runs and 32 RBIs, while Lonnie Smith was hitting .297 and had slipped to second in the league with 48 runs, and third with 25 stolen bases. Iorg was up to .324 and McGee .319, but neither hit for power. As the team had excess outfielders, Green was sent to Louisville, despite batting .325.

The pitching had been mixed. Forsch was 8-2 with a 3.58 ERA while Andujar had a fine 2.35 ERA, but was just 6-4. Mura was 5-

5 with a 4.90 ERA and LaPoint, though 3-1 had a 4.14 ERA. Sutter's ERA had climbed to 3.71, although he was 5-3 with 15 saves.

Despite all the injuries, hitting slumps, and erratic pitching the Cards remained in first. They were 38-28 followed by Montreal (35-27), New York (34-30) and Pittsburgh (33-30), as Philadelphia had seemingly dropped out of the hunt.

The race was tightening as St. Louis had just a one-game lead on Montreal and Philadelphia. Montreal was starting to play like the forecasters had predicted and Philadelphia had come from the back of the pack to move into serious contention. Herzog expected a dog fight for the division title.

The Cardinal big hitters took a snooze during the month of June. After a successful West Coast trip, the team returned home late in May and the slump began. They were just 14-16 in June, averaging just 3.5 runs per game. If you discard an 11-6 win over San Francisco they averaged 3.3 runs per game.

By late June, Sutter finally had shaken a long slump. On May 12th; he was 1-0, 1.71 ERA and 10 saves. On June 20th, he was 5-5, 5.00 ERA and 15 saves. In that 28 inning stretch, Sutter allowed 33 hits, 22 earned runs. The low point hit in St. Louis on June 18th when he blew a 3-0 lead in the ninth inning of a 5-3 loss to the Mets. Two days later he gave up two runs in the 10th inning to lose 5-4.

"If he doesn't do it, we ain't gonna have a very good season," said a puzzled Herzog. "He's the key to the whole thing. And he ain't getting it done. He just isn't getting the ball down." Sutter came to two conclusions. First, he needed to mix more fast balls instead of almost totally relying on his split-fingered pitch. Secondly, he needed consultation with Mike Roarke, former Cubs pitching coach, who monitored him when in Chicago.

On June 21st, after going two scoreless innings in a 7-5 win over the Phillies, he called Roarke. Roarke had seen the game on television and told Sutter a couple of things he was doing wrong. He said it wasn't anything major, he was just overthrowing the ball. He had this problem last year and Roarke helped him then.

Herzog had given permission for Roarke to help, as Cardinal pitching coach Hub Kittle said Roarke could do more for Sutter than he could. Roarke's advice helped, and in a doubleheader against the Cubs, Sutter saved both games.

Stuper pitched his first complete game when he defeated the Phillies 3-2. On June 27th, he suffered his first loss in a 4-2 defeat by the Cubs, making his record 2-1. His promotion had been a shot in the arm for the pitching staff. Mark Littell, one time relief ace, was designated for assignment and relief pitcher Jeff Lahti was recalled.

Finally, on June 29th, the Cardinals exploded with 15 runs against Philadelphia. However, in the previous seven games against the lowly Cubs and contenders Philadelphia, they had scored just 14 runs. "I think I could pitch a four-hitter against this team," said Porter, one of the chief slumpers, "especially if Porter and Hendrick were in the line up."

Porter would play from 1981-85 in St. Louis, but could never really win the hearts of the St. Louis fans. In replacing Simmons, he had displaced an excellent hitting catcher who was one of the most popular players on the team. Porter had one great season for the Royals in 1979. He batted .291 with 101 runs scored, 23 doubles, 10 triples, 20 home runs, 112 RBIs, and a league high 121 walks. A great season for anyone, but an exceptional one for a catcher.

Porter developed severe drug and alcohol problems and was almost out of the game, but proper treatment saved him and he was able to continue his career until he retired at the end of the 1987 season. Unfortunately, the fans had expected to see him hit like he had in 1979 or like Simmons, but that never happened. When it didn't, the fans just couldn't accept him.

At one point during this slump, Porter was two for 33 and Hendrick was 11 for 68. Hernandez, although driving in runs, was not the extra base hitter of prior seasons. Thus, many of the times Lonnie Smith and McGee got on base were wasted. "The three, four, five, and six men (Oberkfell hit sixth) have got to do it for us," said Herzog.

In the 15-run game at Philadelphia, Hernandez got his third home run and three RBIs while Hendrick got seven RBIs, including his third grand slam of his career. That marked just the third time in the month the two had RBIs in the same game. Prior to the June 29th outburst, Hendrick had just 10 RBIs since May 16th.

The Cardinals had also been doing some bad base running. In Chicago, with the bases loaded, McGee singled to the outfield. Landrum didn't break right away and had to be held at third. Lonnie Smith, running with his head down, ran to third. Landrum was then run down between third and home and tagged out. McGee, panicking, raced from past second base back to first. If the Cubs had appealed, McGee would have been out as he had failed to touch second on his way back to first.

The next night, in a 1-0 loss to Philadelphia, Herr got picked off first base with a 3-0 count on Ozzie. "If I were Whitey I'd fine me $500," said Herr. Mura suffered the heartbreak loss. He had been winless for a month.

Meanwhile, Lonnie Smith continued to haunt his old team-mates, batting .377 against Philadelphia. If he could hit that way against Montreal and Cincinnati, he would terrorize the league. He had now taken over the league lead in runs with 66 and stolen bases with 37.

The hitting slump had affected the pitching as well. Forsch, after his fine start, was still stuck at eight wins and was now 8-4. Even more alarming, his ERA has jumped to 4.30. Meanwhile Andujar, had trouble winning, not because of his pitching, but failure of his teammates to score runs. He had a fine 2.25 ERA, but was just 7-5, while Mura had slipped to 5-7 with a 4.45 ERA.

Nearing the mid-point of the season, things weren't looking all that bright for the Redbirds. They had fallen out of first place and trailed Philadelphia by one game. Philadelphia was 44-34, the Cardinals, 44-36, Montreal was 41-37 and Pittsburgh was 40-37 and moving up. Take away the Cardinal 12-game winning streak, and they were 32-36. That streak had kept the team atop the division since the first week of the season.

Stuper and LaPoint had picked up the pitching slack, as they were 4-1 and 4-2 respectively. They replaced Martin (4-4) and Rincon (2-2) in the rotation. Mura went 47 days with a victory, from May 26th to July 6th. He got win number six (one more than last season with San Diego) when he beat Cincinnati, 3-1 on a four hitter.

Hendrick had a seven-game hitting streak, during which he was 12 for 27, while Porter thought he was out of his slump with a three hit-game against Philadelphia. However, he went hitless in the Cub series.

To loosen up the clubhouse, trainer Gene Gieselmann played the old "mongoose trick" on rookie McGee. He placed a box labeled "wild mongoose" by McGee's locker. When McGee opened it, out pooped a fake furry critter. McGee was last seen trying to climb atop a locker. It didn't affect his hitting, as he was still at .335. Hernandez, although not hitting for power, continued to drive in runs and had 47 RBIs. He also had 12 game-winning hits and 12 stolen bases.

Lonnie Smith was at .307 with a league high 69 runs and 41 stolen bases, while Hendrick had pushed his average up with his hitting streak to .268 with 12 home runs and 51 RBIs. However, Herr continued to have trouble with his batting, hitting just .239. Fortunately it had not affected his fielding, as he was playing a flawless second base.

Andujar continued to have a frustrating season. He had made 21 starts and had an excellent 2.30 ERA, but just a 7-7 record. He easily could have had 14 or 15 victories. Forsch, with a 4.28 ERA, was 8-4 in 19 starts. Sutter had 19 saves, as he continued his improved pitching.

By the All Star break, Philadelphia continued to lead with a 47-38 mark, St. Louis was one game back at 48-39, and Pittsburgh was 44-40, followed closely by Montreal at 43-42.

Porter must produce in the second half. The Cardinals couldn't play Tenace behind the plate. He couldn't throw like Porter. A new prediction said the race would now finish Philadelphia, Montreal, and St. Louis. For the Cardinals to win it, they needed another starter, a middle relief pitcher, and a power hitter. That was a tall order. Where was a team going to get that in mid-season, and what would they have to give to get it?

Ozzie was a hero in the All Star game. He was not an offensive star, but was the defensive player of the game. In the eighth inning, Lance Parrish hit a dribbler over the mound and Ozzie made a great play to throw him out. Instead of the bases being loaded with two outs, the inning was over. Andujar was mad that Dodger manager Tommy Lasorda left him off the All Star team. Based on his record, it seems he should have been picked. He had the second best ERA in the league and it cost him a bonus of $25,000 to $50,000 because he didn't make the All Star team.

The Cardinals had dropped their first three series to Houston, each two games to one. Bob Knepper was 2-0 against the Cards, but 1-10 versus the rest of the league. "He looks like Rube Waddell when he faces us," said Herzog.

Lonnie Smith had set a goal of 60 stolen bases at the start of the season, but now that he had at 41, set a new goal of 80. He continued to lead the league in runs scored as well as steals. He said, "when I over try, I have problems. I just have to let things happen naturally."

Forsch dropped his third game in a row and fell to 8-5, while Anduĵar just couldn't win and was now 7-8, despite a 2.40 ERA. The Cardinals continued to trail Philadelphia by one game.

Just when everybody thought he was washed up, Kaat, at age 43, bounced back with a new pitch. Early in the season, he and Littell bore the brunt of fans' dissatisfaction. The low point came on May 1st. Dan Driessen of Cincinnati hit a grand slam home run off his quick pitch, which had been so successful with the White Sox in the 1970s. It wasn't working now.

He began to experiment with a side arm delivery and it brought his ERA down to 3.20 and his record improved to 4-1 with a save. Since the May 1st debacle, he had allowed just seven earned runs in 32 1/3 innings over 24 games. Herzog no longer had to fear putting him in game situations. Their middle reliever had been found.

Hendrick's 15-game hitting streak ended. He didn't play against either Joe or Phil Niekro, as they both made life miserable for him. In previous meetings against either of the two, Hendrick had fail to hit them, and stayed messed up for the next several games. Therefore, if they were going to pitch against St. Louis, Whitey sat Hendrick down.

Anduĵar's frustration showed on his his record versus Atlanta this season. He had faced them four times and allowed just nine earned runs in 27 2/3 innings, but had only a 1-3 mark to show for his efforts. There was some concern because it looked like Atlanta would win the West and would be the opponent in the playoffs. Of course, right now the Cardinals had to worry about winning the East.

The Cardinal subs, especially Tenace, Ramsey, and Iorg, continued to perform superbly. Lonnie Smith continued to lead in runs and stolen bases, while Hernandez had the most game winning hits at 14. Anduĵar continues to be jinxed, as his ERA was 2.52, but his won loss record was just 7-9. Forsch broke his three game losing streak and was 9-5. Sutter had lowered his ERA to 4.18 and had 20 saves. The Cardinals continued to trail the Phillies by one game, with Pittsburgh 3 1/2 behind St. Louis.

Tenace had a .544 on base percentage based on his 21 for 57 hitting, plus 20 walks and two hit-by-pitch. Tenace only had a .242 career batting average, but he was a feared hitter with a career .384 on base average. Five times in his career, he had hit more than 20 home runs, with a high of 29. Six times he has drawn more than a 100 walks, leading the league twice in that department.

Even with several key individual performances, the Cardinals success had been a team effort. At this juncture, the bench was hitting .284 and the regulars .274. Finally a break went Andujar's way and he gained a victory, breaking his personal four game losing streak. Mura continued his turn around, going 3-0 in July, all complete game wins. In his last five starts, his ERA was 1.70, lowering his season's ERA to 3.71.

The Cardinals reached the height of frustration in a 17-inning loss to Pittsburgh, 4-2. They set a major league record with 24 men left on base. Each player felt he could wear the goat's horns as all had chances to chase home the winning run, but none didn't. Herr had five hits in the game, part of his seven game hitting streak, during which he went 15 for 34. To say the fans in St. Louis were frustrated that night would be putting it mildly.

Hernandez had slumped to .276, but still had 64 RBIs with 15 game winning hits and 16 stolen bases. Herr's hitting streak raised his average to .262 and he had 16 stolen bases. Hendricks was at .266 with 16 home runs and 70 RBIs, as the Cardinals pressed for two men to have 100 or more RBIs. McGee, Iorg, and Lonnie Smith were over .300 and the latter still led the league with 86 runs scored and was second with 48 stolen bases. Smith's goal of 80 stolen bases looked a little out of sight.

Forsch was now at 11-5 with two thirds of the season gone. His goal of 15 victories looked quite obtainable. Andujar was 8-9 with 2.72 ERA, while Mura was now 9-7, and Sutter was 7-5 with 22 saves. Despite all these efforts, St. Louis continued to trail Philadelphia by one game. Pittsburgh and Montreal had picked up the pace and each was just two behind St. Louis.

During the first half of the season, Herr wasn't of great value to the team. He had a torn muscle, walking pneumonia and other ailments. He hit just .235. When Herr couldn't hit, he couldn't run, and that was a great part of his offensive game. Since the All Star game, Herr had been the lead-off hitter and had raised his average to .262. Lonnie Smith now batted second.

Just when it looked like the team was ready to come together and make a typical Cardinal drive, they hit the skids. After a six-game winning streak, they dropped 7 of the next 11. Herzog felt the team didn't have the intensity that a pennant winner needed. They lacked the killer instinct. "We need a take charge guy on the field," says Herzog. Tenace was that type, but he didn't play regularly.

McGee continued to punish the ball and was hitting .320. Herr batted .393 in 14 games, while Iorg had been a Montreal killer in the past three years. He was 42 for 93, .452 against them. Lahti had been a splendid addition, going 3-2 since joining the team. His most recent effort was six scoreless innings against the Mets.

The Cardinals had pushed back into first place and enjoyed a one game lead over Philadelphia with Montreal and Pittsburgh right behind. Andujar, Forsch, Mura, LaPoint, Stuper, and Sutter were leading the way from the pitching mound.

Being a third string catcher on a baseball team is like being a permanent KP in the Army. There is little glory, but a lot of potatoes to peel. Brummer was the Cardinals' third string catcher and knew the feeling well. Until Sunday, August 22nd.

The Cardinals and San Francisco were all knotted up at 4-4 at

Busch Stadium in the bottom of the 12th. The bases were loaded with Brummer at third and two outs. The count was two strikes on Green. Nobody knew Brummer was running. The next thing everyone knew, he was sliding across home plate with the winning run. A new hero had been born.

For days this play was all St. Louis talked about. Did pitcher Gary Lavelle throw strike three, nullifying Brummer's steal? Did catcher Milt May receive it before it went over the plate? Did he step in front of the plate, which would have caused a balk? What was Brummer thinking?

He shocked everyone. "He's now captain of the shock troops," said Herzog, who normally choreographed such aggressive base running. Brummer did it on his own. He thought "why prolong the game. It's the 12th inning, let's end it." And he did. He had now stolen home one more time than Lou Brock did in his entire career.

With McGee batting .336, there was talk about the possibility of him leading the league, however, even if he could keep his average up, he would probably fall 30 or 40 plate appearances short of the 502 requirement. McGee, Herr, and both Smiths had at least 20 stolen bases each. Hernandez had 18. The Cardinals could have five players with 25 or more stolen bases each.

The Cardinals almost had a disastrous west coast trip. They won six of the 10 games, but their starters made it past the sixth inning only three times. The bullpen saved the day. In 49 innings, the starters allowed 32 earned runs, whereas the bullpen allowed just 13 earned runs in 42 innings, six coming in an 11-3 loss in Los Angeles.

Sutter saved five of the six wins and the Redbirds were 68-3 when leading after eight innings. If the Cardinals starter could go seven or eight innings and were leading, the game was over. Give the ball to Sutter, and that was it. Lahti and Bair had also done a good job coming out of the bullpen. LaPoint and Stuper were 13-7 since replacing Martin and Rincon in the rotation, and Stuper had the second best ERA among starters at 3.66.

With just over three weeks to play, the race was heating up as the Cardinals had just a half game lead over Philadelphia with Montreal and Pittsburgh not far back.

If it was going to take power to win the title, count the Redbirds out. With their lowest home run total since 1942, they had a power outage. The Cardinals home run total of 55 was the lowest in the major leagues by a wide margin. No major league team had ever won a division title by finishing last in home runs. Before divisional play, only the 1965 Los Angeles Dodgers, 1906 Chicago White Sox, 1924 Washington Senators, and 1959 Chicago White Sox had won pennants while finishing last in home runs. The Cardinals were bucking baseball tradition.

The Cardinal team was built on speed. The dimensions of Busch Stadium were conducive to team speed and defense. Herzog knew his best chance was to build a team strong on defense, speed, and pitching. The team would have to manufacture its runs. They could not rely on the three-run home run to win ball games for them. So far it had worked, as they were in first place.

The title chances received a real jolt when Ozzie Smith sufferd a leg injury on September 11th. Ozzie was kneed by San Francisco catcher Bob Brenly who was trying to break up a double play. Ozzie was told he would be out for nine games.

The Cardinals had won just 10 more than they had lost at home. If they were going to win it all, they had to improve their play during this last stretch of the season.

The season-long problem the Cardinals had was hitting in the clutch. This was especially critical for a team that lacked any real home run threat. Only Lonnie Smith (.367), Hernandez (.315), and Hendrick (.307) were hitting over their average with men on base. The rest of the lineup was batting below average; Porter (.188), Oberkfell (.237), Ozzie(.246). Hendrick, one of the only two real home run threats the team had, received little protection from Porter. At home, Porter was hitting just .200 and only .140 during day games. Overall he was batting .230, but just .188 with runners in scoring position. He and Lonnie Smith had eight home runs each and Tenace and Hernandez had seven.

With a 12-game hitting streak, Hernandez was at .300 for the first time since June 12th. Andujar got his fourth shutout of the season to tie for the league lead. Mura, after two bad outings, was dropped to the bullpen and replaced by Lahti. However, Lahti's first effort was a losing one to Montreal, 7-4.

With just three weeks to play, the Cardinals clung to a slim one-half game lead over Philadelphia. Just when it looked like another season was going down to the final day of the year, the team got hot and blew the race open, winning eight in a row. They swept New York in five then took three straight from the Phillies. During a nine-game stretch their pitching staff allowed just nine runs. In typical Cardinal tradition, they came roaring down the stretch.

Forsch was one of the chief drivers in this September push. After eight years in the league and with a 20-win season behind him, Forsch finally had gained the respect he deserved. Only three National League pitchers (Steve Carlton, Phil Niekro, and Steve Rogers) had been with their teams longer. And only three pitchers in the National League Carlton, Tom Seaver, and John Candelaria had more than 50 victories and a better winning percentage. Pretty good company, considering the first two were future Hall of Famers.

Forsch was 15-9, making his career mark 107-83 as of September 19th. He was in the middle of a six-year, $3,500,000 contract. In September, Forsch had allowed just three runs in 24 innings, but was just 1-1 for his efforts. He had a no decision against San Francisco when he left leading 2-1. In his other games, he shut out Montreal 1-0 and lost to Carlton, 2-0.

It looked like the Cardinals would be the division winner. The question was who they would play. For months it looked like it would be Atlanta, who started by winning their first 13, then hit a huge slump in August. The Cardinals were 7-5 versus Atlanta and Los Angeles, but only 5-7 versus San Francisco. Based on those records, it would seem the Redbirds would prefer Atlanta or Los Angeles.

In the Cardinals nine-game pitching streak, there were three shutouts, three one run games and three two run games. Except for a five-walk outing by Mura, Cardinal pitchers gave up just 13 walks in eight games. Sutter retired 18 consecutive batters over four games. Lahti had six innings of one run relief for a victory. Bair had two saves with six innings of shut out ball. Stuper won two games. Andujar had 29 2/3 scoreless innings and Forsch allowed just two runs in 31 1/3 innings.

The Cardinals finish at 92-70, three games in front of Philadelphia, six ahead of favorite Montreal, and eight in front of Pittsburgh. They clinched the flag on September 27th with a 4-2 win over Montreal. Stuper got the victory and Sutter the save.

Why did they win? There were many reasons. The 12-game winning streak in April gave them a cushion that carried them for several months. Then there was the eight-game winning streak when they blew the race open in September. The team never lost over three in a row. They never quit or panicked, even when they fell out of first place for a short while in mid-season.

Sutter certainly was a key too. Since the All Star break Sutter had three wins, 18 saves, and a 1.47 ERA. The bullpen produced 31 wins and 47 saves. Reserves played a big part, getting key hits and playing when regulars such as Herr, Ozzie, Porter, and others were down with injuries.

Lonnie Smith was the only .300 hitter at .307 with a league-leading 120 runs scored. He was second with 68 steals. Hernandez finished at .299 with 94 RBIs, while Hendrick hit .282 and led the team with

19 home runs and 104 RBIs. Herr had a strong second half to finish at .266 with 83 runs scored and 25 steals in 135 games. Forsch was 15-9, Andujar 15-10 and Mura 12-11. LaPoint (9-3) and Stuper (9-7) were life savers in the second half. Sutter led the league with 36 saves.

The National League Championship Series

The Cardinals were scheduled to open the best of five National League playoff series in St. Louis against Atlanta. In game one on October 6th, Niekro held a 1-0 lead over Andujar with one out in the fifth when the heavens opened up. It rained for two hours and the game was finally called. There had not been a rain out in St. Louis since 1979. This play-off series would see two.

The game was rescheduled for October 7th and this time the Cardinals won, 7-0 behind Forsch. McGee hit a triple and should have had an inside the park home run, but he stopped at third. He scored on an Ozzie fly out. The Cardinals blew the game open with five runs on six singles in the sixth inning.

It rained the next day, so game two couldn't be played until October 9th. Niekro was back on the hill for Atlanta and he held a 3-2 lead. Gene Garber came in and the Cardinals tied it in the eighth. Sutter retired the Braves in the ninth. In the Cardinals half ,Green singled, Herr sacrificed, and Oberkfell won it with a base hit.

The scene shifted to Atlanta for game three on October 10th with the Cards up two games to none. The Cardinals broke on top with four in the second. Herr singled, Porter walked, Hendrick singled, McGee had a two run triple, and Ozzie had an RBI single. In the fifth, Hernandez had another RBI. Sutter took the mound in the seventh after Atlanta scored their two runs. McGee hit the only home run of the series in the ninth. The final score was St. Louis 6, Atlanta 2 with Andujar the winner.

The World Series

After the sweep of the Braves, the Cardinals were headed to the Fall Classic for the first time since 1968. The World Series would feature the power-laden Milwaukee Brewers as favorites against the speed-and defense-minded St. Louis.

Game one on October 12th at St. Louis before 53,723 was a rout and humiliation for the home town boys as Milwaukee won 10-0. Paul Molitor had four hits, Robin Yount five hits and Ted Simmons two, including home run. Mike Caldwell stymied the Cardinals on three hits. Forsch took the loss.

The next night before an identical attendance, the Cardinals scrambled for a 5-4 victory. Porter, who had spent the season feeling the scorn of the St. Louis fans, finally heard the jeers turn to cheers. He doubled home two runs in the sixth inning off veteran Don Sutton to tie the score, had a key single in the winning rally in the eighth inning, and threw out Molitor trying to steal in the ninth. Sutter gained the victory in relief.

The third game, on October 15th at Milwaukee, disappointed 56,556 Brewer fans. McGee's bat and glove won the game. He robbed Molitor and Gorman Thomas of extra base hits with great catches in the first and ninth innings. In between, he hit two home runs and drove in four runs to pace a 6-2 victory. Andujar was the winner with Sutter gaining the save.

Milwaukee evened the Series the next afternoon before 56,560 winning 7-5. The Cardinals had broken on top with a 5-1 lead, including the first two-run sacrifice fly in World Series history. It happened when Herr hit a 390 foot fly out to Thomas. When the Brewers outfielder slipped and fell, both McGee and Ozzie scored. It looked like an easy Cardinal victory until LaPoint dropped Herr's throw for an error and opened the gate for six unearned runs in the seventh inning.

Milwaukee felt the momentum turn their way and the next night, when, before 56,562, Caldwell again beat Forsch, this time 6-4. Yount was the hitting hero with four hits, including a home run. Hernandez had been hitless in the Series, going 0 for 15, but broke out with three hits and two RBIs.

The situation looked grim for the Redbirds as they headed home for game six, down three games to two. However, all we have to do is look at Cardinal history to see that they had been there before and rallied. The Cardinals came from behind in 1926, 1934, 1946, 1964, and 1967.

The Cardinals got a brilliant game from Stuper, who pitched a four-hitter, and the Cardinal hitters exploded for 12 hits and 13 runs to win 13-1. Herr, Hendrick, and Hernandez each had two hits with Porter and Herr earning two RBIs and Hernandez four. Porter and Hernandez each had a home run.

Once again, it all came down to game seven. Familiar territory for the Cardinals. Only once in seven tries had they lost in a seven-game series and that was in the heart breaking loss in 1968. As October 20th dawned, another 53,713 hearty St. Louis fans were ready to cheer their Redbirds on to victory.

The team would not disappoint their fans. Milwaukee had grabbed a 3-1 lead with their ace Pete Vukovich pitching. In the bottom of the sixth, the Cardinals rallied for three runs to take the lead. Tenace pinch hit and walked and Ramsey ran for him. Ozzie singled, Lonnie doubled, and Hernandez had an RBI single to tie the game. Hendrick then singled to put the Cardinals ahead 4-3. They added two insurance runs in the eighth on RBI singles by Porter and Braun. Sutter retired the last six men to gain his second save and give Andujar his second win.

The Cardinals were World Champions for the ninth time and the first since 1967. Hitting stars were many. The designated hitter, which was the American League's concoction, saw Milwaukee's go just three for 24, while the Cardinals were 12 for 28. Iorg was nine for 17 with a .882 slugging percentage as the St. Louis DH. Porter was voted the

MVP of the series, edging out Hernandez with his eight RBIs, Sutter with his two saves and a win, and Yount who became the first player to have two four hit games in a single World Series.

Epilogue

After the 1982 world championship, once again there were parades, celebrations, and jubilation in St. Louis. The fans looked at the youth of the ball club and thought they saw another dynasty in the making. Unfortunately it didn't happen that way. The next season the team collapsed.

Hernandez was traded about one third through the season to New York for Neil Allen, a journeyman pitcher. It stunned the St. Louis fans, because he was the guts and heart of the St. Louis team. Herzog refused any comment and for several years would take the heat for trading an extremely popular ball player.

It wasn't until several years later when a drug scandal in baseball broke, that the real reason for the trade of Hernandez was known. He had been involved in the use of drugs and to Herzog that was taboo. Yet, Herzog kept quiet and endured the slings and arrows of the fans. After the truth was known Herzog's popularity greatly increased while Hernadez' declined.

Lonnie Smith was also involved in a drug rehabilitation program, although he hit .321 in 130 games in 1983, he wasn't the catalyst of 1982. Herr had a knee injury and was limited to 89 games. LaPoint and Stuper each won 12 games and the aforementioned Allen picked up 10 wins. However, Andujar and Forsch were off their 1982 performance.

Andujar went from 15-10, 2.47 ERA to 6-16, 4.16 ERA, while Forsch dropped from 15-9, 3.48 ERA to 10-12, 4.28 ERA. Their reversal meant a drop in the standings of 12 games. Sutter slipped to 9-10 with just 21 saves and 4.23 ERA. Thus, the three top pitchers of 1982 all had losing records and ERAs of over four runs per game in 1983. The club finished fourth, 11 games out, with a 79-83 mark.

It would take some more rebuilding of the pitching department, a new catcher, a power hitting first baseman, and improved outfield before the Cardinals would once again challenge.

Tommy Herr

George Hendrick

Willie McGee

Whitey Herzog

Rosters and Statistics

The following tables show the full-year statistics for every Cardinal player from the Glory Years discussed in this book.   You can also use this section as an index since whatever year in which a player wore the Birds on the Bat, he will be mentioned in the corresponding chapter of the book.   By including all the tables for each year in one section, you can follow certain trends in baseball, such as the evolution of the save, which came at the expense of the complete game. You will also see the increased emphasis in other areas, such as team speed by noting the increasing number of stolen bases.

Following are the abbreviations used:

Ave . . . .Batting Average

AB . . . . .At Bats

H . . . . . .Hits

2b . . . . . .Doubles

3b . . . . .Triples

HR . . . . .Home Runs

R . . . . . .Runs Scored

RBI . . . .Runs Batted In

SB . . . . .Stolen Bases

SLP . . . .Slugging Percentage

G . . . . . .Games Pitched

GS . . . . .Games Started

CG . . . . .Complete Games

W . . . . . .Wins

L . . . . . .Losses

PCT . . . .Winning Percentage

ERA . . . .Earned Run Average

Saves . . .Saves

K . . . . . . .Strikeouts

1926 Cardinals Roster & Statistics

Manager: Rogers Hornsby

Player	Ave	AB	H	2b	3b	HR	R	RBI	SB	SLP
Jim Bottomley	.299	603	180	40*	14	19	98	128*	4	.506
Rogers Hornsby	.317	527	167	34	5	11	96	93	3	.463
Tommy Thevenow	.256	563	144	15	5	2	64	63	8	.311
Lester Bell	.325	581	189	33	14	17	85	100	9	.518
Billy Southworth	.317	391	124	22	6	11	76	69	13	.488
Taylor Douthit	.308	530	163	20	4	3	96	52	23	.377
Ray Blades	.305	416	127	17	12	8	81	43	6	.462
Bob O'Farrell	.293	492	144	30	9	7	68	68	1	.433
Chick Hafey	.271	225	61	19	2	4	30	38	2	.427
Specs Toporcer	.250	88	22	3	2	0	13	9	1	.330
Wattie Holm	.285	144	41	5	1	0	18	21	3	.333
Heinie Mueller	.267	191	51	7	5	3	36	28	8	.403
Jake Flowers	.270	74	20	1	0	3	13	9	1	.405
Art Reinhart	.317	63	20	2	2	0	7	11	1	.413
Ernie Vick	.196	51	10	2	0	0	6	4	0	.235
Bill Warwick	.357	14	5	0	0	0	0	2	0	.357
Jack Smith	.000	1	0	0	0	0	0	0	0	.000
Totals	.286	5,381*	1,541*	259	82	90*	817*	756	83	.415*

Player	G	GS	CG	W	L	PCT	ERA	Saves	K
Flint Rhem	34	34	20	20*	7	.741	3.21	0	72
Bill Sherdel	34	29	17	16	12	.571	3.49	0	59
Jesse Haines	33	21	14	13	4	.765	3.25	1	46
Art Reinhart	27	11	9	10	5	.667	4.22	0	26
Vic Keen	26	21	12	10	9	.526	4.56	0	29
Grover Alexander	23	16	11	9	7	.563	2.92	2	35
Herman Bell	27	8	3	6	6	.500	3.18	2	22
Allen Sothoron	15	4	1	3	3	.500	4.22	0	19
Eddie Dyer	6	0	0	1	0	1.000	11.57	0	4
Bill Hallahan	19	3	0	1	4	.200	3.65	0	28
Duster Mails	1	0	0	0	1	.000	0.00	0	1
Sylvester Johnson	19	6	1	0	3	.000	4.22	1	10
Walter Huntzinger	9	4	2	0	4	.000	4.24	0	9
Ed Clough	1	0	0	0	0	.000	22.50	0	0
Totals		156	90*	89*	65	.578*	3.67	6	365

*Denotes led league.

1931 Cardinals Roster & Statistics

Manager: Gabby Street

Player	Ave	AB	H	2b	3b	HR	R	RBI	SB	SLP
Jim Bottomley	.348	382	133	34	5	9	73	75	3	.534
Frankie Frisch	.311	518	161	24	4	4	96	82	28*	.396
Charley Gelbert	.289	447	129	29	5	1	61	62	7	.383
Sparky Adams	.293	608	178	46*	5	1	97	40	16	.390
George Watkins	.288	503	145	30	13	13	93	51	15	.477
Pepper Martin	.300	413	124	32	8	7	68	75	16	.467
Chick Hafey	.349*	450	157	35	8	16	94	95	11	.569
Jimmie Wilson	.274	383	105	20	2	0	45	51	5	.337
Ripper Collins	.301	279	84	20	10	4	34	59	1	.487
Jake Flowers	.248	137	34	11	1	2	19	19	7	.387
Andy High	.267	131	35	6	1	0	20	19	0	.328
Joe Benes	.167	12	2	0	0	0	1	0	0	.167
Ray Cunningham	.000	4	0	0	0	0	0	1	0	.000
Eddie Delker	.500	2	1	1	0	0	0	2	0	.000
Ernie Orsatti	.291	158	46	16	6	0	27	19	1	.468
Wally Roettger	.285	151	43	12	2	0	16	17	0	.391
Taylor Douthit	.331	133	44	11	2	1	21	21	1	.466
Ray Blades	.284	67	19	4	0	1	10	5	1	.388
Joel Hunt	.000	1	0	0	0	0	2	0	0	.000
Gus Mancuso	.262	187	49	16	1	1	13	23	2	.374
Mike Gonzales	.105	19	2	0	0	0	1	3	0	.105
Gabby Street	.000	1	0	0	0	0	0	0	0	.000
Totals	.286	5,435	1,554	353*	74	60	815	751	114*	.411

Player	G	GS	CG	W	L	PCT	ERA	Saves	K
Bill Hallahan	37	30	16	19*	9	.679	3.29	4	159*
Burleigh Grimes	29	28	17	17	9	.654	3.65	0	67
Paul Derringer	35	23	15	18	8	.692*	3.36	2	134
Flint Rhem	33	26	10	11	10	.524	3.56	1	72
Sylvester Johnson	32	24	12	11	9	.550	3.00	2	82
Jesse Haines	19	17	8	12	3	.800	3.02	0	27
Jim Lindsey	35	2	1	6	4	.600	2.77	7	32
Allyn Stout	30	3	1	6	0	1.000	4.21	3	40
Tony Kaufmann	15	1	0	1	1	.500	6.06	1	13
Totals		154	80	101	53	.656*	3.45	20*	626*

* Denotes led league

1934 Cardinals Roster & Statistics

Manager: Frankie Frisch

Player	AVE	AB	H	2b	3b	HR	R	RBI	SB	SLP
Ripper Collins	.333	600	200	40	12	35*	116	128	2	.615*
Frankie Frisch	.305	550	168	30	6	3	74	75	11	.398
Leo Durocher	.260	500	130	26	5	3	62	70	2	.350
Pepper Martin	.289	454	131	25	11	5	76	49	23*	.425
Jack Rothrock	.284	647*	184	35	3	11	106	72	10	.399
Ernie Orsatti	.300	337	101	14	4	0	39	31	6	.365
Joe Medwick	.319	620	198	40	18*	18	110	106	3	.529
Spud Davis	.300	347	104	22	4	9	45	65	0	.464
Burgess Whitehead	.277	332	92	13	5	1	55	24	5	.355
Pat Crawford	.271	70	19	2	0	0	3	16	0	.300
Chick Fullis	.261	199	52	4	1	0	21	26	4	.317
Buster Mills	.236	72	17	3	1	1	7	8	0	.361
Kiddo Davis	.303	32	10	1	0	1	6	4	1	.485
Gene Moore	.278	18	5	1	0	0	2	1	0	.333
Bill DeLancey	.316	253	80	18	3	13	41	40	1	.565
Francis Healy	.308	134	4	1	0	0	1	1	0	.385
Lew Riggs	.000	1	0	0	0	0	0	0	0	.000
Red Worthington	.000	1	0	0	0	0	0	0	0	.000
Total	.288*	5,502*	1,582*	294*	75	104	799*	748	69*	.425*

Pitcher	G	GS	CG	W	L	PCT	ERA	Saves	K
Dizzy Dean	50	33	24*	30*	7	.811*	2.66	7	195*
Paul Dean	39	26	16	19	11	.633	3.43	2	150
Tex Carleton	40	31	16	16	11	.583	4.26	2	103
Bill Walker	24	19	10	12	4	.750	3.12	0	76
Wild Bill Hallahan	32	26	10	8	12	.400	4.26	0	70
Jesse Haines	37	6	0	4	4	.500	3.50	1	17
Burleigh Grimes	4	0	0	2	1	.667	3.52	0	1
Jim Mooney	32	7	1	2	4	.333	5.47	1	27
Flint Rhem	5	1	0	1	0	1.000	4.60	1	6
Dazzy Vance	19	4	1	1	1	.500	3.66	1	33
Jim Lindsey	11	0	0	0	1	.000	6.43	1	7
Jim Winford	5	1	0	0	2	.000	7.82	0	3
Clarence Heise	1	0	0	0	0	.000	4.50	0	1
Pepper Martin	1	0	0	0	0	.000	4.50	0	0
Totals		154	78*	95*	58	.621*	3.69	16	689*

*Denotes led league

1942 Cardinals Roster & Statistics

Manager: Billy Southworth

Player	AVE	AB	H	2b	3b	HR	R	RBI	SB	SLP
Johnny Hopp	.258	314	81	16	7	3	41	37	14	.362
Jimmy Brown	.256	606	155	28	4	1	75	71	4	.320
Marty Marion	.276	485	134	38*	5	0	66	54	8	.375
Whitey Kurowski	.254	366	93	17	3	9	51	42	7	.391
Enos Slaughter	.318	591	188*	31	17*	13	100	98	9	.494
Terry Moore	.288	489	141	26	3	6	80	49	10	.391
Stan Musial	.315	467	147	32	10	10	87	72	6	.490
Walker Cooper	.281	438	123	32	7	7	58	65	4	.434
Creepy Crespi	.243	292	71	4	2	0	33	35	4	.271
Ray Sanders	.252	282	71	17	2	5	37	39	2	.379
Harry Walker	.314	191	60	12	2	0	38	16	2	.398
Coaker Triplett	.273	154	42	7	4	1	18	23	1	.390
Ken O'Dea	.234	192	45	7	1	5	22	32	0	.359
Buddy Blattner	.043	23	1	0	0	0	3	1	0	.043
Erv Dusak	.185	27	5	3	0	0	4	3	0	.296
Sam Narron	.400	10	4	0	0	0	0	1	0	.400
Estel Crabtree	.333	9	3	2	0	0	1	2	0	.556
Gus Mancuso	.077	13	1	0	0	0	0	1	0	.077
Jeff Cross	.250	4	1	0	0	0	0	1	0	.250
Totals	.268*	5,421	1,454*	282*	69*	60	755	680	71	.379*

Pitcher	G	GS	CG	W	L	PCT	ERA	Saves	K
Mort Cooper	37	35	22	22*	7	.759	1.78*	0	152
Johnny Beazley	43	23	13	21	6	.778	2.13	3	91
Howard Krist	34	8	3	13	3	.813	2.51	1	47
Max Lanier	34	20	8	13	8	.619	2.98	2	93
Harry Gumbert	38	19	5	9	5	.643	3.26	5	52
Howie Pollet	27	13	5	7	5	.583	2.88	0	42
Ernie White	26	19	7	7	5	.583	2.52	2	67
Murry Dickson	36	7	2	6	3	.667	2.91	2	66
Lon Warneke	12	12	5	6	4	.600	3.29	0	31
Bill Beckmann	2	0	0	1	0	1.000	0.00	0	3
Bill Lohrman	5	0	0	1	1	.500	1.42	0	6
Whitey Moore	9	0	0	0	1	.000	4.38	0	1
Clyde Shoun	2	0	0	0	0	.000	0.00	0	0
Totals		156	70	106*	48	.688*	2.55*	15	651*

* Denotes led league

1944 Cardinals Roster & Statistics

Manager: Billy Southworth

Player	AVE	AB	H	2b	3b	HR	R	RBI	SB	SLP
Ray Sanders	.295	601	177	34	9	12	87	102	2	.441
Emil Verban	.257	498	128	14	2	0	51	43	0	.293
Marty Marion	.267	506	135	26	2	6	50	63	1	362
Whitey Kurowski	.270	555	150	25	7	20	95	87	2	.449
Stan Musial	.347	568	197*	51*	14	12	112	94	7	.549*
Johnny Hopp	.336	527	177	35	9	11	106	72	15	.499
Danny Litwhiler	.264	492	130	25	5	15	53	82	2	.427
Walker Cooper	.317	397	126	25	5	13	56	72	4	.504
George Fallon	.199	141	28	6	0	1	16	9	1	.262
John Antonelli	.190	21	4	1	0	0	0	1	0	.238
Augie Bergamo	.286	192	55	6	3	2	35	19	0	.380
Debs Garms	.201	149	30	3	0	0	17	5	0	.221
Pepper Martin	.279	86	24	4	0	2	15	4	2	.395
Ken O'Dea	.249	265	66	11	2	6	35	37	1	.374
Bob Keely	.000	0	0	0	0	0	0	0	0	.000
Totals	.275*	5,474	1,507*	274*	59	100	772*	722	37	.402*

Pitchers	G	GS	CG	W	L	PCT	ERA	Saves	K
Mort Cooper	34	33	22	22	7	.739	2.46	1	97
Max Lanier	33	30	16	17	12	.586	2.65	0	141
Ted Wilks	36	21	16	17	4	.810*	2.65	0	70
Harry Brecheen	30	22	13	16	5	.762	2.85	0	88
George Munger	21	12	7	11	3	.786	1.34	2	55
Al Jurisch	30	14	5	7	9	.438	3.39	1	53
Freddy Schmidt	37	9	3	7	3	.700	3.15	5	58
Harry Gumbert	10	7	3	4	2	.667	2.49	1	16
Blix Donnelly	27	4	2	2	1	.667	2.12	2	45
Bud Byerly	9	4	2	2	2	.500	3.40	0	13
Bill Trotter	2	1	0	0	1	.000	13.50	0	0
Mike Naymick	1	0	0	0	0	.000	4.50	0	1
Total		157	89	105*	49	.692*	2.67*	12	637*

* Denotes led or tied for league lead

1946 Cardinals Roster & Statistics

Manager: Eddie Dyer

Player	AVE	AB	H	2b	3b	HR	R	RBI	SB	SLP
Stan Musial	.365*	624*	228*	50*	20*	16	124*	103	7	.587*
Red Schoendienst	.281	606	170	28	5	0	94	34	12	.343
Marty Marion	.233	498	116	29	4	3	51	46	1	.325
Whitey Kurowski	.301	519	156	32	5	14	76	89	2	.462
Enos Slaughter	.300	609	183	30	8	18	100	130*	9	.462
Terry Moore	.263	278	73	14	1	3	32	28	0	.353
Harry Walker	.237	346	82	14	6	3	53	27	12	.338
Joe Garagiola	.237	211	50	4	1	3	21	22	0	.308
Dick Sisler	.260	235	61	11	2	3	17	42	0	.362
Lou Klein	.194	93	18	3	0	1	12	4	1	.258
Jeff Cross	.217	69	15	3	0	0	17	6	4	.261
Nippy Jones	.333	12	4	0	0	0	3	1	0	.333
Erv Dusak	.240	275	66	9	1	9	38	42	7	.378
Buster Adams	.185	173	32	6	0	5	21	22	3	.306
Bill Endicott	.200	20	4	3	0	0	2	3	0	.350
Del Rice	.273	139	38	8	1	1	10	12	0	.367
Clyde Kluttz	.265	136	36	7	0	0	8	14	0	.316
Ken O'Dea	.123	57	7	2	0	1	2	3	0	.211
Del Wlber	.000	4	0	0	0	0	0	0	0	.000
Walter Sessi	.143	14	2	0	0	1	2	2	0	.357
Danny Litwhiler	.000	5	0	0	0	0	0	0	0	.000
Emil Verban	.000	1	0	0	0	0	0	0	0	.000
Totals	.265*	5,372	1,426*	265*	56	81	712*	665	58	.391*

Pitcher	G	GS	CG	W	L	PCT	ERA	Saves	K
Howard Pollet	40	32	22	21*	10	.677	2.10*	5	107
Murry Dickson	47	19	12	15	6	.714*	2.88	1	82
Harry Brecheen	36	30	14	15	15	.500	2.49	3	117
Al Brazle	37	15	6	11	10	.524	3.29	0	58
Ted Wilks	40	4	0	8	0	1.000	3.41	1	40
Johnny Beazley	19	18	5	7	5	.583	4.46	0	36
Max Lanier	6	6	6	6	0	1.00	1.93	0	36
Ken Burkhart	25	13	5	6	3	.667	2.88	2	32
George Munger	10	7	2	2	2	.500	3.33	1	28
Red Barrett	23	9	1	3	2	.600	4.03	2	22
Freddie Martin	6	3	2	2	1	.667	4.08	0	19
Freddy Schmidt	16	0	0	1	0	1.000	3.29	0	14
Blix Donnelly	13	0	0	1	2	.333	3.95	0	11
Johnny Grodzicki	3	0	0	0	0	.000	9.00	0	2
Howard Krist	15	0	0	0	2	.000	6.75	0	3
Totals		156	75*	98*	58	.628*	3.01*	15	607

* Denotes led league

1964 Cardinals Roster & Statistics

Manager: Johnny Keane

Player	AVE	AB	H	2b	3b	HR	R	RBI	SB	SLP
Bill White	.303	631	191	37	4	21	92	102	7	.474
Julian Javier	.241	535	129	19	5	12	66	65	9	.363
Dick Groat	.292	636	186	35	6	1	70	70	2	.371
Ken Boyer	.295	628	185	30	10	24	100	119*	3	.489
Mike Shannon	.261	253	66	8	2	9	30	43	4	.415
Curt Flood	.311	679*	211*	25	3	5	97	46	8	.378
Lou Brock	.348	419	146	21	9	12	81	44	33	.527
Tim McCarver	.288	465	134	19	3	9	53	52	2	.400
Phil Gagliano	.259	58	15	4	0	1	5	9	0	.379
Jerry Buchek	.200	30	6	0	2	0	7	1	0	.333
Dal Maxvill	.231	26	6	0	0	0	4	4	1	.231
Charlie James	.223	233	52	9	1	5	24	17	0	.335
Carl Warwick	.259	158	41	7	1	3	14	15	2	.373
Bob Skinner	.271	118	32	5	0	1	10	16	0	.339
Johnny Lewis	.234	94	22	2	2	2	10	7	2	.362
Doug Clemens	.205	78	16	4	3	1	8	9	0	.372
Jeoff Long	.233	43	10	1	0	1	5	4	0	.326
Bob Uecker	.198	106	21	1	0	1	8	6	0	.236
Ed Spezio	.333	12	4	0	0	0	0	0	0	.333
Joe Morgan	.000	3	0	0	0	0	0	0	0	.000
Totals	.272*	5,625	1,531*	240	53	109	715	654	73	.392

Pitcher	G	GS	CG	W	L	PCT	ERA	Saves	K
Ray Sadecki	37	32	9	20	11	.645	3.68	1	119
Bob Gibson	40	36	17	19	12	.613	3.01	1	245
Curt Simmons	34	34	12	18	9	.667	3.43	0	104
Ron Taylor	63	2	0	8	4	.667	4.63	7	69
Roger Craig	39	19	3	7	9	.438	3.25	5	84
Mike Cuellar	32	7	1	5	5	.500	4.50	4	56
Gordie Richardson	19	6	1	4	2	.667	2.30	1	28
Ray Washburn	15	10	0	3	4	.429	4.05	2	28
Ernie Broglio	11	11	3	3	5	.375	3.50	0	36
Bob Humphreys	28	0	0	2	0	1.000	2.53	0	36
Lew Burdette	8	0	0	1	0	1.000	1.80	0	3
Glen Hobbie	13	5	1	1	2	.333	4.26	1	18
Barney Schultz	30	0	0	1	3	.250	1.64	14	29
Bobby Shantz	16	0	0	1	3	.250	3.12	0	12
Harry Fanok	4	0	0	0	0	.000	5.87	0	10
Dave Bakenhaster	2	0	0	0	0	.000	6.00	0	0
Jack Spring	2	0	0	0	0	.000	3.00	0	0
Dave Dowling	1	0	0	0	0	.000	0.00	0	0
Totals		162	47	93*	69	.574*	3.43	36	877

* Denotes led league

1967 Cardinals Roster & Statistics

Manager: Red Schoendiest

Player	AVE	AB	H	2b	3b	HR	R	RBI	SB	SLP
Orlando Cepeda	.325	563	183	37	0	25	91	111*	11	.524
Julian Javier	.281	520	146	16	3	14	68	64	6	.404
Dal Maxvill	.227	476	108	14	4	1	37	41	0	.279
Mike Shannon	.245	482	118	18	3	12	53	77	2	.369
Roger Maris	.261	410	107	18	7	9	64	55	0	.405
Curt Flood	.335	514	172	24	1	5	68	50	2	.414
Lou Brock	.299	689*	206	32	12	21	113*	76	52*	.472
Tim McCarver	.295	471	139	26	3	14	68	69	8	.452
Phil Gagliano	.221	217	48	7	0	2	20	21	0	.281
Ed Spezio	.210	105	22	2	0	3	9	10	2	.314
Ed Bressoud	.134	67	9	1	1	1	8	1	0	.224
Steve Huntz	.167	6	1	0	0	0	1	0	0	.167
Jim Williams	.000	2	0	0	0	0	0	0	0	.000
Bobby Tolan	.253	265	67	7	3	6	35	32	12	.379
Alex Johnson	.223	175	39	9	2	1	20	12	6	.314
Dave Ricketts	.273	99	27	8	0	1	11	14	0	.384
Johnny Romano	.121	58	7	1	0	0	1	2	1	.138
Ted Savage	.125	8	1	0	0	0	1	0	0	.125
Totals	.263	5,566	1,462	225	40	115	695	658	102*	.379

Pitcher	G	GS	CG	W	L	PCT	ERA	Saves	K
Dick Hughes	37	27	12	16	6	.727*	2.67	3	161
Nellie Briles	49	14	4	14	5	.737	2.43	6	94
Steve Carlton	30	28	11	14	9	.609	2.98	1	168
Bob Gibson	24	24	10	13	7	.650	2.98	0	147
Ray Washburn	27	27	3	10	7	.588	3.53	0	98
Al Jackson	38	11	1	9	4	.692	3.95	1	43
Larry Jaster	34	23	2	9	7	.563	3.01	3	87
Ron Willis	65	0	0	6	5	.545	2.67	10	42
Joe Hoerner	57	0	0	4	4	.500	2.59	15	50
Jack Lamabe	23	1	1	3	4	.429	2.83	4	30
Hal Woodeshick	36	0	0	2	1	.667	5.18	2	20
Jim Cosman	10	5	0	1	0	1.000	3.16	0	11
Mike Torrez	3	1	0	0	1	.000	3.18	0	5
Totals		161	44	101*	60	.627*	3.05	45*	956

*Denotes led league

305

1982 Cardinals Roster & Statistics

Manager: Whitey Herzog

Player	AVE	AB	H	2b	3b	HR	R	RBI	SB	SLP
Keith Hernandez	.299	579	173	33	6	7	79	94	19	.412
Tommy Herr	.266	493	131	19	4	0	83	36	25	.320
Ozzie Smith	.248	488	121	24	1	2	58	43	25	.314
Ken Oberfell	.289	470	136	22	5	2	55	34	11	.370
George Hendrick	.282	515	145	20	5	19	65	104	3	.450
Willie McGee	.296	422	125	12	8	4	43	56	24	.391
Lonnie Smith	.307	592	182	35	8	8	120*	69	68	.434
Darrell Porter	.231	373	86	18	5	12	46	48	1	.422
Mike Ramsey	.230	256	59	8	2	1	18	21	6	.289
Julio Gonzales	.241	87	21	3	2	1	9	7	1	.356
Kelly Paris	.103	29	3	0	0	0	1	1	0	.103
Dane Iorg	.294	238	70	14	1	0	17	34	0	.361
David Green	.283	166	47	7	1	2	21	23	11	.373
Tito Landrum	.278	72	20	3	0	2	12	14	0	.403
Steve Braun	.274	62	17	4	0	0	6	4	0	.339
Gene Roof	.267	15	4	0	0	0	3	2	2	.267
Gene Tenace	.258	124	32	9	0	7	18	18	1	.500
Glenn Brummer	.234	64	15	4	0	0	4	8	2	.297
Orlando Sanchez	.189	37	7	0	1	0	6	3	0	.243
Totals	.264	5,455	1,439	239	52*	67	685	632	200*	.364

Pitcher	G	GS	CG	W	L	PCT	ERA	Saves	K
Joaquin Andujar	38	37	9	15	10	.600	2.47	0	137
Bob Forsch	36	34	6	15	9	.625	3.48	1	69
Steve Mura	35	30	7	12	11	.522	4.05	0	84
Dave LaPoint	42	21	0	9	3	.750	3.42	0	81
John Stuper	23	21	2	9	7	.563	3.36	0	53
Bruce Sutter	70	0	0	9	8	.529	2.90	36*	61
Doug Bair	63	0	0	5	3	.625	2.55	8	68
Jim Kaat	62	2	0	5	3	.625	4.08	2	35
Jeff Lahti	33	1	0	5	4	.556	3.81	0	22
John Martin	24	7	0	4	5	.444	4.23	0	21
Andy Rincon	11	6	1	2	3	.400	4.73	0	11
Jeff Keener	19	0	0	1	1	.500	1.61	0	25
Eric Rasmussen	8	3	0	1	2	.333	4.42	0	15
Mark Littell	16	0	0	0	1	.000	5.23	0	7
Totals		162	25	92*	70	.568*	3.37	47	689

* Denotes led league

Index of Cardinals Players & Managers

The Glory Years

Hobbie, Glen 1964
Hoerner, Joe 1967
Holm, Wattie 1926
Hopp, Johnny 1942, 1944
Hornsby, Rogers 1926
Hughes, Dick 1967
Humphries, Bob 1964
Hunt, Joel 1931
Huntz, Steve 1967
Huntzinger, Walter 1926
Iorg, Dane 1982
Jackson, Al 1967
James, Charlie 1964
Jaster, Larry 1967
Javier, Julian 1964, 1967
Johnny, Beazley 1942
Johnson, Sylvester 1926, 1931
Johnson, Alex 1967
Jones, Nippy 1946
Jurisch, Al 1944
Kaat, Jim 1982
Kaufmann, Tony 1931
Keane, Johnny 1964
Keely, Bob 1944
Keen, Vic 1926
Keener, Jeff 1982
Klein, Lou 1946
Klutz, Clyde 1946
Krist, Howard 1942, 1946
Kurowski, Whitey 1942, 1944, 1946
Lahti, Jeff 1982
Lamabe, Jack 1967
Landrum, Tito 1982
Lanier, Max 1942, 1944, 1946
LaPoint, Dave 1982
Lewis, Johnny 1964
Lindsey, Jim 1931, 1934
Littell, Mark 1982
Litwhiler, Danny 1944, 1946
Lohrman, Bill 1942
Long, Jeoff 1964
Mails, Duster 1926
Mancuso, Gus 1931, 1942
Marion, Marty 1942, 1944, 1946
Maris, Roger 1967
Martin, Pepper 1931, 1934, 1944
Martin, Freddie 1946
Martin, John 1982

Maxville, Dal 1964, 1967
McCarver, Tim 1964, 1967
McGee, Willie 1982
Medwick, Joe 1934
Mills, Buster 1934
Mooney, Jim 1934
Moore, Gene 1934
Moore, Terry 1942, 1946
Moore, Whitey 1942
Morgan, Joe 1964
Mueller, Neinie 1926
Munger, George 1944
Mura, Steve 1982
Musial, Stan 1942, 1944, 1946
Narron, Sam 1942
Naymick, Mike 1944
Oberfell, Ken 1982
O'Dea, Ken 1942, 1944, 1946
O'Farrell, Bob 1926
Orsatti, Ernie 1931, 1934
Paris, Kelly 1982
Pollet, Howard "Howie" 1942, 1946
Porter, Darrell 1982
Ramsey, Mike 1982
Rasmussen, Eric 1982
Reinhart, Art 1926
Rhem, Flint 1926, 1931, 1934
Rice, Del 1946
Richardson, Gordon 1964
Rickets, Dave 1967
Riggs, Lew 1934
Rincon, Andy 1982
Roettger, Wally 1931
Romano, Johnny 1967
Roof, Gene 1982
Sadecki, Ray 1964
Sanchez, Orlando 1982
Sander, Ray 1944
Savage, Ted 1967
Schmidt, Freddy 1944, 1946
Schoendienst, Elbert "Red" 1946, 1967
Schultz, Barney 1964
Sessi, Walter 1946
Shannon, Mike 1964, 1967
Shantz, Bobby 1964
Sherdel, Billy 1926
Shoun, Clyde 1942
Simmons, Curt 1964

Bibliography

"The Sporting News" selected years from 1926-1996

"Baseball The Sports Encyclopedia" by David S. Neft
and Richard M. Cohen

"Total Baseball" Edited by John Thorn and Pete Palmer

"Stan Musial 'The Man's' Own Story" as told to Bob Broeg

"From Ghetto to Glory: The Story of Bob Gibson" by Bob Gibson
with Phil Pepe

"Stranger to the Game" The Autobiography of Bob Gibson
with Lonnie Wheeler

"Diz: The Story of Dizzy Dean and Baseball During
the Great Depression" by Robert Gregory

"The Cardinals: The Complete Record of Redbird Baseball
Every Season Through 1982"

The Sporting News Cooperstown
Where Baseball's Legends Live Forever

"The Cardinals Encyclopedia" by Mike Eisenbath

About The Author

Mel R. Freese is a lifelong Cardinals fan having followed baseball since he was seven. He has published two other books on baseball. "Charmed Circle" chronicles the history of 20-game winning pitchers in the 20th Century. "Magic Numbers" does the same thing for hitters who have achieved super seasons of 30 home runs, 100 RBI, and .330 batting average. He credits his involvement with the Society of American Baseball Research (SABR) with helping to make his a successful baseball author. After earning a Masters at St. Louis University, Mel went on to a successful career as a marketing executive and professor of economics. Since retiring, he keeps busy teaching business part time at Webster University. He and his wife Martha live in St. Louis.

About the Publisher

Palmerston & Reed is a St. Louis-based publisher featuring the works of local writers on local topics. We have a variety of titles designed to provide information and reflections on aspects of our community's past, present, and future that are unavailable anywhere else. Our writers live in the community they write about, giving them the personal insight and experience that our readers want. Our publishing procedures and capabilities give us the opportunity to produce books on more narrowly targeted subjects than larger publishing houses. This allows more responsive revisions and less costly updates, so we can provide better and faster new editions.

For more information on Palmerston & Reed,
feel free to contact us. 1524 S. Big Bend Blvd.
St. Louis, MO 63117
877-99-BOOKS (toll-free)
www.StLouisBooks.com

Other Books By Palmerston & Reed

Pitching Isn't Rocket Science

by John Stuper

This new book is a very complete guide for teaching and learning how to pitch. Young pitchers and their coaches alike will learn not only how and when to make certain pitches, but also why. They will also understand the pitcher's many roles on a ball club. Stuper, a former St. Louis Cardinal pitcher and the current Yale coach, called on other ex-Redbirds for help. The book features a series of drills by Greg Mathews, who runs a youth baseball clinic, and a foreword by Bob Forsch, who hurled two no-hitters while a Cardinal. The book is edited by experienced authors and accomplished sportswriters Rob and Sally Tippett Rains.

Illustrated

ISBN 0-911921-37-0

The St. Louis Cardinals Almanac 2000

by Tim Steele

The definitive book on the history of one of the most successful and storied franchises in the history of professional sports. The book is divided into several sections to provide the kind of in-depth coverage based on extensive research that will appeal to the casual and ardent fan alike. Steele, a lifelong fan of the game, takes the reader through the year-by-year history of the club from its founding in 1892 as the St. Louis Browns to the exciting Mark McGwire's inspiring home run drives of 1998 and 1999. He also offers biographical information about everyone who has worn the Birds on the Bats along with year-end statistics for every season.

Illustrated, 1,100 pages

ISBN 0-911921-55-9

Keeping Your Kids Grounded
When You're Flying By the Seat of Your Pants
by Tim Jordan, M.D. & Sally Tippett Rains
In this "ground-making" book, you will learn practical tools that will enable you to create more time, closeness, and cooperation within your family despite all the external pressures. Dr. Tim Jordan, a licensed family therapist and father of three, and Sally Tippett Rains, a professional writer and mother of two, have written this book to help families deal with today's hectic pace. You will learn how to add deposits into your goodwill account with your kids, establish and revisit family traditions, cope with the teenage years, slow your family down, bring spirituality into your home, and cut corners to create more time together.
Illustrated, 165 pages. $14.95
ISBN 0-911921-42-7

Pushcarts & Stalls: The Soulard Market History Cookbook
by Suzanne Corbett
Soulard Market is a St. Louis tradition. Its history spans from the days of horse-drawn wagons and carts to pickup trucks. 'Pushcarts & Stalls' celebrates the history and the experiences of cooking from St. Louis' oldest public farmers market. Preserving the regional food ways of our grandmothers, culinary historian Suzanne Corbett features more than 150 heirloom recipes, plus vintage photographs illustrating Soulard Market throughout its most colorful era – the 20th century.
Illustrated, 240 pages, wire-bound. $16.95
ISBN 0-911921-38-9

A Mosaic of Governments: Why St. Louis Has So Many
by E. Terrence Jones

St. Louis is a rarity in that its metropolitan area is split not only into the usual political parties, but into a large number of political entities as well. Citizens here distrust government but seem to love governments.The book begins with the split between the City and County of St. Louis in 1876 and goes on to how St. Louis went from one dominant government, the City of St. Louis, to more than 300 in the region today. It will also touch on the ramifications of having that many individual municipalities, some tiny and some huge. It also explores the suburban explosion, the rise of regional districts, and the outlook for the future. E. Terrence Jones is a renowned professor of political science and public policy administration at the University of Missouri – St. Louis and a nationally known expert in local government. Since 1969, he has served as a consultant to more than 40 local municipalities.
ISBN 0-911921-53-2

And Men Don't Talk - The Writings of a Modern African-American Man
by Eric Vickers

Written by prominent St. Louis attorney Eric Vickers, this book of short stories, poems and essays provides an interesting and entertaining insight into the inner thoughts of a modern African American man. Mr. Vickers has long been a civil rights attorney, championing the cause of minorities and women. Through the prose and poetry in this book, he gives the reader a compelling look at his inner most thoughts and feelings. 'And Men Don't Talk' is a rare work, sure to intrigue, provoke, and entertain all readers.
150 pages. $14.95
ISBN: 0-911921-57-5

Insider's Guide to The Pope's Visit To St. Louis, Missouri, USA
by David Klocek & Sally Rains
A memorable book about Pope John Paul II and his historic 1999 visit to St.Louis. Klocek and Rains have written a very readable book that is a wonderful keepsake from the Pope's visit. This book provides some interesting personal history about Pope John Paul as well as other papal history. It includes details about the Pope's visit, the preparations for his visit, the chronicles of personal experiences of some St. Louisans with Pope John Paul II, including Stan Musial, Johnny Londoff, Gene McNary, and many others.
Illustrated, 100 pages. $7.95
ISBN 0-911921-50-8

Notorious St. Louis Crimes
By David Linzee
"Notorious St. Louis Crimes" is a masterful presentation of some of the most heinous and well-known crimes from the St. Louis police blotter. All were quite notorious in their time, dominating local and national headlines whether they were tumultuous public events or domestic dramas no one knew about until they turned violent. They are still talked about today, even though many are decades and even centuries old. These dramatic crimes - usually murders but also robberies, kidnappings, swindles, and other assorted mayhem - make good stories in themselves and collectively, they cast a light on the larger life in St. Louis over time. This book also offers a whole new look into St. Louis's past as it includes a crime representative of every era in the city's history. David Linzee is a prominent local writer whose work regularly appears in St. Louis Magazine. He is also a mystery novelist and fourth-generation St. Louisan.
ISBN: 0-911921-58-3

The Magic of the Chilli

by Chris Toney

It's all about chili. To the true aficionados, chili has certain magical powers that no other food can come close to. "The Magic of the Chilli" explores the origins of chili and chili parlors in the Midwest, the people responsible, and why there are sometimes two ls in chili. The book is divided into eight chapters, each featuring a well-researched aspect of the history of chili from the glory days the local chili parlor, through the development and refinement of commercially produced chili, to the stories of regional and national chili competitions. Best of all, there are more than 100 chili recipes to give the readers a chance to cook something special to please family, impress company, or win cookoffs. "The Magic of the Chilli" is a fun book that will make you want to put it down and start cooking a pot of your own. Christine R. Toney is a well-known writer of all things chili and has done extensive research into the history of chili. She has competed in chili competition since 1976 and won more than her share most of the time.

Illustrated

ISBN: 0-911921-56-7